MW00562902

More Praise for *All That Glitters*

"A muse to as well as a long-term lover of David Bowie, singer and fashion icon Ava Cherry, despite her influence, has been until now one of the more neglected characters in his colourful history. Her refreshingly down-to-earth and unpretentious memoir (co-written with Lisa Torem) is an illuminating and inspiring account of the 1970s and 1980s rock and soul scenes and beyond."

—John Clarkson, Editor, pennyblackmusic

"Ava Cherry is the power behind the throne. They called it 'plastic soul' but this was authenticity based on the fact that Luther Vandross and Ava Cherry were there. *Young Americans* was one of the top albums of my youth."

—Joe Shanahan, Founder, METRO

"We, Sigma Kids, had front row seats to the *Young Americans* release. *All That Glitters* has the details...David definitely loved Ava's sense of style! How amazing it must have been for Ava to share her clothes with David! After nearly fifty years, five decades, still being in touch with Ava is a gift! There will always be a soul connection with David, Ava, the Sigma Kids and Philly!"

—Marla Kanevsky, "Sigma Kid"

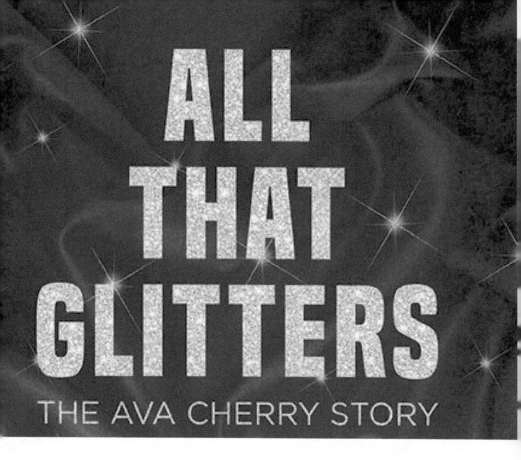

ALL THAT GLITTERS

THE AVA CHERRY STORY

AVA CHERRY and LISA TOREM

AQUARIUS PRESS
Detroit, Michigan

All That Glitters: The Ava Cherry Story

Editor: Lisa Allen
Cover photo: Ava Cherry

ISBN 978-1-7367677-6-4
LCCN 2021950919

Disclaimer: This book is the author's own personal recollections of actual events, persons and institutions.

Several interviews in *All That Glitters* were excerpted from *pennyblackmusic.co.uk.*, courtesy of Lisa Torem.

Cover design by Aquarius Press
Back cover photo by Anne Nieves, courtesy of Wake Up! Music.
Interior photo credits: page 7 © Bob Krasner, courtesy of Tony Zanetta; page 9 courtesy of Tony Zanetta; pages 76 and 147 © Bob Gruen, "Ava Cherry & David Bowie"; pages 226-227 and 229 © Bobby Talamine; page 230 courtesy of Joe Shanahan. All other photos courtesy of Ava Cherry.

Aquarius Press LLC
PO Box 23096
Detroit, MI 48223

www.AllThatGlitters.media

Printed in the United States of America

Contents

FOREWORD

"Time may change me
But I can't trace time."

David Bowie—CHANGES, 1971

The early 1970s was the moment of GLITTER and GLAM:

New York Dolls. Lou Reed. Iggy Pop. Bette Midler. Jackie Curtis. Candy Darling. Andy Warhol's PORK. Mercer Arts Center. Max's Kansas City. Reno Sweeney.

Pop culture was exploding. It was a very exciting time in New York to be young, outrageous and fabulous. The experimentation of the Sixties was continuing at full speed but the style had definitely evolved.

Photo courtesy of Tony Zanetta

© bob krasner

This new style featured flamboyant costumes, makeup and hairstyles and incorporated 1950s rock 'n' roll, Cabaret and Art Rock. Gay and Feminist cultures were on the rise. The 1960s hippie Style was officially Dead. No more plaid flannel shirts and denim dullness. In its place was a fascination with the Glamour of 1930s and 1940s Hollywood along with a bit of Sci Fi. There was a glorification of decadence and superficiality. Androgyny and gender ambiguity were being embraced...the boys were wearing more makeup than the girls.

7

It was into this colorful milieu that a beautiful, free-spirited, very young black model from Chicago made her entrance into New York. With her platinum blonde, very short Fro, shaved eyebrows and perfectly stylized makeup, Ava Cherry was the personification of the new Glamour and the ideal Post-Pop, Space Rock, Boogie-Woogie Queen…just waiting to be discovered. And the night she met David Bowie, Glam's newly-anointed King (Queen), it seemed she was well on her way.

After nearly ten years of false starts and failed attempts, Bowie was having a moment of Great success, touring the world as his alter ego, ZIGGY STARDUST. He had recently completed his first tour of the United States and was about to hit the road with Tour # 2. Ziggy Stardust had conquered the US. The tour was scheduled to travel to Japan and then back to the UK to do a record-breaking 72 shows!

For this tour, he had added horns and additional percussion to his band, THE SPIDERS FROM MARS.

Meeting Ava immediately inspired David to ask her to join the tour singing backup. He had already added several musicians to the four-piece SPIDERS FROM MARS and was eager to include backup singers. Ava would be perfect! She was stunning and had just the right look, had great stage presence and could sing! Besides her impeccable style and sophistication, Ava's beauty and charisma had everything to do with her youth and incredible sweetness. She was a very pure Spirit who emanated good energy. Ava had star Quality!

I was Ziggy's Road Manager and all-around assistant to Tony DeFries, Mr. MainMan himself. MainMan was the rights management organization that supported and helped develop the careers of various artistes and orchestrated Bowie's road to Superstardom. MainMan would also work with Iggy Pop, Mick Ronson, Mott the Hoople, Lou Reed, Dana Gillespie, Amanda Lear, Wayne/Jayne County, John Cougar Mellencamp and eventually, Ava Cherry. I had met David the year before and become fast friends when I was appearing in Andy Warhol's play PORK in London.

And now here I was…Ziggy Stardust's Road Manager. It was my job to find the city and make sure that the band got to the gig. And sometimes deal with not so pleasant tasks . . .

David often made plans and promises that he was not always able to carry out. Unfortunately, promising Ava a spot on the tour was one of them. After giving up her job and apartment in New York and returning to Chicago to wait for the promised ticket to Japan, I had to inform her that the gig had fallen through. Defries had refused to add any more personnel to the tour and so Ava was out. I always felt bad about that and tried to make it up to her in later years. But Ava was not to be deterred. Her spirits remained high and she continued with Plan B.

Plan B would bring her to Paris and Fate would bring her back into the arms of David, who was recording at the Chateau D'Herouville just outside of Paris.

I would next meet Ava in London in the Fall of 1973. I had gone to London to produce Bowie's 1980 FLOOR SHOW for American television. There was Ava! Ava was now a part of David's latest project, THE ASTRONETTES. Her perseverance had paid off.

Six months late, but the promised backup gig had materialized! Not only that but David had created a singing Group starring Ava, Geoff MacCormack and Jason Guess, THE ASTRONETTES.

Photo courtesy of Tony Zanetta

THE ASTRONETTES did record an album...but...it would not be released for another 25 years. David easily lost interest and MainMan had other priorities at the time. His interest in Ava, however, remained strong. They would stay together for the next few years. Ava would become a MainMan Artiste and be supported by the Company. She was moved into a MainMan apartment in Greenwich Village, was given a clothing allowance and weekly subsistence salary. She was sent to a vocal coach and dance classes. The Company committed to producing a solo LP for her. Once again, it looked as if her Star was on the rise.

But again...The Company relied a little too heavily on David for direction of her career and consequently accomplished very little on her behalf. MainMan produced a single and video, I AM A LASER, had some stunning photos taken of her and dubbed her the Black Barbarella . . . none of which did much to propel her career...But as David's interest in Soul Music and R&B piqued, Ava proved to be an invaluable asset. David considered her the epitome of U.S. Soul Culture. Together, they attended the Apollo Theater in Harlem. And through Ava, David began meeting musicians who would become integral to his next project, YOUNG AMERICANS.

Being particularly a fan of the Philly Soul sound, recording time was booked in Philadelphia at Sigma Sound Studio with Carlos Alomar, Robin Clark and a very young Luther Vandross. Ava, Robin, Luther and Geoffrey McCormack would sing backup vocals on the album and the upcoming tour. David had entered his PLASTIC SOUL period with Ava firmly at his side.

The PLASTIC SOUL TOUR commenced in St. Paul, Minnesota on October 3, 1974, winding up in Atlanta on December 1. It was David's ode to the Apollo soul reviews Ava had taken him to and opened with each backup singer doing a solo. This was David's gift to Ava, Geoff, Luther Vandross and Robin Clark. A very young and impressionable Luther would remember Ava later when he was planning his own tours. She would work with him for many years.

As the tour came to an end in December of 1974, we did a final show on American television. I had booked THE DICK CAVETT SHOW against Tony Defries's wishes. David wanted to do it and I thought TV coverage would be great. The appearance is still considered controversial, but brilliant. David was obviously high as he continuously sniffled throughout the interview...but the band and the performance was incredible. Of particular note and still exciting to watch is the shot of Ava dancing. Ava stole the Show. Her dancing to YOUNG AMERICANS is truly memorable. The camera (and cameraman) loved her!

That show was the last time any of us would work together. Professional and personal differences between Bowie and Defries had come to a boiling point. David left the Company. Ava was dropped by the Company, David and Ava soon parted and I also left the Company. It was truly an end of an Era. Glitter and Glam had faded and morphed into Punk, New Wave and Disco.

It's always made me sad that David and I did not stay in touch after this. He had some bitterness about MainMan and chose to erase it as much as possible from his history. Of course, we have all seen what happened to him.

I am so happy to discover more about Ava's journey. I have been fortunate to watch Ava's career from afar and have had the pleasure of seeing her from time to time. I am always very pleasantly surprised and happy that after so many years she remains upbeat and enthusiastic. She is just as sweet as she was at 20. Her great spirit has carried her through an exciting life that has not been without its challenges. And of course, she is still GORGEOUS after all these years!

I have learned that the one constant in life is Change. As Bowie would say, "Ch- ch- ch- ch changes." To watch Ava change and evolve into the mature woman and seasoned performer she has become has been truly an inspiration. Her good spirit and grace and inner light have served her well. It's tough to survive in the Music Business. To be able to thrive and still be performing and making music after nearly 50 years in the Business is absolutely phenomenal. Long Live Ava Cherry!

—**Tony Zanetta**, *former President of MainMan Ltd.*

And Another Foreword...

I met Ava back in 1987 whilst she was on tour in London, through mutual friend David Drew.

Her electric personality, beauty and class were intoxicating. We became instant friends from that day onwards.

Part of our initial conversation was "Darren, you must come to LA, I will introduce you to Luther and he will love you." Little did I know then that those words would change my life.

Fast forward to July 1989. I was working for Gianni Versace boutique on Rodeo Drive in Beverly Hills as a sales executive and in walks the man himself, Mr. Luther Vandross.

As I was wrapping up his first sale, I plucked up the courage and said, "Luther, does the name Ava Cherry ring any bells?" to which he didn't miss a beat and responded, "Ya know that bitch?" in jest of course, and we all roared with laughter.

From that day forward, I would be intrinsically linked to Luther Vandross, Ava and Gianni Versace as salesperson to the stars, at the height of Versace's dominance in fashion worldwide.

The first show of Luther's that I went to was in Anaheim, California, and it was the beginning of many that I would experience of them all performing together. VIP tickets that Luther generously gave me also extended to all the staff at Versace.

That show was magical and magnificent. Ava's stage presence in her form-fitting black-beaded pantsuit, coupled with a jewel-encrusted bustier, looked like it just came off the Versace Atelier runway from the Ritz in Paris, and I was spellbound.

Ava's performance was magnetic and mesmerizing, from the shapes she created with the Lester Wilson choreography to the perfect hair and makeup by Jeff Jones, like that of a *Vogue* cover.

This was also the first time I had heard Ava sing, and what was created during that show was a true ensemble collaboration of sheer talent; the best of the best in the world.

It was hypnotic. Ava had it all: beauty, vocal talent, class, poise, sophistication and elegance.

How Luther had managed to master and frame all those elements was truly an art form, and you just didn't want the show to end.

On another occasion, Luther invited me, Ava and her boyfriend at the time, Herman, to his Beverly Hills mansion on Chanross, just off Laurel Way, for champagne. He would serve Cristal Rosé flown in from Paris in Lalique champagne flutes that were exquisite.

That evening was memorable, not only for the fabulousness, but also the laughter, conversations and fun that we all shared behind closed doors away from prying eyes and the cameras. It was a private soiree without any need to be guarded. To see Ava and Luther interact was just like seeing any normal brother/sister relationship.

All That Glitters is an adventure: The experiences Ava has had throughout her career, on stage, in the recording studio, in front of the camera and performing for thousands globally, and her association with countless singers, musicians and celebrities…

Once you have met Ava Cherry, you know it and will never forget her; the driving force of her personality and sheer talent will make this book a page turner to the end.

—**Darren Margo**, *former manager of Versace Beverly Hills during the time Ava Cherry worked with Luther Vandross*

INTRODUCTION

David Bowie Is, Museum of Contemporary Art, November 25, 2014

The only reason I nabbed a good seat was that I arrived fashionably early for the press event that preceded the multi-media *David Bowie Is* exhibit held at Chicago's Museum of Contemporary Art in November of 2014. But as more and more press arrived, the remaining seats started to go fast, with more down jackets demanding "dibs."

A slender and elegant woman of color with blonde, curly hair and immaculately tailored clothes scanned the crowded room. The speakers were about ready to start their presentation; she needed to sit down quickly.

I realized that I had left my own coat on a neighboring chair, so I removed it, caught the woman's eye, smiled and pointed to the unoccupied space. Truthfully, I didn't know who Ava Cherry was then, but I was drawn to this charismatic soul. She had that look of someone you really want to know.

We chatted and ended up exchanging information. When she learned I was a writer, she mentioned that she'd been thinking about writing a memoir. We said we'd stay in touch. But as the days zoomed by, we both got busy the way folks do.

Then, after a few false starts, meeting for interviews and water or smoothies (Ava prefers goji berries to caffeine), we took a hiatus due to busy schedules, but finally committed to a series of interviews about Ava's life, which would focus not only on her experiences with David Bowie and Luther Vandross, but the equally significant before and after.

Conversations with Ava

And what a life! Ava's early years on the South Side of Chicago, where she was raised by an open-minded mother and trumpet-playing World War II vet father who worked for the postal service, were as essential to her success in show business as the royals, former Beatles, David Bowie, the Rolling Stones and a slew of other celebrities she would later meet.

Tracing the Cherry family has been a living history project in and of itself; many of Ava's ancestors played the game of "policy," a betting game which would eventually morph into the Illinois Lottery System, and which, sadly, did not monetarily benefit the African American communities which created the initial rules.

Her father, Antonio Cherry, and uncle, Isaac Cherry, played trumpet in the popular swing band, Benny Layton and the Rhythm Kings. Her mother, Erma, turned her on to astrology and even though she and her sister, Toni, were "polar opposites," they came together to belt out "Maria" from *West Side Story*.

For that reason, Ava's family-life heroes figure prominently in *All That Glitters*. In fact, they're the backbone of the story and the source of this former fashion model's resilience, inner drive and sense of style.

When Ava reminisces about the "street lights" and "double-dutch jump rope" or how she mirrored the Fanny Brice character in *Funny Girl* when searching for David Bowie, her passion for life filters through.

There were the stunning girl groups that Ava crooned to, the Old Town head shops, the glamorous parties in Hugh Hefner's Playboy Mansion, the starched shirts and pleated skirts of a prestigious, white-dominated Catholic school and the bustling urban high school where Black Studies ranked high among the curriculum choices.

And when Ava continues her life's journey, forging and fine-tuning her career with David Bowie in the 1970s and Luther Vandross in the 1980s, finding hope and heartache along the way, those formative traits become kindred souls.

All That Glitters is a one-off memoir. Ava did not become a victim of substance abuse, as did many of her peers. But she did need to draw from her reservoir of inner strength, time and time again, when she reimagined her life as a solo artist, a single woman in Paris, or when performing in genres as different as Fado and hip-hop to keep up with the music industry's seismic shifts.

The lives of David Bowie and Luther Vandross have previously been discussed and documented and Ava was important to both men's careers, yet her own gifts—which include a unique sense of style, sharp songwriting and evocative vocals—have too often been relegated to the sidelines. In addition, her life-affirming stories or quotes have frequently been taken out of context. With *All That Glitters*, Ava exposes her truth, thereby setting her story straight once and for all.

All That Glitters is comprised mainly of Ava's own voice, but many of her contemporaries joined the conversation. Award-winning producers, Bowie authors and fans, graphic artists, nightclub owners, tribute bands and world-class musicians all shared their perspectives on her art and her life.

In homage to her birth city, Ava's story begins on the South Side of Chicago, acclaimed for its rich, cultural history, although many community landmarks that she grew up with—such as the original Regal Theater— have been demolished.

During her parents' time, opulent jazz clubs, such as the De Lisa, were torn down and now solely exist as inter-generational asides. The ghosts of these essential meeting places bring to mind years of disinvestment, a topic that the Black Lives Matter Movement has helped bring to light. That said, *All That Glitters* is as much about Ava Cherry's entertainment trajectory as it is about her progressive political awareness as she reflects back on her life and times.

Still, with sincere affection for her neighborhood's families, Ava recounts exciting moments at the Regal. We feel her presence in that gilded hall as much as we do in the neighborhood movie theater.

But her story gets much deeper: As a black female entertainer, Ava faces barriers when trying to establish herself as a rock artist, rather than a R&B artist. In fact, she ultimately discovers that label mate, Tina Turner, recorded her breakthrough album, *Private Dancer,* in the U.K. because of the restrictions this American vocalist faced in the U.S.

In Ava's words, "Pop music was very hard to crack."

Ava's deepest wish has been to inspire posterity. *All That Glitters* was written during the COVID-19 pandemic, when the livelihoods of music professionals were decimated overnight. Despite this setback, Ava comes back stronger.

But before beginning, here's a brief portrait of Ava working the crowds today …

—**Lisa Torem,** *co-author*

BELLE OF THE BAR

Ava sweeps onto the stage of an Uptown bar on a Saturday night. The pink ribbons of petite ballet shoes tie snugly around her ankles and her svelte form is swathed in a glittery ensemble. Ava's soft eyes flaunt smoky-lidded shadow.

She's performing an impromptu set with a local band but in record time she has the crowd moving to the front of the room, transfixed. Some of the locals passing through from the nearby Greta Van Fleet concert elect to stay, perhaps intrigued by Ava's alternating current. The set includes "Love is Good News" penned by the late fellow Chicagoan, Curtis Mayfield, who was one of Ava's beloved mentors and early producers. In full possession of the cramped stage, Ava's gestures mirror the life-affirming R&B lyrics.

What follows is more in line with a tribute to David Bowie. Ava sings several of her own favorites: the transcendental "Moonage Daydream" and the truculent "Rebel Rebel." She's up against the quintessential drinking crowd. A few find it a challenge to chug a brew and punch a fist in tandem, but those elbowing their way to the front figure it out fast.

In this noisy watering hole, people freely float in and out. Their sweats and baseball caps reflect the hood's loosey-goosey ambiance. Some have heard all about Ava; others are witnessing her act for the very first time, but collectively, they get that she's a starlet because of the self-assured way she finesses the clientele.

A simmering contralto with flawless skin and tousled, blonde-streaked curls, Ava flirts with cadence and mood. Her repertoire reveals a sense of wonderment, longing and vulnerability. On occasion, a sandpapery toughness slips out.

She closes the set with a *femme fatale* rendition of Led Zeppelin's "Whole Lotta Love." Here, especially, Ava's a fire tickled by lighter fluid. She sparkles, yet if one dares to disarm her, she *will* inflame.

Outside, the grumbling Red Line, well within sober earshot, grinds across an archaic, ill-equipped track. Street sounds seep through the storefront transom. Inside, there's no perfumed, green room or lit makeup mirror, like back in the day to return to, but Ava has the crowd up on their feet, wanting more…

The applause was genuine; the setting, underwhelming. Ava Cherry, however, carries herself with confidence, no matter where life takes her, no matter how big or small the room, she carries herself and approaches life like a star.

This story began on the other side of the city, the South Side, perhaps an hour away from the neighborhood of Uptown on that rickety Red Line, where a pair of doting parents raised two polar-opposite but equally spirited girls.

1.
GOUSTER

M y dad, Antonio Cherry, a trumpet player, was originally from South Carolina. He and his twin, my uncle Isaac, also a trumpet player, were very musical. They gigged in New York in the 1940s with Benny Layton and the Rhythm Kings, an 11-member swing band which originated out of Richmond, Virginia. Mr. Layton doubled as the band leader and a tenor saxophone player. They must have been something. I heard they opened once for the great Count Basie in Pederson, Virginia (or maybe New York).

Mr. Layton's daughter, Catherine, is a singer in upstate New York. She told me that the late jazz pianist and award-winning educator, Billy Taylor, began his career with the band. In his autobiography, Mr. Taylor talked about playing piano with Benny Layton (after their own pianist got drafted) during his college freshman year. He admitted that the other members were "more seasoned" and spoke highly of his day with this big band.

"I gained a great deal of insight from learning to be a part of an ensemble," Taylor wrote in his memoir, "from having to listen and respond as part of a larger musical team, which was a very different musical experience than playing solo or playing with some of the small combo groups I'd experimented with…"

During that time, Mr. Taylor found out that he could purchase song arrangements like "Tuxedo Junction" and "Take the A Train" for only a dollar. When he discovered that a professional musician could transcribe the solo parts directly from the record, that must have been a big deal. And there was always room for creativity. Taylor said about that: "Even though the solos were right there on the page to read, we always added our own original touches." Ms. Layton said that the Benny Layton Band did make a vinyl recording, which was, unfortunately, "lost to a fire in Billy Taylor's studio in the 1970s."

The band members dressed formally in starched, white shirts with turn-down collars and black suits with bow ties and pocket squares, a sign of the fashionable times. Their stands were decorated with forward-facing dancing eighth notes with the moniker "The Rhythm Kings" scripted across the wood finish. The *wah-wahs* for the trumpets were placed between the players for easy access.

This particular ensemble included three trumpets, slide trombone, a stand-up bass, a simple drum kit and saxes. All I have is one black-and-white picture from those days, but I can feel the warmth and enthusiasm in the band members' smiling faces. So, music must have been a driving force in the Cherry home even before I got there…

Black musicians rode in segregated trains; it was a hard existence, but hopefully, the work was rewarding. Ms. Layton also revealed, "They were an all-black band that played for white audiences, but my father was proud of demanding good wages for their performances. The band ended when my father was drafted."

Dad and Uncle Isaac were drafted into World War II, which put a halt to their own professional musical careers. During wartime, there was a strict rationing of rubber and shellac, which affected the logistics of driving from club to club and the manufacturing of records. Plus, there was a two-year musicians' strike in the 1940s—musicians were afraid that the recorded music on the radio would threaten the future of live music. These factors led to fewer opportunities for professional musicians all across the board.

So, once Dad and Momma were settled in Chicago and raising my sister Toni and I, Dad started working two jobs. He became a mail carrier in Uptown on Chicago's far North Side. During that time, many mentally-challenged people lived in the neighborhood. My dad was a kind man, though, and always honored them with patience. In his other job at Marshall Field's (later bought out by Macy's), where he worked for twenty years, he was responsible for bringing in the merchandise. So, by the time I began school, my dad had delved into working these two jobs for the rest of his life.

But before he attended Roosevelt University in downtown Chicago to study music theory, my dad attended a private military school in West Virginia. *How did that happen?* His mother, my grandmother, Naomi, had been the housekeeper for the major boarding school there, so that's where he and Isaac learned how to shoot and to play archery and tennis. My dad had the privilege of being on campus at a predominately white school. Now, black people weren't allowed to go to that school in general, but *they* were because of his mother's job.

Momma's marriage to my dad was rock-solid. She was proud of my dad because he fought in Normandy during World War II. It must have been scary, keeping watch in those foxholes, but fortunately he was there with Isaac—after that time, the Army separated siblings.

Now, even after his time gigging, my dad took pride in being a stylish dresser, but one of the reasons he kept looking so sharp was because my momma always dressed him. See, that's because he kept his clothes from the 1940s, and so my momma would get him all dressed up in his suit and camel-hair coat…He often wore one special zoot suit from the 1940s, "gousters" with baggy pants.

Let me tell you about that suit: Years later, when I worked with David Bowie, the rock star would ask if he could wear my dad's suit! See, David was not only attracted to the style, he was curious about the unique fit.

I'd show up for rehearsal, wearing an article of clothing from my dad's closet, and David's twinkly blue eyes would follow me around the room. Eventually, I'd show him a photo of the zoot suit and he'd have to know: "Why is your dad's suit baggy like this?"

That's when I told David that in the 1940s, when guys in America wore the zoot Suits with the baggy pants, they called themselves "gousters." When I was growing up, some of the younger kids took it up, too.

"See, David," I'd explain, "they wore baggy pants and were calling themselves gousters, just like the adults. They would go to dances and parties. They would slow dance. In other words, they would 'gouster dance.'"

That's how the whole thing really started, with David getting more curious and excited every time we talked about my father's wardrobe.

"Oh, gousters!"

The next thing I knew, *The Gouster* was going to be the title of what became the *Young Americans* album. It also became a popular term that other people and the press were using. Now, David never said where the term originated from or gave a definition of it, and that's because I gave it to him. The influence didn't stop there. Several tracks of that unreleased *The Gouster* were restructured for 1975's *Young Americans* and then became part of an archival David Bowie box set called, *Who Can I Be Now?* (1974-1976).

David's obsession with my father's clothes didn't end there, either. I ended up giving him different articles of clothing from my father's closet, like one big zoot suit and chains. David was completely taken with my father's 1940s image.

Whether I wore a silk tie or a vest, everything came from that same era, when my father was working the jazz clubs, and I loved wearing them all. See, I resembled my father. I have his skin tone. I have his cheekbones.

I've always been slender. And so, I loved to wear his suits. So, even before knowing about the actual zoot suits, the accessories piqued David's interest.

When David glanced at me from across the room, I knew he appreciated my sense of style. In fact, the first thing he'd say was, "Now, who's a clever girl?" in that crisp British accent. David used to come over for dinner sometimes and never actually looked through the closet, of course, but by then, he already knew so much about these suits, so I took things to the next level …

"Dad, do you think I can let David borrow one of your zoot suits and ties? Or something like that?"

Now, my dad liked David, but I didn't know if he would actually allow him to wear one of his suits. I was standing there, wondering how I could convince him, but it turned out that I didn't actually have to because my dad's reaction was so sweet—he just turned around and smiled.

"Yeah, I don't mind, Ava. I'm not wearing them anymore and they're just sitting in the closet." You see, my dad was always so easy-going.

So, one day I took a suit down to David and he was so excited. "Wow. Oh, man," he said as he grabbed the garment from me. Now, he was shorter than my dad but the suit still fit because David was so thin, and yeah, it looked a little baggier on David than on my dad, but by the time I saw him in it, he had already taken it in.

Do you want to know the next thing that happened? David walked onstage for a minute. He looked so good; he asked his then-chief designer, Freddie Burretti, to make a knock-off of my father's suit that was even more "Bowie-esque" with more pronounced shoulder pads, and things like that, but even though it came from my father's closet, David never gave the suit back. And that wouldn't be the last time…

See, I also had this one forest-green army flight suit with lots of patches. It was a trend; everybody back then wore one of those.

"Where did you get *that* suit, Ava?" David asked. By this time, I knew he was being more than just curious. Now, I *knew* I'd never get it back. And we wore the same size shoes! See, I was wearing these cool, white shoes.

"Ava, can I wear those, too?" David asked, charming me once more with that boyish grin. And I *knew* I'd never get those back…

So, I let David wear the suit for a photo session where he was holding up a glass of milk. And those were my white shoes he had on, too! As far as the flight suit? My friend, Lester Hyatt, a New York designer, used to go with me to shop at the Army-Navy surplus stores. When we wore that army-green stuff, everyone in New York would stop and ask where we got our suits. Of course, we never admitted where we got them! (I still have Lester's silk leopard flared skirt and army-green pedal pushers in my closet. Even though that skirt is forty-years-old, people still ask me about it.)

Now, you have to understand how much I loved that flight suit. It was a one-of-a kind. I still remember asking David for it back and how he responded so firmly ...

"No, Ava, once I wear it, you can't have it back because it has become part of *my* style." Meanwhile, I was thinking, *I'm adding to your style. Right*? But after that conversation, I never asked David for anything back again.

But it all started with that zoot suit in my father's closet. My momma still remembers the details. It was navy blue surge, and the baggy pants with those deep pockets ... We both loved my dad's vintage ties and vests, but especially that zoot suit.

I don't think my momma understood that David would look so good in that suit onstage. She just didn't know. Of course, my momma would be quick to point out, "My husband was taller than David," but David and my dad had so many other things in common. Both were hard-working, talented musicians. They both had a great sense of style. A nip and tuck or a hem, and yeah, that transformation was complete.

But what I'm trying to tell you is that, when I gave David that word "gouster" and shared my father's clothes, this is what opened him up to a new world of fashion and a more inclusive way of thinking about American culture.

2.
INNER DRIVE

I f my momma, Erma Cherry, had big dreams when she was young, those dreams would have been difficult, or maybe impossible, for an impoverished black woman to achieve. Maybe that's one reason I worked so hard at my career—my momma didn't have a lot of opportunities.

She grew up in Oklahoma. Now, Oklahoma was kind of backwards in those days, but that hadn't always been the case. By the 1920s, a prosperous black middle class had established a thriving business community, but the majority population put a quick end to that.

Momma's family was poor. She was an only child who became independent at an early age. In fact, she did all of the cooking for her family. But in the 1950s, when she got to be about seventeen, my momma decided to leave. She wanted to be on her own, find her own way and move to the big city. My aunt Juanita already lived in Chicago, so when my momma got here, she stayed with my aunt and found a job at an army base called Fort Sheridan.

A friend of a family member introduced my momma to her future husband, Antonio. During their courtship, he'd talk to her about those New York hot spots where he played with Benny Layton and the Rhythm Kings. Once, she even spoke a little to Benny, but you have to understand; that was only a one-off conversation. See, my momma was a prim and proper girl. Women didn't talk much about those things back then to men they didn't know.

My friends called her "Queen Erma" because she had that royal demeanor and a little girl quality that was priceless. Even though she didn't have a lot when she was growing up, she swore that her children would have more. She worked so hard. And over the years, even with her prosthetic knee, she kept right on dancing.

My momma went to the movies all of the time. She was a real movie buff and so I became one, too. She likes to remind me that I especially loved Elizabeth Taylor in her portrayal of Cleopatra, as well as any movie with Marlon Brando. She was such a huge fan of the glamorous actresses that she named Toni and I after Ava Gardner and Lana Turner.

You see, Ava Gardner was one of my momma's idols. On my sister's birth certificate, it says, "Thondelayo," but her nickname is Toni. Why did momma name my sister that? Because in the movie, *White Cargo*, Lana announces, "My name is Thondelayo."

My momma's music people were Sarah Vaughan, whom she idolized, and Ella Fitzgerald, but Frank Sinatra was also her idol. She adored "Old Blue Eyes" because he had a beautiful voice. Momma had dreams about meeting Frank in which he'd be "so nice to me…"

She still recalls the first movie he made; she heard his "perfect, perfect voice." She loved Sinatra so much that she fell into a deep depression when he died. Because of my momma, I know every line of every Sinatra song and all of the phrasing. See, my dad was a trumpet player, but my momma was the one who set me up for a musical background.

Later on, when I performed professionally in Chicago, Luther Vandross made sure the spotlight was on my parents as he introduced them. He once pulled my momma up on stage at the Arie Crown Theater in August of 1985 during The Night I Fell in Love Tour. Everyone told me how much they loved my mother and how beautiful she was. She always had such a good vibe when she came to the show. If you asked her, she'd smile and say, "I sure did."

Before that show, we went out to Oak Street and I bought her a beautiful short black dress. It was so sexy. And when she stepped into that concert hall, she was looking sharp as a tack.

I was very fortunate that both of my parents believed in me. After I left home and every time I grew homesick on the road or needed advice, I called my momma. She is everything to me.

Then, and even now, I call her every single day and ask her: "Momma, did you take your Vitamin D3 and zinc? Did you drink your apple cider vinegar?"

****

I was born in a three-flat building in Woodlawn on the South Side of Chicago. At the time, it was an all-black neighborhood. It wasn't the best neighborhood and it wasn't the worst. St. Ansel was my grade school and Holy Cross was my other Catholic school. I was just a regular South Side kid, a nothing special, innocent kid.

I come from a large family. I had nine great-aunts. Aunt Helen and Uncle Henry worked as a maid and butler team in Hollywood for the actress Betty Grable, and her husband, orchestra leader Harry James (another horn player!) in the 1940s. And when my uncle Isaac played the racetrack and poker, let me tell you, he always won.

HOLY CROSS SCHOOL

My Aunt Juanita, Aunt Helen and Aunt Betsy played the racetrack, and a betting game, called "policy," too, but Aunt Juanita, she was always the one who won big. All my aunts had money.

29

They were considered upper-middle class black people. They had the best clothes and married men who had good jobs.

My family lived big. Like, if they were cooking, they'd have a big feast. They could make something out of nothing. We shared these wonderful dinners together. I don't remember ever going hungry.

My parents worked so hard … That's why I thought I was rich until one neighborhood kid dared to set me straight. "You're not rich. You're a city kid."

Every day, my momma would painstakingly fix our hair. Because every hair was so perfectly in place, the kids called us "tight-heads." She would dress us pretty much the same, but Toni would come home with every hair in place and my shoes would always be scuffed. I'd always get dirt on my dress, too. No wonder the kids would say, "You guys are as different as night and day." They got that right.

My mother was a stickler for fine clothing. She knew how to buy the best material. She loved herringbone and velvet and the clothes she bought lasted for years, like those beautiful circle skirts that looked so great with sunglasses.

Like I said, my father worked two jobs all my life. He went out at four in the morning and didn't get home until nine or ten at night, ever. Even though he worked hard as a postal carrier for forty years, he always made time for us. He'd help us wash up; he'd lift us up in the air, and affectionately call Toni and I, "my little soldiers." He'd clean the meat and help my momma cook. He was a good cook and a loving, caring, do-anything-for-his family person.

Our neighborhood was a little more affluent than the surrounding neighborhoods. A lot of the kids in the other neighborhoods were poor, but because my parents let me take piano lessons and dance lessons and let me be a Girl Scout, I thought I was middle class. Of course, then I'd be haunted by those taunts: "You're not rich, you're poor."

My momma was always there for me. What she saw in me was that I was mature for my age. What she saw in me was that I was hanging out with people who were a little older than I was. At sixteen, I was hanging out with eighteen, nineteen or twenty-year-olds.

Now, some parents might have had some trouble with that, but she felt that I was mature because of the way I would talk to her. I'd ask her if I could do something; she would listen carefully, and if I explained why, more than likely, she'd let me do it.

My momma was always confident that I could do what I set out to do and she was right. I mean, she disciplined me, as needed, but was definitely more lenient than a lot of the other parents of that era.

On my block, everybody cared about everyone and watched out for each other's kids. This was the city; there was gang activity, but the gangs never bothered regular people.

I did everything I wanted to do. I was a Girl Scout; I went camping. My parents bought us the best-made clothes. If my mother was going to buy us shoes, they were the kind that would last a few seasons. One thing I learned early on—you can fool people with things.

"You always dress so nice, like you have money." That's what people said about our family. That's how I was brought up.

You know what the teachers said about us? "They wear the most beautiful clothes." But that required time and effort. My momma would be washing on her hands and knees, she'd make sure our blouses were bleached, she'd be polishing our shoes so they wouldn't be scruffy.

I didn't look at it like I was better than anybody else. I didn't realize that I was a kid brought up in the inner city. This was the South Side. I always thought I had a lot.

I was a constructive kid who was interested in skating, basketball and sock hops. I was in skating shows and I even had a skate master. I had a girl group. I did normal, fun, young lady things.

We played double-dutch jump rope out on the sidewalk in the hot summers. Those ropes could smack the pavement so fast, but in no time, I figured out how to gauge the distance and jump back in. As far as inside the house, my momma bought me a tea set, so I was always having parties.

The streetlights gave us our curfew. The rule was, you could play outside, but you had to be in before dark, as soon as the city streetlights came on. Sometimes, we would be busy playing and it would get dark and my mother would come out frantically and look for us. I'd see that look of worry on her face and then run in. *"Don't worry, momma. I'm home."*

So, there were lots of families on our block and we looked out for each other. When I was twelve, there would always be the five and six-year-olds, running around, playing games outside. We were a tight community.

My parents raised me to be independent. My father revered my mother and called her "love" until the day he died. When he was dying, he only opened his eyes when she talked with him.

My home was a matriarchy. With nine great-aunts, everyday life was very women-heavy. The women ruled in our family. The guys loved them to death, but the women ruled.

But outside our home? If any of the girls threatened to beat me up after school, I'd go outside and make a quick decision: to fight or not fight. Sometimes Toni would try to fight for me. We had to be tough when we were growing up.

I have always been fearless, honey, fearless. When I was about four, my mother used to pay this crossing guard to wait until she could pick me up from school. The crosswalk was right next to a busy drugstore.

One day, my mother wasn't there and didn't show up for about twenty minutes. The crossing guard wasn't looking, so I thought, *I know the way home.* I waited for the light and looked both ways and went home all by myself.

My mother got there about ten minutes after I left. The crossing guard explained that she didn't know what happened. She just said, "She disappeared." Of course, my mother was freaked out because this woman was supposed to be looking after me, right? Now, my mother was always very careful with us and always made sure she only put us with people she trusted…She went home and there I was. Playing. Her best friend, Ace, was beside her. My momma was crying and all upset.

Ace intervened: "Don't whip her, Erma, she's smart." My momma responded, "I'm not going to whip her, but I'm just shocked that she found her way home all by herself."

I just started walking—I knew the way home. Finally, my momma sat me down and calmly asked, "How'd you find your way all by yourself?"

I said, "Momma, we go this way every day." And that's when she knew that I was sharp and that she could let me do things. Girl power…Toni remembered that incident, too.

TONI

Ava must have thought that my mother wasn't going to show up, which was the first and only time that ever happened. Ava was precocious and that act showed bravado. She's been that way ever since. She loved to travel and wouldn't be afraid to travel to far-out places as an adult and not know anybody there. You know, going off to Paris or Rome or London… In contrast, I've lived a very buttoned-up life and Ava's always been very adventurous and not afraid and I always admired that quality in her.

AVA

My mother was always inviting my white friends from the North Side to come over for dinner. Now, this was during the time of the Civil Rights

Movement and before Dr. Martin Luther King, Jr. got killed. Our families lived on opposite sides of the city but my momma treated everyone the same.

My friends that were white were never racist. They were always sweet and nice, not a racist bone in their bodies. In fact, they were always trying to figure out why some people were so mean to people of color. But we tried not to pay attention to the bad stuff. We knew what was going on, but we didn't want it to affect our friendships.

Years later, I experienced racism from people I wasn't expecting to experience racism from. In Santa Monica, some gay people would say things to me that were racist and mean, like, "Get off the street, bitch." Why were they saying this to me when they were being oppressed, too?

But it was everybody's street. I have so many gay friends that I love. But some, at that time, would see me with a guy they were attracted to and get angry.

Fortunately, I never experienced the bad part of racism when I was growing up. My parents brought me up to believe that everyone is equal; that they were individuals regardless of race. What I saw on TV stressed me out: the images of Selma, Alabama, black people being beaten up and hosed, the bombing of churches, but I never saw it myself. I was innocent.

Toni is one year older. Toni and Ava—we were both Scorpios. We had bunk beds. I was on the top. And of course, like all sisters, we had our share of rivalry. We were as different as night and day, so I'll let Toni tell you her side of the story.

TONI

Ava's the funny one. For example, when we were little, she would put her shoes on the wrong feet—you know, the toes go inward, and I was always the one that was buttoned up. I'm not trying to give you the impression that I'm perfect, no, I wasn't perfect at all, but we are both Scorpios. And yet even though we share the same astrological sign, we are as different as night and day.

Ava has more of a Sagittarian nature. She's always been very free-spirited. She lived life like a loose garment. I was the worrier, the one who was taking care of my little sister.

34

My dad used to take a lot of pictures of us when we were little. If I had on my trousers, I would lift them almost up to my armpits. I was a very rigid child. But Ava? Her shoes would always be untied.

She was always losing things. In the winter, she was always losing her mittens. Always. I never lost my mittens, but I wanted to protect her so I'd give her my mittens and let my hands freeze.

I would do anything for Ava, but as a child, she was not very generous in return, especially not with her candy. At the little store across the street, we could get big bags, but whenever I would ask her for something that I had bought, she would have to take my share out of the bag for me, instead of allowing me to put my hand inside the bag. My whole life with Ava was always about protecting her, even though she was bravado …

From my window in Bronzeville, I can see the White Sox Park and the Illinois Institute of Technology, but I can also see beautiful sunsets. Once I had this dream that I kept looking at this orange sun. It was the daytime, but soon it started turning to dusk. Then the orange sun began to turn into a ball of fire and finally into a fiery tornado, like that scene from the film, *The Ten Commandments*, where Charlton Heston blocks the other characters. So, there I was in this bad dream. As the fiery tornado started coming toward the building, this message came into my mind: *Oh my God, I have to find Ava.*

I felt that my mother in Michigan City and daughter were going to be safe, but I still didn't know that Ava would be safe. The fiery tornado was coming at me so quickly that all I wanted to do was run out of that building and try to find Ava…

My sister and I both have powerful personalities and sometimes we don't agree, especially when it comes to politics, but the one thing I feel about her is that I want to protect her. I know that she doesn't need protecting, but it's just something inside of me. Even if we have an argument or we don't see each other for a while, she's always in my subconscious.

AVA

See, Toni and I would eventually travel in different circles. I remember her arching her eyebrows: "How did you get involved with these people, A?" Over the years, Toni would quiz me about my show business connections.

See, she was always corporate. I was always creative. We were two different poles, and believe me, Toni had her little idiosyncrasies.

But we had a few things in common. Fun things, like, we both loved to sing. Now, we didn't have a fire escape, but once we discovered that there was a nice echo in the basement, we would belt out the ballad "Maria" from the film, *West Side Story* at all hours of the night.

My dad died twenty years ago, but before that, Mom and Dad enjoyed a long and happy marriage. The best part for us kids? The holidays.

Christmas was the happiest time of my life. I wanted a bike so bad… But one Christmas, I was worried that this would never happen. I knew money didn't come easy, but I was heartbroken when my momma gently whispered, "Ava, I don't know if Santa can do this."

Things were lean that particular Christmas. One night, though, through the closed door, I overheard my momma say to my dad, "I don't care what you do, you'd better come back with that money."

I watched him come out; he didn't say a thing. He quietly put his coat on, put his shoes on and said, "I'll be back." Wherever he went, he got the money.

But fortunately, I got distracted, listening to the records of Frank Sinatra singing "Merry Christmas" and of course, we could never get enough of Ella Fitzgerald and Nat King Cole. Because we had such a close and loving family, holidays were always wonderful, but especially Christmas, with our beautiful tree on which we hung sparkling decorations. And my momma had a great sense of Feng Shui. You could tell this by the way she strung the shiny rows of holiday lights against the frosted windows.

That one year still sticks out in my mind. Just two days before Christmas, the closet door was cracked open just enough so I could spot some shiny, blue metal. Now, I carefully closed that closet door and took a deep breath. Sure enough, that was the bike I wanted…That turned out to be the happiest Christmas ever.

Mealtime was the most exciting time. My momma was the most wonderful cook; the best cook in the world, such a clean cook with clean herbs and vegetables and onions. I can't ever tell you how good it was. I'd be sleeping or getting ready for school and I'd inhale those fragrances and race Toni down the hall, so I could inhale all of those sweet kitchen smells.

I don't care whose house I went to; nobody cooked better than my momma. My whole family consisted of cooks and bakers and they made incredible meals. They'd make pies and pastries. They were a cooking family.

You remember my aunts. They were all gourmet cooks. On Sunday mornings, they'd make a really good breakfast. My great-aunt Juanita would make fried chicken with grits and biscuits from scratch that were dripping with butter.

Now, I come from a family of great cooks, but my momma was the best of them. She'd make ham with pineapples and cloves. She'd make ham sandwiches and my friends would shout, "WHO MADE THIS HAM?"

My parents built up so many memories over the years. As a family, we shared so many emotions. But life never stands still, so when Momma passed along the kitchen baton, I prepared the first of many special meals.

For somebody who had cooked the most delicious meals every day to all of a sudden stop in her early eighties…Now, I'm a pretty good cook, but everything I learned, I learned from her.

Just like that movie, *Soul Food*, where the families sit around a big table and share stories and dishes…That's how I felt when I tasted my mama's cooking. This was home. The smell of food made me feel so secure, whether it was nice, crisp bacon or toast and jam.

When I tell you my mother cooked clean, I mean it. She didn't use any lard and she used lots of beans and corn bread—there were always large bowls of red beans and black-eyed peas on the table. She worked with garlic and onions; no bad ingredients. She only used pure vegetable oil. She made the best macaroni and cheese. Just the right consistency. You had to take a spoon.

I still make those same things in a healthy way. I don't eat as much as I used to. In fact, I hardly eat pork or beef anymore…

But enough is enough. When she got to be 81, my momma announced, "I'm never cooking again!" Then it was up to me. So, when my momma celebrated her next birthday, I took over as cook in that spotless kitchen. We talked about when she made ham, meatloaf and all those things that are really good and I knew I had big shoes to fill.

That kitchen brought me back to those days of growing up. Then, it seemed so easy. We sat down at the table once the streetlights flashed on. But in those later years, Momma would worry. See, I was an ambitious daughter, so anxious to forge my own path.

Like when I started my all-girl group. I had even warned my momma that when we girls got older, we would fly off to France. And just the other day, I reminded her about the friend who invited me to Monaco years ago. That trip dramatically altered both of our lives. Me, staring out of the compact airplane window at that fairy tale city, where I would boogaloo with *Doctor Zhivago* actor Omar Sharif.

I can still imagine momma shaking her head. "Eight months, I didn't see Ava for eight months." She counted the days. but never once kept me from my dreams.

My momma and I are *like this.* I even look like her. She has been so inspirational to me my whole life. There are so many things I wouldn't have had the opportunity to do if it hadn't been for her.

When I smoked my first joint, she said, "Just be careful, A." Instead of chastising me or getting angry, she just explained the possible effects. I told her everything; I trusted her.

My momma would boost my confidence by saying, "You have that *it* factor," and then I would excitedly respond to that energy around me.

She always encouraged me to do what my heart felt, yet I realize now, sometimes she was really worried about me, even though she tried not to show it. We both always had that independent streak, and sometimes she'd have to explain to friends or family members: "Oh, yes, Ava always seemed to go her own way."

She encouraged me to reason. I could never understand people who don't stand up for what they believe. See, if I see something that isn't right, I speak up. And sometimes that worried my momma, too, but she always had my back. When I asked if I could do something, she would more than likely let me do it. She was confident that I could do what I set out to do and she was right.

Like when I first told her, "Hey, Momma, I think I'm going to go to New York"—of course, she was a little nervous, thinking about her younger daughter in a strange, new place. She'd say, "What?" or "Why?" But she always listened. She always let me explain: "See, if I go out there, Momma,

I think I can meet some people, maybe get a part in a movie ..." And she did end up sharing a contact with me in L.A. Sure, she was worried, but she trusted my judgment.

She'd say, "Well, if that's how you feel, A." You see, my momma never tried to hinder me from doing what I felt in my heart. If you second-guessed her, she'd look you straight in the eye and say, "Ava always had a good head."

My momma has been my heartbeat. Her energy and warmth have sustained me. One of the greatest joys of my life is knowing she's been there for me. During a rough patch with Luther Vandross, she reassured me: "While I'm alive, you're not going to go down."

When I would be with David, I'd call her at three a.m. and ask her (after I checked to see if I woke her) to look in her astrology book for someone's rising sign.

My momma is why I set my sights so high, why I've always been self-motivated and why I've always had inner-drive. And that trust gave me the confidence to pursue my dreams, like when I spent eight months trying to track down David Bowie—I was obsessed. Yet I knew I would find him. I knew I would never give up. It was my fate. What fueled that confidence? I owe it all to my momma.

Now, before my music business adventures and meeting David and Luther, there was my time in Catholic school—that experience radically changed the direction of my life.

3.
TURNING POINTS

My parents sent me to all-girl Catholic schools, first St. Anselm on 61st and Indiana, and then Academy of Our Lady aka Longwood High School on 95th and Throop, because they felt that public schools had too many bad kids. My mother and father made sacrifices. They even converted. They became Catholic because they wanted me to go to a Catholic school, but originally, my mother was a Seventh Day Adventist, which was what my grandmother Inez was, and my father had been born a Baptist.

For most of those early years, the school was a good fit. I learned in Catholic School. The nuns kept you focused. We learned discipline. Every day, we had to wear starched white shirts, blazers and pleated skirts. Ours was a uniformed, 85-percent white, all-girls Catholic school with a long, educational history. It was a boarding school until 1935 and shut its doors for good in 1999.

I'll always remember the statue of the Sacred Heart that stood on the grounds. If you walked further and planted yourself in front of Hackman Hall, there was a lagoon teeming with lily pads that spelled out the school initials.

At the time I was there, most of my friends were white. I never saw any race fights or anyone even standing there fighting. I never saw that. A.O.L. was a pretty peaceful school. It really was.

Now, St. Anselm had a recreational center right across the street from the school and that's where they held all of our skating events and basketball games. They also hosted school dances where we heard all the favorite hits of the day. Smokey Robinson was my favorite, and of course, Diana Ross.

The nuns wore full habits. I loved them because they were so nice to me. In eighth grade, Sister Joelle, who was still in her 20s, would ask me to clean the nuns' quarters. So, every Saturday, I would clean, just to be around her. I admired her so much that one day I blurted out, "Sister Joelle? I want to be a nun."

When she paused and then laughed a little bit, I wondered, *Did I say the wrong thing?* But Sister Joelle's tone was reassuring when she replied, which put me at ease:

"Ava, I don't think God intended for you to be a nun. You have too much energy and way too much zest for life to be a nun. It's not that exciting." But if Sister Joelle would have told me to become a nun, I would have become a nun.

Sister Joelle made me feel. Before I went to school, I didn't know nuns could be cool like that. Just like my mother, she was so nurturing. And Sister Erma—I was so surprised that she had my mother's name. She would nurture and protect me, too. Even though I was bad at math—it was my worst subject, yet they passed me.

They'd say to each other, "I love Ava. Don't fail her." Still, school was a challenge. The hours were strenuous. By first period, I'd be falling asleep.

There were two things that made me change schools. Who knows who I would have become if I had stayed? But here's what happened:

There was an event in high school which opened my eyes to the world at large. Like I said, Longwood was top-of-the line in terms of all-girl Catholic schools and fit the bill for many students, but the curriculum didn't allow for much change.

Most subjects were taught by nuns, but a few were taught by lay teachers. One of them, Mr. Rosatti, also an art teacher, taught a class about religions of the world in which he explained all of the philosophies. This was one of the most interesting classes I had.

So, I went back to school the following year as a junior and wanted to take Mr. Rosatti's class again, but when I asked him about it, he took me aside. He told me that the Catholic Church had made the decision to take any classes out of the curriculum that taught about any religion other than Catholicism.

Now, this decision really disturbed me. I had learned so much about different religions in class and I was really interested in what made people *want* to worship. I kept asking myself, "What?" and "Why?" I appreciated

Mr. Rosatti teaching us about these philosophies; I took the subject matter seriously.

I didn't see anything terrible about the point-of-view, but I guess that's not how the school administrators felt. Right then and there, I started changing my ideas about religion and God and all of that. So, that was a huge turning point. That decision changed my mind about being Catholic. I wasn't going to let anybody make me be Catholic if I didn't want to be Catholic.

Why don't they want you to know about other religions? It doesn't mean that you're going to go to those other religions! (Then again, at one point later on, I became a Buddhist).

The second thing that happened was even more dramatic. That's when my closest friend disappointed me. In my Catholic school, I had been friends with some girls since kindergarten, but this one girl, Mickey, was my best friend. We did everything together. We went to sock hops, basketball games and skating. We put together a little girl group as well. She had a beautiful voice. We sang the Supremes and Smokey Robinson. We were like Motown fanatics.

But one day when we got to high school, Mickey decided she wasn't going to hang out with me anymore. I was freaked out because we had always been so close. To make matters worse, she started hanging out exclusively with this other girl. I finally mustered up the courage to ask, "Mickey, what's wrong? Did I do something wrong?"

But Mickey just wouldn't talk to me anymore. If she saw me, she would shove me, or when she'd see me coming down the hall, she would walk away in a huff with this other girl. She really hurt me, because I had been so close to her. I had spent the night at her house all the time. I was really close to her family.

I didn't want to be in this situation that Mickey was putting me under any longer. I had tried so hard to remedy the situation. I'd been pleading with her, "*Please Mickey, tell me what I did.*" But every time I got close to her, she kept on running away from me. It was the kind of hurt I could never forgive.

Years later, I would reflect back on those days without remorse. But at the time, I remember thinking over and over: "*You did this to me, Mickey.*

I'm never seeing you again."

Now, I was a virgin, but I soon found out that Mickey wasn't. She was sleeping with a guy and she couldn't bring herself to talk to me about that. See, we never talked about sex; we just talked about girly things. So, it turned out that she was afraid to tell me that she'd started having sex with this guy. And then, she got pregnant…

But before I found this out and before Mickey started doing all this, I would just start crying. Here was my best friend, shutting me out of her life, replacing me with her boyfriend's sister. So, I had to make a quick decision. I marched down to the office to confront the administrators.

"I want to transfer out of this school," I blurted out. The administrator's response was firm: "You've got to ask your mother and father if you want to move from here."

I was determined to leave that school, but worried. How would my parents react? They had worked so hard to get me into Longwood. They'd even become Catholics. How could they understand?

From across the dining room table, I leaned in. My palms were sweaty but I couldn't spit the words out fast enough. Of course, momma already knew I was suffering.

"Momma, listen," I began. "I can't go to this school anymore. Mickey's treating me so badly and I can't concentrate. I'd rather be away from here and not anywhere around her."

Mickey had been making me *so* uncomfortable that year, but this I knew—I had to leave that school to be who I wanted to be. Leaving Longwood would upset my high school career, but things had come to a head and I had no choice.

My best friend deeply disappointed me. To make matters worse, when I found out the truth, she didn't apologize. Yet, in hindsight, that painful incident ultimately moved me forward. Ironically, Mickey's actions had a positive effect.

Let her go ahead and have babies, I told myself; *I'm going to be someone.* In fact, I became more serious than ever about wanting a career as a model, wanting to travel around the world and do things that you could only dream of—after that treatment from Mickey, all I wanted to do was get away, and I did.

I hadn't anticipated then that getting away from Mickey would open up my world in such a positive way. How could I have known that I'd be hitchhiking in L.A. off of Sunset Blvd. in the near future, before working as a fashion model in New York?

But, I wasn't free yet. I still had to finish high school. I was headed into the unknown and would have to make new friends, but the minute I got away from Longwood, I really did adapt. It was like magic.

I ended up going to night school downtown at Central Y.M.C.A. High and I graduated from there. Now, that was a big contrast. Gone were the manicured shrubs and starched uniforms. The building was right smack in the middle of The Loop, around State and Lake St., near the crowded Greyhound Bus Station and a white-washed building with an old-world clock that housed Ronny's Steak House, where you could get breakfast, lunch and dinner. We were steps from the dazzling Theater District marquees. You could hail a yellow taxi, hop on the El or hang out at the submarine sandwich shop.

And this school attracted a whole different crowd. The "Cardinal" Alums included blues guitarist Michael Bloomfield, Linda Leilani Brown, of *Dream Girls* fame, and Robert Sengstacki, who worked with the *Chicago Defender*, one of the last published African American newspapers. He was also famous for photographing Martin Luther King, Jr., Muhammad Ali and poet Gwendolyn Brooks.

At this school, white people were the minority. I made new friends, and for the first time, I had the opportunity to take a Black Studies class and learn all about black history: Martin Luther King, Jr., The Black Panthers and the Civil Rights Movement, important things that I never would have studied at Longwood.

It was a big change. Like I said, I had always gone to Catholic schools, first, St. Anselm and then Longwood High School. It had been a great opportunity for me educationally, but not emotionally, and my momma understood.

More and more, I was opening myself up to change. But that was only the beginning because then I met a bunch of people who were Sabians: Nina, and her husband Paul, worked at the North Side temple on Sheffield Ave., and then there was Ordune, the "Obeah," whose position is equivalent to that of the temple priest.

See, the Sabian religion is based on African traditions. In South America, it's called Santeria. The different gods that are involved are based on saints: St. Christopher, St. Francis of Assisi and Mary Magdalene.

One of the guys who was involved in the practice was called Obatala, he would be equivalent to Jesus. A five-eight, light-skinned Cuban, or what you call a "white Cuban," Obatala was so smart and so creative. He put on ballets and played the drums. He was a spiritual leader who talked about the elements of the universe. Obatala was the head of all the Gods, and although I'd never been exposed to something like this before, I didn't see anything wrong with this practice; I saw it as all positive.

I soaked it up. I was able to work out so many of my problems once I learned about this philosophy. I used to go to the North Side temple and meditate with them. Ordune became almost like my step-father. I mean, I loved my father, but Ordune became like another father figure to me. Whenever I called him up for advice, he would freely give it.

When Tina Turner embraced Nichiren Buddhism and started to chant Nam Myoho Renge Kyo, it seemed like her newfound spirituality gave her the strength to promote a successful solo career, despite the sexism and racism she'd experienced. Astrology and Santeria did that for me.

I guess my mind, too, has always been open to change. My momma first started buying books about astrology when I was about fifteen—I'm a Scorpio. I'm interested in metaphysics.

Together, we started reading about what the different signs meant: the oppositions, the different transits of the planet, the eclipses, all kinds of different things and what they mean based on an individual's horoscope. There are twelve planets that rule you in an astrological horoscope. You have to know the time of the person's birth and where to get their rising sign so it's very intricate.

In order to know how you're going to get along with another person, you have to know their signs. This is how you find out the negatives and positives between you—astrology helps you to understand.

Many times, throughout my adulthood, I would call my mother up and talk to her about important people in my life, especially about David, about certain signs that he had in his chart. For instance, like I said, I was a

Scorpio and he was a Capricorn. We were compatible because I was a Virgo rising which is Earth, and Capricorn is an Earth sign, so we both felt very grounded and down-to-earth. We both were about climbing up the ladder to become successful. That had been a great starting point. If only it had been that simple…

4.
COMING OF AGE IN WOODLAWN/
SWEET INSPIRATIONS

Music was a major influence and my momma lit the fire. Growing up, I'd blast the volume on my huge transistor radio, which was, oh my God, as big as a boom box. If I leafed through a teen magazine, I wouldn't pay attention to the gold lamé gowns and shiny heels or hair piled high in a bouffant or beehive. I would put my own stuff together. I was a fashionista, on my own. I didn't really follow fashion trends. People were like, "How'd you do that? Where'd that combination come from?" I just wore whatever I thought looked good on me.

I was still young when I found my second home in a palatial building. This special place, close to the Savoy Ballroom and just steps from the soot and exhaust of the Dan Ryan Expressway, was a cultural, South Side treasure. Over the years, comedians Flip Wilson, Red Foxx and Richard Prior polished their monologues in front of sold-out crowds, but for me and my friends, the live soul music was the big draw.

Acts like soulful Gladys Knight and the Pips and handsome, caped baritone Gene "Duke of Earl" Chandler sang heartfelt to light songs. Of course, hundreds of other vocalists cut their teeth or grew their careers on that stage, too.

All this happiness occurred at the Regal Theater on 47th and Grand Boulevard/South Parkway (which would be renamed Dr. Martin Luther King Jr. Drive in 1968). It was designed in the Moroccan Revival Style by architect Edward Eichenbaum.

Mott's Pekin Theater on 27th and State, which featured vaudeville and jazz acts, goes on record for being one of America's first black-owned theaters. After owner Robert Mott died in 1911, the building was taken over by white proprietors and turned into a dance hall which got demolished in the 1930s. Nevertheless, Mott's ingenuity had sowed a creative seed.

The Regal opened in the late 1920s and became a cultural gathering place for the mostly African-American population living in bustling Bronzeville.

The design was "atmospheric." The ceiling swelled overhead like a giant canopy. It was connected with shiny, gold poles. You could look up through a narrow opening and get lost in the deep blue sky, sparkling stars and floating clouds. Because of the thick carpeting and lush velvet drapes, the acoustics were always perfect.

The Regal had enough comfortable seating for 3,000 patrons. Now, there was a huge Wurlitzer organ and spacious orchestra pit, but all we kids wanted to see was the act on the stage!

The South Side had a lot of incredible theaters then that had mostly been built in the 1920s. We still had *so* much history in our neighborhood when I was growing up. In the 1940s, The Marx Brothers lived on King Drive in a white-stone building with high ceilings.

A lot of times, people compared the Regal to Harlem's Apollo Theater, which opened in 1934 and also featured black entertainers, but the Regal had a different kind of pull. The management could solicit bigger stars and the theatre could seat twice as many fans.

The Regal closed officially in 1968 and it was demolished in 1973. Sitting there now, is the Harold Washington Cultural Center, named after Chicago's first black mayor who served from 1983 to 1987. (On May 20, 2019, Lori Lightfoot, was sworn in during the city's inauguration ceremony at Wintrust Arena. She became Chicago's first black female mayor.)

There was a South Side showplace, rebuilt in the mid-1980s, named the "New Regal Theater" in homage to the original, but it suffered from years of neglect and its future was a big question mark. So, when entrepreneur Jerald Gary bought the building, he planned to use holographic technology and encourage community involvement and investment. But even with these changes, the thrill of the original Regal disappeared.

My real love for show business started at the Regal Theater—seeing the shows and talking about all of the fantastic performances that we had just seen. That theater brings back some of the happiest times of my childhood. The sea of neighborhood kids, wall-to-wall kids; they were so excited, pouring out of their homes, racing down King Drive, trying to get to the Regal before show time. And then, when you got there, you were so concerned about getting a seat up front.

Every other Sunday, which was when the shows occurred, people would first go to church and then attend the performance. And it was like you were watching television. From the minute the show started, you couldn't keep your eyes off of the act on the stage.

And when we faced that stage, as I watched those entertainers, I thought, *I want to be up there. I want to be that.* I'd be wearing my fringed bell-bottoms and gym shoes—see, I was a pseudo-hippie, and of course, lots of fringe, I was fringed-out.

And there was even a soul food restaurant we could stop at before we went home. It was called Gladys's—it's no longer there now, but it served collard greens and chicken. Yummy. Everyone went to that soul food restaurant. I'm telling you, it was the best in the city. We would go to a show and then we would eat and talk about the acts, Aretha or Michael Jackson or whatever.

According to an NBC online report, the Bronzeville luncheonette, on 4527 S. Indiana, was demolished. In 1997, the original owner, Gladys Holcomb, couldn't run the "South Side institution" due to "failing health," but during its long run, Gladys's client list included Dr. Martin Luther King, Jr., Lou Rawls, Della Reese and Gladys Knight.

So, going to the Regal was a treat. Just watching those kids in droves trying to get to the show before it started made me happy. Oh, and the anticipation when the announcement came: "Tonight we're going to see Michael Jackson." Back then, Michael Jackson was just a kid. He was only eight.

Or "Tonight we're going to see Smokey Robinson," who was my idol. Smokey still is, because he's so cute. When I had my little girl group, I would sing "More Love." When I was growing up, Smokey Robinson was definitely my favorite one.

Now, I loved Diana Ross and all that, but when we used to slow dance with the boys, who we met at the basketball games and church dances, we never missed an opportunity to slow dance to Smokey. It was a beautiful theater, but the focal point was *who you came to see, who you came to hear.*

So many great acts came out of Chicago, like The Dells and Curtis Mayfield and the man with the deepest voice, Lou Rawls, who started singing with his church choir at seven, and for a spell, sang with Sam Cooke in the Teenage Kings of Harmony. His biggest hits were "You'll Never Find Another Love Like Mine" and "Lady Love."

The all-girl trio The Emotions had a hit with "Best of My Love" in the late '70s. They started out as a Gospel group, the Hutchinson Sunbeams, and it was through their association with songwriter/producer Maurice White of Earth, Wind & Fire that they found fame.

The Dells actually got started in Harvey, Illinois. In 1966, they opened for Ray Charles, enjoyed repeat standing ovations and got fired! A few years later, "There Is" featured the great baritone Marvin Junior, who was a major influence on Teddy Pendergrass—more about Teddy, later. I mean, this quintet had such soulful, soaring harmonies...

We lived about twenty blocks from the Regal. Back then, it seemed far to us kids, but it wasn't really that far away. Only a quick bus ride. See, the Regal was our Chicago Apollo.

The Apollo audience had a different set of expectations. They let you know immediately what they thought. One night, they booed entertainer Al Green. Now, he looked like he was dressed very gay or something. He was throwing roses into the audience and they booed him. I don't know why—he was singing so good.

But the Regal wasn't like that. People were so happy just to be in there during the great art of our day. Nobody ever booed. Now, there were tears and screams of "Ah!" but never that critical kind of reaction; it just wasn't that kind of vibe.

The concerts were mostly attended by youngsters unless your mom wanted to go with you, but my momma never went along. It was mostly kids that loved the The Supremes and Smokey. By the time the show was over (and there'd been six or seven acts that you wanted to see), they just wore you out and you were ready to go home. There was nobody waiting for autographs outside the stage door. I just wanted to go to Gladys's and get some soul food.

I spent time at the Tivoli Theatre on South Cottage Grove, too, which was one of the other beautiful Chicago theaters. My momma took us to see biblical movies like *King of Kings* and *The Ten Commandments* and *Ben-Hur*. I loved going to the movies. I was in awe of how architects designed such intricate theaters in those days. We'd sit there with our hot-buttered popcorn and take it all in.

You could look around, see the gold leaf in the ceiling, the colored marble and the ornate features engraved in the sides of the seats. The lobby had a painted ceiling, like the one that I'd later see at the Palace of Versailles. But like so many of the South Side treasures, the Tivoli was shut down in 1963 and then completely demolished.

Of course, times have changed. I'm telling you, I don't feel that same way when I go to the multiplex movie theaters these days, with their vending machines, boxy seats and processed snacks.

I had a number of favorite actresses and musicians when I was growing up, some of whom I got to meet when I got older.

Chaka Khan was one of my early inspirations. I knew her from watching Lock and Chain perform on the South Side, before she performed in Rufus. Now, we weren't bosom buddies—Chaka was older than I was when we met—I was still in school. We crossed paths early on when I dated a man named Finis Henderson, whose father managed Sammy Davis, Jr. and Lena Horne during the last fifteen years of their lives. Now, Finis opened for Chaka Khan when she was with Lock and Chain. I'll never forget those acts, or Chaka's range and soulful voice.

But we really got to know each other when Chaka first started her career because of a mutual friend, Gavin Christopher, a dedicated Rufus band member, who has now passed. Gavin told me that he and Chaka performed in Chicago a lot and encouraged me to drop by the shows.

Gavin wrote the funky 1975 hit "Once You Get Started" which appeared on Rufus's third album, *Rufusized* and co-wrote "Stars in Your Eyes," released on Herbie Hancock's 1980 recording of *Monster*. He was acclaimed for his rich vocals on "One Step Closer to You."

Gavin was like my big brother and my friendship with him didn't end then. When I ended up in L.A., Gavin told me that they needed someone to record a demo. I was in the studio and he asked, "Can you do this demo so Chaka can hear the structure?"

The song was "Hollywood." I did those background harmonies at the end. Chaka liked my part but ultimately redid all of the vocals.

Chaka used to come around years later when I was performing with Luther Vandross and sometimes sang a song with him, too. The reason Chaka influenced me from the beginning was because her voice was the voice of the time.

Now, Aretha's voice was incredible, and people tried to copy her all of the time, but then Chaka came along, and her voice was a little bit deeper and she could go high, too, so yes, she could do songs in a low voice and then go high.

I used to copy her low range because I was a second alto. Sometimes, I would take bits of her songs and use them. "Everlasting Love" was one of my favorites, but I used to copy all of her songs. Hers was the voice I used to emulate; I had real admiration for Chaka Khan.

And of course, since Rufus performed in Chicago a lot, I used to go to their gigs and say hello to Chaka whenever I could.

But another female star that I equally admired was the actress Marilyn Monroe. Ever since I was a kid and I watched her films, I admired her screen presence. Marilyn had this sweetness, this little girl quality about her, as well as the sensuality and the talent.

Critics tried to imply that she was stupid, but she was not. Marilyn was a brilliant comedienne. She was also so good at drama, like in *Niagara Falls*. And I just loved *Gentlemen Prefer Blondes*, *How to Marry a Millionaire* and all of those films where she was drop-dead sexy but also "little girl" sexy.

Jayne Mansfield seemed to be more of an "older woman" sexy. Both actresses were the same age yet Marilyn came off as, "I know I'm sexy," but it was never an offensive sexy. It was like a kitten and it was just wonderful.

I watched her perform and do the dance routines and sing the song "River of No Return," which was one of my favorites. I admired her professionalism on stage, especially the way she moved. She rehearsed all of the time and was always taking dancing and singing lessons, whatever. That's me. She was always trying to perfect her craft.

So, I dreamt about being someone like Marilyn Monroe when I got old enough to be in show business. In some of my photographs, I think, I captured a sexy, little girl quality like hers and I was really pleased to see that I'd done that. My admiration for Marilyn Monroe was amazing and I still love her so.

My mother instilled in me such a strength of confidence and purpose in myself that I never thought, *Oh, they're putting a white woman up there.* I saw Marilyn as a three-dimensional, vulnerable woman. It was her sincerity that made me love her.

Now, I might have had a little criticism of the black artists of the time because they were trying so hard to be accepted by the white community; they felt they had to be accepted in order to be happy.

I admired Marilyn for ethical reasons. When she saw injustice, she took action. For example, when Ella Fitzgerald wanted to perform at The Mocambo, the owners refused to hire her because she was black. At that point, Marilyn immediately stepped up.

"If you don't let Ella perform there, I won't ever perform there either," she reportedly said. "But if you let her perform, I'll come every night."

Then, Marilyn took a picture with Ella, hugging and kissing. That image touched me so much. I already knew Marilyn wasn't a person who was a racist, but when she said, "If you don't let Ella perform, I won't perform there either and bring all of those people," that gave me the extra love and respect for Marilyn Monroe that I still have.

So, Ella Fitzgerald opened at this West Hollywood, California nightclub on March 15, 1955, but only after Marilyn Monroe "lobbied the owner for the booking." (Wikipedia) The owner, Charlie Morrison, closed the club's doors in 1958.

Then there was entertainer Barbra Streisand. I know every word from the score of *Funny Girl*. I enjoyed singing along to all of the songs. In fact, I saw that film thirteen times. My mother would ask, "How many more times are you going to see that?" When I was a little girl, I'd go all by myself.

Barbra inspired me so much because she was kind of an ugly duckling. She wasn't really beautiful—I'm not saying I was an ugly duckling, but when I first saw her, I didn't realize that she was going to blossom into this beautiful woman that she became in the end.

There was something else about that story line in *Funny Girl* that stuck with me. The main character, Fanny Brice, was completely devoted to her love interest. I think that my idea— to follow David Bowie to Europe—was similar to the way in which Fanny Brice followed Nick Arnstein, after he told her he loved her. So, she's with the Ziegfeld Follies and just picks up and decides that she wanted to be with this guy.

All her friends said, "Why are you doing this?" and she just said, "Because I love him" and that's why I followed David, too. So, I kind of took a page out of that book when I was old enough and remembered that Fanny Brice did that for the guy she loved. And since David was one of the biggest loves of my life...

There was Barbra's pure talent—you saw the hunger she had and how much she wanted to get an Academy Award for this part, because she was just brilliant from beginning to end. She was such a professional; every arrangement was written out. I saw her bravado and that she wanted this so bad. She really impressed me so much when I was growing up.

My momma used to say that I could be a comedienne, too. Sometimes, I play the glamorous thing. I know how to do that, like when I was with Luther and when I was with David, but I know how to play the "Funny Girl," too.

In fact, right now, I'm thinking about studying "improv" with Second City, the Chicago-based acting studio that launched the careers of John Belushi, Gilda Radner and Eugene Levy.

I come up with stuff that's about life. You can only be funny when you experience life and you see those stories. I always considered myself that. I *can* be funny and Marilyn Monroe glamorous, too. I think of myself as a chameleon. I could be all of those things.

Doris Day was another one of my idols. At first, she was a dancer, then a singer. I loved her beautiful voice and the role she played in the comedy *Pillow Talk*.

Much later in my life, I'd look at Hollywood through a different lens.

Sammy Davis, Jr. was one of the greatest black talents, black or white. He could sing, tell jokes and dance. He was a full-spectrum entertainer, much like Michael Jackson.

At first, they tried to paint in our minds that Davis was a traitor, because he was working with Frank Sinatra. I didn't really know what to make of it, but I thought their working relationship was great. There were stories about Sinatra and Davis; they couldn't stay in the same hotels in Las Vegas and I did wonder about that. But it wasn't about Davis "trying to be white," it was about Davis being so talented, then meeting Sinatra, who really liked him, not only as a professional colleague, but as a friend. Sinatra used his influence, as a white entertainer, to help Davis move along in his career. I studied that. And Sinatra, like Marilyn Monroe, took a stand. He wouldn't perform at hotels where Davis wasn't allowed to stay.

There was so much Hollywood film footage that didn't include black people. For all these years, I never thought much about it one way or another, but now I am. We were definitely not treated fairly in Hollywood. We were left out of so many films that I loved. We had no rights, nothing in those days.

Now, I see at least one of us in everything and that's how it should be. I didn't realize how wrong things were until I was grown.

There were a few black actors that made it through back in the day, but they played the role of nannies and house servants, like Hattie McDaniel, who won the Academy Award for Best Supporting Actress as "Mammy" in *Gone with the Wind*.

Hattie McDaniel was the first black American to win an Oscar, but her success was bittersweet. The ceremony, held at the Ambassador Hotel, had a no-blacks policy, so producer David Selznick had to get special permission just so McDaniel could enter the room. These awards ceremonies started in 1929. Since then, 3000 awards have been given out, but only 43 black artists have come away with Oscars.

The first movie that I saw with an all-black cast was based on a musical. The 1943 film *Cabin in the Sky*, directed by Vincente Minelli and Busby Berkeley, featured singers Ethel Waters and Lena Horne. Duke Ellington contributed arrangements. The film suffered setbacks; some American theaters, especially in the South, refused to show films starring black performers.

But *Cabin in the Sky* was made about black people and for black people and it was beautiful. It showed folks dressed up and going to the clubs at night. That film gave us a chance to be seen as just regular people.

Another early inspiration? Those girl groups! In 1962, Patricia Holte, Sarah Dash, Cindy Birdsong and Nona Hendryx created magic. They were originally called The Odettes, but then the quartet changed their name to Patti LaBelle and the Bluebells. They stayed together for five years. Then, they branched out into solo careers, but Patti's range inspired new talent for decades.

Berry Gordy's "Motown Sound" was my biggest motivator. When I was a teenager, Motown was my heart. Gordon cranked out hits for The Supremes: Florence Ballard, Mary Wilson and Diana Ross. When the glam trio joined up with Dick Clark's *Caravan of Stars* on a cross-country tour, "Where Did Our Love Go" became a number one smash. In 1965, "Baby Love," "Come See About Me" and "Back in My Arms Again" followed. A year later, girls sang along to "Jimmy Mack." In 1967, "Nowhere to Run," well, that cast a more serious spell.

Now, that was an era with great songwriters. Lamont Dozier Holland, Brian Holland and Eddie Holland were hit-making machines who penned tunes for Martha and the Vandellas, like the sizzling "Love Is Like a Heat Wave" and "The Hunter Gets Captured by the Game."

But I was also a Beatles fan. They began their recording career by turning out covers originally recorded by black artists, like "Please Mr. Postman" for 1963's *With the Beatles*.

Recorded by The Marvelettes, "Please Mr. Postman" was first heard on American radio in 1961 and became the first No. 1 hit in Motown's pop history. The Beatles were inspired by other black acts, too, like Little Richard and Chuck Berry; they came up with great harmonies on their cover of his "Roll Over Beethoven."

I was a big, big Beatles freak. I loved "A Hard Day's Night" and "If I Fell in Love with You" and one day, I would love to redo "And I Love Her" in Spanish with flamenco guitar. Even though they used Spanish guitar on that arrangement, I would really like to make a version that is even more Spanish-sounding.

That ballad was so beautifully recorded. It made me feel sad, but good inside. I can't explain it. The Beatles really were a phenomenon that changed the face of how I listened to music.

Paul McCartney was my favorite Beatle in those days, but later on when David Bowie and I met him, I didn't feel he was very nice to David, so John Lennon ended up becoming my favorite. More about that later; John was so sweet when we recorded "Fame" and "Across the Universe."

The Beatles were a huge part of my early youth. We would be standing there huddled together in the school yard, singing Beatles songs. They made me feel special, I'm not sure what you call that feeling ...

On August 20, 1965, I was at a Beatles concert with Toni and a couple of friends in the nosebleed section at Comiskey Park. Even though we were far away, we could still see the boys moving down there, shaking their long hair. Of course, you couldn't hear anything because all of the girls were screaming and crying so loud. It really was mania.

Now, Comiskey Park, located on the South Side, was renamed Cellular Field in 2003. Older Chicagoans think of it as the home of the Chicago White Sox baseball team. In 1990, the "old" Comiskey Park was replaced with the new, obstruction-free stadium.

We played *Meet the Beatles* to death, until it was all scratched up. My momma used to bring home all of these incredible records and we would fall in love with her choices, because she had really good ones.

Of course, I grew to love rock and soul: Jimi Hendrix, the Stones, Led Zeppelin, Gladys Knight, Aretha Franklin, Chaka Khan, of course ... I became more obsessed with the solo artists, than the groups. Some of the Stones became my friends, as I will tell you later.

And years later, when I performed with David Bowie and Luther

Vandross, my parents were elated because I was finally realizing my dream. In her sweetest voice, my momma would say, "Ava, that was fantastic. You were really something." And my dad cried in the first row when he first saw me perform with David Bowie.

But what started me on the road to meeting David Bowie and performing with Luther Vandross was a perfunctory photo shoot with a world-famous photographer.

5.
BEYOND THE LENS:
STARTING WITH SKREBNESKI

Growing up, I was always aware that I was thin like my dad. That's why my momma would always let me get banana splits after school so I could gain weight. Toni was always meatier. I would sometimes think, *Maybe I'm not as attractive as other girls; other girls have more developed bodies.* But I began to notice that when I walked down the street, guys would say something positive to me.

So here I am, thinking that I was too thin, yet guys would try to hit on me when I passed them by. Maybe I'm not as thin as I thought, maybe I was attractive. They'd say, "How are you doing, cutie?" Sometimes they'd say, "Hey, Slim" or "Cute Slim" or something like that. They called me "Slim." I did know I had something, but I didn't exactly know what it was yet.

I thought, *I must be cute,* but I never dressed like other people dressed. I wore what I liked, what I wanted. If I wanted to wear blue lipstick, I'd wear blue lipstick. If I wanted to dye my hair purple, I'd dye my hair purple.

For some reason, I always had a sense of style. My hair was either blonde or short, so people got used to seeing me that way. I also cared about nutrition. I was always used to eating healthy. I never ate crap or drank a lot.

I think it's messed up when people are so serious about themselves. You have to allow for change. I started modeling and then I started developing and that's when I really began to see the beauty that I had. One thing led to another. I got to know a few photographers well and then I got interested in having my professional pictures taken. With Victor Skrebneski, I hit the jackpot.

Victor Skrebneski had been leaning toward a career in painting or maybe sculpture—he studied both mediums at the Art Institute, but after a friend gave him darkroom equipment, he got riveted by the rewards of photography. He had a mentor, Harry Callahan, at the Institute of Design, who persuaded him to show his innovative shots to New York magazine editors. His creativity and command of the camera impressed the editors of *Esquire* and others.

At that point, Victor was fully prepared to work on the East Coast, but after returning to the Windy City, he was besieged by assignments, especially for the then-named retailer Marshall Field's, which would later be bought by New York's premiere department chain, Macy's. His black-and-white posters for the Chicago International Film Festival are collector's items.

In 1952, Victor opened up his own studio in Chicago. Ten years later, he signed an exclusive agreement with the fragrance company Estee Lauder. His fashion photography subjects eventually included Cindy Crawford, Audrey Hepburn, Diana Ross and Hubert de Givenchy.

Victor greatly influenced young talent. I will always be grateful that he gave me my start. I was beside myself when I found out that he died at ninety-years-old on April 4, 2020.

For me, it all just fell into place. I called the studio one day and said that I wanted to get some test shots. Victor's secretary called back and said, "Let's see what you look like," and that was it.

So, the session mostly consisted of my getting these test shots, but I was fortunate to get these results. Victor did this picture of just my face—a close-up of my eyes, and then he solarized the photo. Although the pictures were taken in black and white, with solarization, they looked more like sepia.

After I saw what he did, I looked at myself in the mirror and thought, *Wow, I do have a really good bone structure.* That's when I became really fanatical about wanting to be a model. Nobody had ever taken a picture of me like that before.

Victor Skrebneski was a master, so he knew exactly how to tell me to move to get the picture he wanted. He'd say, "Chin up. Turn your face to the left. Move your body around just a little bit. Now turn around."

I loved when Victor told me to do different moves and I acclimated myself to it. I still remember exactly how I felt when he told me how to move. So, when I first started modeling, I was lucky enough to have help—photographers were guiding me as to how they wanted me to present myself.

Through the years, I took pictures with a million photographers. I can't remember all of their names, but Victor always stood out. He became famous, and because he was one of the first photographers who ever worked with me, he helped me gain confidence. After that experience, I knew I could model for other photographers who were less famous, but I always kept in mind that Victor was a great one. He set the bar high.

Victor set my career in motion. After working with him, I had the opportunity to work with photographers from all over the world, from London to Paris and Spain.

Like I said, I was really thin. I didn't start to gain weight for a long time. Some of the designers would give me their samples that were size one or three. I could wear them all. I had lots of clothes.

But now, I'm starting to get a little hippier after all these years because I'm taking after my mom, who had sexy hips. She was a little bigger than me. I always took after my dad, being super-thin, but now that I'm getting older I'm taking after my mother's shape.

6.
POLITICS, WOODSTOCK &
THE ROLLING STONES

I love glamorous movie stars and vocalists, but I've also been deeply affected by American politics. A strong memory of a particular event still sticks out in my mind. I was on my aunt Bessie's balcony—I used to spend a lot of time at her house on 52nd and King Drive, right across the street from Washington Park. We used to go there every holiday—my family would cook, but this time, Aunt Bessie specifically invited us for a parade—it might have been the annual Bud Billiken Parade. And that year, something incredible happened. While we were sitting out on that balcony, my mom looked out and screamed, "There's JFK!" We loved John F. Kennedy.

Much later, I'd be influenced by the turbulent politics of the times. A couple of guys from the neighborhood went to Vietnam. After they came home, they used to come to our house and have dinner. They acted very nice, but I could tell by their body language that they'd been through a lot.

One, in particular, really opened up. He told us about the horrors that he saw during the war. We found out a couple of months later that he committed suicide. I remember that incident touching me very much—I saw these boys going over there and just dying for nothing, for that useless war.

I cried when I heard he did that. I thought, *Wow, he was such a nice guy.* I'd had such long talks with him and then he did that. I guess that after you see so much horror, you can't handle it anymore.

Just like most of the people during that time, even though I was younger, I was thinking, *No war. Get out of Vietnam. We don't want to be there. It's not good.*

I wasn't unhappy with people who said that they weren't going to go and who ended up going to prison. I didn't see them as cowards; I saw them as, *Why go into a useless war? Why kill people or end up being killed?* A whole generation of our boys were getting killed off in Vietnam. I was very anti-war.

And then Woodstock touched me so much because I was like a mini-hippie. I was just making it to a teenager. All this love and black and white getting together and not dealing with race ...

I cried when Joe Cocker sang "With a Little Help from My Friends" because at the time that he did that song, it was just the right thing for him to sing. He took the Beatles' song, and I loved how they did it, too, but I love even more how Joe Cocker interpreted it. It was very emotional for me.

And all of the other artists there, like Richie Havens singing "Freedom." The people really meant it when they sang those songs. Woodstock was really about coming together as a movement. I just can't say how much it touched me.

Of course, I always loved the Rolling Stones. I met the Stones way, way back when I was with David; Mick Jagger, David, Ronnie Wood and I would hang out all of the time after David befriended Ronnie.

I remember talking to Keith when they were rehearsing for their Steel Drums Tour. Sitting at the breakfast table, we had the nicest conversation. Keith always knew what he wanted. He was a person who would say how he felt, especially when he felt very strongly about something. Charlie (Watts) was quiet and didn't say a whole lot but he was always nice. Mick was sexy and I really liked being around him.

About four or five years ago, the Stones invited me backstage. Lisa Fischer was singing with them so I asked her if she could get me a few tickets. She got a few and a backstage pass to their party—they give the most amazing parties before the show with food and drink and wine, the best screen, the best sound, the best stage. I really take my hat off to the Stones for having class and style.

I was walking down the hallway of the United Center and Ronnie and Keith were standing there as I was coming toward them. This was about an hour or two before the show, when they were having dinner backstage. They shouted my name and started putting their arms around me. It was such a nice feeling until I realized that the security people were staring at me; they'd never seen me before. They had no idea that I'd known the Stones for that long, more than twenty years since the time I'd been with David.

You don't know how that feels, when they greeted me that way. If you offend the Stones and they don't like you, it can be much different.

Some guy had just made Keith a beautiful new guitar. We were sitting there; Keith was playing. A crew was there shooting a documentary. Someone tried to push me out of the scene…

"Could you please, move?"

Keith had my back. "She doesn't have to move. You sit right there, Ava. This is my dressing room."

I had never felt so wonderful, and then after the show, they invited me back up. We listened to records. I think, American singer-songwriter Bobby Womack was there, too. They remembered me from the past and it was really nice. I'm looking forward to seeing them tour this summer.

Then my favorite act, besides Jimi Hendrix, was Led Zeppelin. Of course, The Rolling Stones are in my heart because every time I go to one of their gigs, I know every word to every song. Their songs are great; they have outlasted so many. Still, Keith's my main man.

7.
HUGH HEFNER'S HUTCH & FEMINISM

See, before I met David Bowie, I had already been around people who had money and who were successful. Eventually, I lived in the mansion with Hugh Hefner where all the parties occurred and where all the celebrities came. So, David Bowie was not the first person I met of that kind, even though when we met, I was still very young.

My momma still remembers how my interest in entertainment started: "Ava didn't walk around singing into a hairbrush like Ronnie Spector. Her first experience in show business was as a Bunny at the Playboy Club. I took her to her first open house."

What an experience that was! Who could have guessed that one day I'd shake the hand of the Shah of Iran at the Playboy Mansion?

I liked the vibe there and I'll always remember how I got a picture of my mother in her go-go boots. I had them on, too. Everybody always dressed cute like that. They had to be prepared in case they got picked for a show.

When I went to work at Playboy, I was sixteen-years-old. I want to stress that fact for a reason; it's why I wasn't stunned when I later met people like John Lennon. In fact, I was very comfortable because I'd already been around Warren Beatty and the other celebrities that used to come to the mansion. Now, I never revealed my real age at the time, but my parents were on board. They had always let me try new things.

My momma had already worked for Chicago's *Playboy* magazine in the corporate office for a couple of years, which is another reason why I was already familiar with the "Jet Set" and accustomed to that lifestyle by the time I became a Bunny and moved into the Playboy Mansion in the Gold Coast.

Before that, I met eighteen-year-old girls who kept telling me, "You have to come to the mansion. Hefner does dinner and a movie every other Sunday."

That's when I first started going there. And why Hugh Hefner asked: "You're here all the time. Why don't you move in?"

Hugh knew I was more innocent than most of the girls there who were more seasoned and that was fine. Hefner was doing whatever he did. He'd have people in town, like Warren Beatty, and they'd all be wanting to go to the Roman Baths.

But when I became a Bunny, I had my own set of issues. I was worried about my chest. The staff told me not to worry. I remember one time when they were trying to put me into a costume, they stuck a stocking into a really big hole in the outfit and it made whatever you had sit up properly. It made you look like you had breasts. Now, I always had a cute shape, but I just didn't have breasts, so I'll always remember the day I put that costume on; it looked cute and like I really had some cleavage.

Hef never pushed you to be in the centerfold or to be naked or anything like that. And sometimes the photographers didn't especially want you to be stark naked. They'd have me wearing something, though, because I didn't have big breasts.

I was a Club Bunny. The photographers took pictures of me topless and also took pictures of the back of me in hot pants. The only picture I have ever found, though, was the one in which I had those hot pants on. I do remember one photo of me with two ponytails on either side of my head. I looked like I was ten. But when I was in those situations, it was completely my choice.

The original multi-story Playboy Mansion was located at 1340 N. State Pkwy. in the very expensive Gold Coast area. Hugh Hefner, being the CEO of Playboy Enterprises, made the decision to relocate to Los Angeles in 1974 to oversee the "Playboy Mansion West," but kept the original Chicago building as headquarters until 2012.

Guests entered the lower-level grotto and swimming pool by fire pole; they could dive directly from the spacious, sunken living room into the bright, blue waters below. Besides lounging around the pool, they could gather in the steam room or play unlimited games of bowling.

"Live-in" bunnies bunked in the upper two floors and had to abide by specific rules: no male visitors and no unauthorized drinking on the premises. Whatever "Hef" offered in the way of libations, however, was fair game. While he was operating the controls of his circular bed, he could usually be found filing or flirting; there was a thin line between his work and play habits.

According to the official handbook, "bunnies" were given merits or demerits based on their social behavior and how expertly they applied their cosmetics, took care of their hair, nails, shoes and "bunny" costume. We had to be immaculate.

Visitors had their choice of four guest rooms, but the bunnies spent time in that communal living room, where sofas were propped up with lots of pillows and there was a big TV. In our free time, we played backgammon and pinball with friends.

Hef loved to play backgammon, too. Sometimes, I would just sit on the side and watch Hef play. Other times, we'd play together. I used to love playing backgammon with him. Once or twice, he even beat me at the game.

Later on, I'd be playing backgammon in L.A. I'd show up at the clubs and people would ask the very same thing, "Wanna play?" I'd answer: "Yeah. For $500." And that would pay my rent.

I loved Mr. Hefner. He was a wonderful man. I never once saw him get mad or scream at anybody. He was the kind of man who was nice to everyone and everybody loved him.

He would be so funny and so sweet. Sometimes, there would be about fifteen bunnies lounging in the sunken living room watching TV, and Hef would nonchalantly ask, "Say, does anyone want to have some fun tonight?" At the time, I thought, he meant, "Does anyone want to have fun with their lady friends?"

While he was playing backgammon, he'd casually look up from the board, and by the time he looked away from the board and back again, there would be five girls left out of the fifteen; not every girl in the house was into getting together with Hef's "friends."

Some of them just wanted the job, but Hef was never aggressive about these situations. He never pushed any of the girls. He would just throw the idea out there, like any man would, but sometimes, with a little more moxie. That's when Hef would push a button that would open a wall and reveal a bedroom. Now, you have to understand, this was really high tech for the time.

And the five girls that were left? That stayed? I'm telling you, those girls acquired property on State Parkway and were paid very well if they did get involved. They would become Jet Bunnies. Now, I was never in those scenes and Hef never made me feel as though I had to comply. He was always more like a big brother to me; Hef was not a bad person—he liked his women, though.

Nobody could complain that Hef was mean or unfair, is what I'm trying to say. Hef was a sweetie pie. I'll always miss him. As for me, I liked talking, but I wasn't interested in sleeping with any of his friends, either. I might have flirted, but that was it; what I'm stressing is that I loved Mr. Hefner. He was a wonderful man. I never ever saw him get mad or disagree with anybody. He might have been called a lech because he liked to make love to beautiful women but those women were very well taken care of. He never mistreated any of them. I never heard about any violence with any women there.

So, here I was living in the mansion with Hef where all the parties occurred and where all the celebrities came. Besides Warren Beatty, British singer Tom Jones was very nice, too. One of the bunnies, Stevie, really liked him. Downstairs in the grotto, they would often disappear. Like I said, the mansion was really spread out.

I was too young to be expected to identify all the celebrities who showed up. There was another actor in attendance who played a very famous character in a popular American film of that era.

Here's how we met. Sometimes I would stay up late and watch TV with the other bunnies, but other times, I'd be the only one in the living room, even though there were about 25 girls who lived in the house. There were certain times when they'd all be asleep, except for me. One night, when I was alone watching TV, the doorbell rang.

After I let the man in, he started playing the piano. He had an air of confidence. He was well-built with close-cropped, brown hair and dark, alert eyes. I walked over to the bench and quietly sat next to him. I was so curious about him that I finally blurted out, "Who are you? I know Mr. Hefner has people here from all over the world."

He politely introduced himself. "My name is James Caan. I'm an actor."

Then I asked him, "What are you acting in lately?"

He said, "I'm in a movie called *The Godfather*. I'm playing a character named Sonny Corleone, one of the Godfather's sons."

At the time, I didn't know anything about the book or the film, so I didn't know what he was talking about, but this seemed like a big deal, so I said, "Oh, wow." James sat down and continued to play piano beautifully and I stayed and talked to him for another minute.

Warren Beatty was especially friendly, too. Warren was so cute, so gorgeous, but also very sharp intellectually. I loved the way he used to speak because he had a very sexy voice. Once, when Warren came to visit, he and I ended up in a closet, kissing. Hef opened the door accidently, mumbled "Excuse me" and shut the door just as fast.

I wanted to be in *Playboy* because I actually thought the magazine was nice. I actually liked some of the articles in it. I thought the women looked sexy and beautiful. I did not look at the content as a way of promoting women-bashing, as many feminists of the day did. In fact, I felt that the magazine brought out my independence.

How did I feel about the feminist movement? As a young girl, I remember watching TV and seeing women burning their bras. I thought it was cool that they were talking about women's rights, for example, the right to take the pill.

Then, when it was time for me to wear a bra, I wasn't big-chested anyway, so it didn't matter very much, but I remember begging my mother to buy me one. When she did, I stuffed it with tissue paper and went out to play basketball. I jumped up toward the hoop and the tissue paper started spilling out of my bra. Everybody started laughing and I felt so embarrassed. At another period of my life, I didn't wear a bra for many, many years.

As I got older and more aware, I recognized that the feminist movement was all about freedom. My whole thing about growing up was freedom, women being allowed to do what they want to do, to be equal to men as far as jobs, and not feel they have to be subservient to a man.

As far as the "Me Too" movement? I'm glad to see women speak up who have been sexually abused, although I was never one of those people. I was ready to tell about whatever happened. If anybody tried to abuse me, I would be telling everybody.

Today, terrible things are happening at schools and kids are afraid. I don't understand somebody threatening to beat you up and saying, "I don't like your hair," or "You're ugly." Nobody ever called me that, but if they did, I would have said, "You don't look so great yourself." I was not afraid of some of the things that kids are afraid of these days.

I reserved the right to appear nude in the magazine if I wanted to. Like I said, we were all independent women. I used my career there as a vehicle and so by the time I started hanging out with people, like Stevie Wonder, I had already been hanging out with celebrities and stuff. The phenomenon wasn't new to me anymore and that advantage helped me a great deal with my future sense of confidence.

8.
SHE'S LEAVING HOME

David Bowie was born on January 8, 1947. His birth name was David Robert Jones, but when the American group The Monkees came to fame, featuring singer Davey Jones, David changed his name at the age of 18, as both men were young British idols and coveted by the press. The name change dispelled any future confusion.

I decided to leave Chicago and go to New York in the early 1970s. I nabbed a job at the Genesis Disco in Manhattan and got a job as a hair model. That's why, when I met David Bowie, my hair was cut short and blonde—I had been doing a hair show.

Before I left Chicago, I had been frequently exposed to people like that, but New York was set up so differently. It took a while to get used to the pace. I was excited about living there, but, of course, I didn't know what was going to happen in my new environment. I was counting on my modeling for Davian Hair Style, the salon that gave me the blonde hair, and what would be my signature image.

When I got to New York, I began dating a man named David Daines and staying in his apartment. As I started working in the nightclub Genesis and doing better, I got my own place on West 28th St. I was partying all of the time. I was going to the Garage every weekend and then there were the fashion shows and the "show" shows and always different concerts.

Genesis was no ordinary venue. It was owned by Hiroaki Aoki, the iconic Benihana restaurateur. As you can imagine, it was a high-scale establishment and served as an incredible people magnet.

One day, my manager excitedly took me aside and showed me an unusual album cover. He said, "I think this David Bowie is going to be huge. He's coming here to play at Radio City Music Hall for his first appearance in America."

I went home and listened and honestly, I fell in love because this music was so different from anything that I had ever heard before. I listened intently to the lyrics of "Moonage Daydream" and I liked that this artist was thinking about himself in second person, as an alien. It was fresh.

As far as possibly meeting David after just seeing his album cover and listening to his music, I was thinking, *How the hell am I meeting this guy*? I was so enamored. I was really over the moon about this whole thing.

I even started falling in love with his picture on the album cover but at that time I was not thinking that I would ever actually meet David Bowie.

9.
STEVIE WONDER
SETS OFF SEARCH FOR BOWIE

Remarkably influential in her career, Stevie Wonder stands as one of Ava's
favorite all-time performers. Here's their backstory.

I can't emphasize enough the importance Stevie Wonder has played in
my career. I met Stevie in L.A. through a mutual friend, a young lady
named Coco. In fact, we were best friends, and at the time I met Stevie,
they were dating. She'd say, "Stevie's doing a session tonight. Do you want
to come along and listen?"

I'd smirk. "Yeah. Are you kidding?"

"Ribbon in the Sky," "Tell You a Story," "Innervisions," "Love in Need,"
"My Cherie Amor," "Isn't She Lovely"... To me, Stevie said so much about
the heart. In his songs, he sang and expressed so many things that I felt
about life. He put me in different moods, moods that I wanted to be in.

I heard a lot of songs from *Innervisions* and as I started going along
more and more, Stevie started liking me as a person. Whenever he would
give a concert, he would invite me. We never did a recording together,
although he would ultimately be very influential as far as my working with
David.

Plus, he was always a good friend. Later, when I was with Luther
Vandross, Stevie came to so many gigs that Luther began asking, "Why is
Stevie always asking for Ava?"

For example, I'd be in a dressing room getting ready to perform. I'd
hear from the crew, "Luther wants to see you in the dressing room." Stevie
would already be in there, smiling at me.

Stevie Wonder was one of the first people to persuade me to work with
David. I'll always remember our conversation. Stevie had asked, "So, you're

going to Europe to find this guy, David Bowie?"

"Yes," I replied, with some hesitation. "But Stevie, should I work with David Bowie? It's a rock act." Being such an intuitive man, he could probably sense my uncertainty, but he assured me that I was heading in the right direction. Later, I would face considerable roadblocks…

But before that happened, Stevie and I got together in New York. Stevie was the most incredible organist; he'd make that instrument sing at Carnegie Hall. His shows were incredible because he had so much energy. Since he was playing there at the time, he suggested that we have an after-party. But where? Finally, we agreed. "How about this place Genesis?"

Stevie's was one of the most incredible concerts I'd ever seen. Carnegie Hall was so packed that you couldn't even stand. The audience loved the performance, too, and Stevie received standing ovation after standing ovation after every song. He was really interacting with the fans. As the concert came to an end, everyone felt really happy that night.

Fortunately, I wasn't very far away from the stage. A band member mentioned that I was there; Stevie shouted out to me. He was excited, knowing that the after-party was definitely going to happen…I'll always remember his warm and exciting acknowledgment from the stage.

So, there we were in New York, with Stevie playing Carnegie Hall that same week that I met David, who was playing at Radio City Music Hall. Little did I know the importance that these two talented men would play in my future life.

After Stevie conferred with his people, all the plans fell smoothly into place. I was so excited. And of course, after the show, all we really wanted to do was party. That night, Stevie was already standing out front greeting people and hugging them by the time I arrived. When he heard my voice, Stevie smiled and excitedly purred, "Hello, Ava."

In walked Aretha Franklin and then Gladys Knight, Peabo Bryson, Marvin Gaye and every major act, every R&B act you could think of, they were down there. We were all down there. Someone started singing this song. I started singing it, too, but at first, only to myself. Soon, everyone in the club was singing along.

My manager rushed over and said, "Ava, guess who's here?" My heart jumped into my throat. I'd been thinking about David so much over the last month or two, but meeting him? Now, that was another thing altogether.

My manager said, "I'm going to get him," and I instinctively held up my hand and said, "No, no, no," but before I could catch my breath, he brought over David, who had just finished performing. I could barely keep from staring at his dazzling blue eyes and matching suit, not to mention his carrot-colored hair.

David said, "How do you do?" I said, "How do you do?" David said, "It's very nice to meet you. Oh, I love your hair. It's kind of like me, huh?" I said, "Yeah, kind of like me." We laughed.

So, what initially made David and I click, I believe, was the hair. Of course, my manager had been talking about this phenomenon all along. Like I said, my short hair was bleached already because of the insistence of my then-boyfriend, who owned Davion Salon. He was in Britain, where they were doing this big project for the *New York Times* about ethnic girls flaunting bleached, blonde hair. They'd asked me if I would bleach my hair and keep it short-cropped specifically for the article, which, of course, I did.

So, yes, it was my hair that David was initially attracted to, plus the fact that I'd been standing there singing with Stevie Wonder, Gladys Knight and everyone else who was dressed-to-the-nines at the party. Given the circumstances, it certainly was no surprise that David asked me, point-blank:

"Are you a singer?"

Now, I wasn't a professional singer, but I *was* a singer, so I enthusiastically nodded yes.

David smiled at my response and continued to captivate me with his impeccable British accent. He told me about his new album, *Aladdin Sane*, and more about his upcoming tour in Japan. Then excitedly, he said the words that would ultimately change the course of my life:

"I have something you might be interested in."

Would I like to be a backup singer for the Japan tour?

Fortunately, I wouldn't have to make a snap decision, he'd be around for a while; David was staying nearby at the Gramercy Park Hotel.

"Let's have dinner tomorrow. I'll introduce you to my manager, Tony Defries," he insisted. *What?* The vocal audition would mean singing in front of David's then-backing band, The Spiders from Mars, so I was already feeling nervous.

But that didn't stop me from enjoying myself at that after-party; in fact, I partied like it was 1999 and it wasn't even 1999 yet! But after the after-party, all I wanted to do was decompress. I went home to my apartment exhausted but understandably elated.

As far as meeting David Bowie after just seeing his album cover and listening to his music—I was overwhelmed. I whispered again and again to myself, *How the hell am I meeting this guy?*

When we went to dinner the following night, the elegant place setting and food were the last things on my mind. I felt completely transfixed by David's mannerisms and good looks. He didn't seem to notice anyone else in the room either; he offered me his undivided attention.

Afterwards, David whisked me away to a small, popular nightclub, (maybe the Blue Note). We went there to see jazz pianist Charles Mingus. The show was really wonderful, even though I had no idea who this Charles Mingus was. David simply said, "We're going to see this legend."

We stayed overnight at the hotel, but believe me, what I was feeling wasn't just lust; it was love. I was so impressed with the whole experience,

with David opening the door for me and offering me his undivided attention. He was a real gentleman, very much on his p's and q's. He was so sweet and interesting. I had never met anyone like him in my entire life.

At this point in his career, David had finished recording *The Rise and Fall of Ziggy Stardust and The Spiders from Mars* and had come to America to promote the album. He'd also moved on to *Aladdin Sane*, the album with that striking thunderbolt face on the cover. He was still considered a rising star, but one that really radiated excitement.

No matter how much we talked, there was so much more to discuss. Curious about my reactions to *Ziggy*, David leaned his thin fingers against a cheekbone as he held my gaze. He was anxious to know, "What's your favorite song on the album?"

I laughed to myself. *After wearing out the needle by hearing the album so many times, why hold back?* I knew every single song by heart. But how could he have known that?

I replied, "Moonage Daydream" and watched David's eyes sparkle in the dim light.

Finally, David revealed more about his plan: "Tomorrow let's meet at the Sound Stage at RCA. I'll introduce you to my manager, Tony Defries. He has to give me the okay so you can join the tour." Everything *was* happening way too fast. I couldn't imagine what was coming next.

****

This glam rock recording, Ziggy Stardust and the Spiders from Mars, *co-produced by Ken Scott and David and recorded at the now defunct (as of 1984) Trident Studios, was released on June 16th, 1972, in the U.K. The cover photo taken by the aptly named Mick Rock shows the rising star with a guitar slung low over one shoulder. He's got an elbow resting on a raised knee. He's on London's Heddon St. Alley, where fans, even today, try to recreate the urban scene.*

Dressed in what looks like denim, he gazes out into the distance; perhaps to take in the industrial expanse. Inches away sit assorted earth-toned crates. But the most imposing feature is the big, brick warehouse that the rock star leans up against and the sign "K. West" which would inspire a host of inquiries. A circular black plaque inscribed with the album name and date sets in stone where the iconic shoot took place.

It had only been a year since Hunky Dory *had come out. David Bowie and The Spiders from Mars now needed songs that would stun a live audience. This new album was a stretch, centered around an androgynous bisexual, the fictional Ziggy Stardust, whose thoughts and feelings were supposed to resonate with extraterrestrials.*

There are lots of theories about who inspired the Ziggy persona. Some say he was a composite of Iggy Pop's attitude and Lou Reed's otherworldly discography. Or was it the Japanese fashion designer, Kansai Yamamoto? He was responsible for seven of David Bowie's most outlandish costumes. Some people pointed out vocalist Vince Taylor because he had these delusional thoughts after having a nervous breakdown. After that, he struggled with this alien/earthling issue.

I was stoked and intrigued by the slender character on the album cover and the unusual lyrics on the eleven tracks. I think David could see right away that I was a straight-shooter, someone who could play the role of the runway model, but also, someone he could count on for the truth. Our connection had been immediate and I believe he valued my opinions.

The Gramercy Hotel, now considered a rock 'n' roll haven, has hosted over the years the likes of Mick Jagger and Bob Dylan, and later the Clash, Bob Marley and Madonna.

On David's previous American tour, he and his entourage enjoyed the ambience of the higher-tiered, posh Plaza. But this time around, RCA Records had held back—there were no guarantees that this tour would result in more money.

David rented a lower, three-story apartment mainly because he had a fear of heights. He must have longed for seclusion after fielding smoke machines and elevated stage sets at his sold-out Radio City Hall concert, on Valentine's Day, 1973, where his audience included Salvador Dali, Truman Capote and Andy Warhol.

On the romantic front, I was headed for the first of many roadblocks. When David and I first met in New York, I fell in love with him, but at that time, I didn't know about his situation. I had no idea. I found out the hard way.

We'd spent the night in the Gramercy Hotel room, luxuriating in our private world, but the next morning, a stranger strolled in. I immediately tensed up. She didn't react the way I would have in that same situation. In fact, she casually brushed away her hair, kissed me on the cheek and whispered, as if we were lifelong friends,

"Hello, darling."

What? After an awkward silence, David quickly pulled me aside. Five soul-crushing words stumbled out of his mouth. "This is my wife, Angie."

I was stunned. David shrugged, mumbled yeah, and explained that he and Angie had an "open marriage." I'd figure out soon enough how common open marriage was during this era, but at that time, I didn't know what the hell it meant.

But by then, I was so in love that there was no way I could end it. Of course, if I had known initially about David and Angie's open marriage, I wouldn't have gotten involved. Their open marriage would eventually dissolve in the 1980s, but during my time with David in the 1970s, the die had been cast. Angie and I would consistently cross paths again, and "open marriage" or not, I'll always remember the discomfort I felt.

To David, his marital status was no big deal. He was more concerned about using Angie as a sounding board for his logistics. In front of us both, he casually announced, "Angie, I'm going back to London tomorrow."

That brief explanation might have satisfied Angie, but for me, that statement was just not enough. *What had I gotten myself into?* I had no choice but to confront David directly.

I braced myself. This was uncharted territory. But even at my young age, I knew there'd be no point playing games.

My voice trembled. "David, why didn't you tell me you were married?"

David turned his face away. "It isn't a big deal. I care about her, but... I'm not in love."

But I *was* in love. I had to face the truth; I had no choice but to let it go...

I'd also gotten some good news, though. When I met with the members of The Spiders from Mars—Mick Ronson, Trevor Bolder and Mick "Woody" Woodmansey. they had asked me to sing a few songs of my own choice. To my surprise, their manager confirmed his approval.

"That sounds great. You're in." David said. His plan was miraculously coming together, or so I thought.

David and I decided we would meet in a month's time. I definitely had a lot on my plate. I had to go back to Chicago to say goodbye to my parents. I also had to quit my job at Genesis and let go of my apartment. But logistics aside, I was so happy.

So, David got me set up waiting for the tour and then left. Before he did, he promised, "We're going to send you the record so you can listen to it. We'll get you tickets. Everything will be waiting for you. Then we'll go." All the words I wanted to hear…

Of course, I immediately got busy preparing for the tour. But not too long after our meeting, the doorbell rang and I was handed a telegram. It was from David Bowie's camp. I figured the telegram contained last-minute details. I eagerly tore the telegram open, but when my eyes skimmed the page, my throat tightened.

Ava, I'm so sorry but we have to cancel the tour. David is ill. We're so sorry for any inconveniences, but we'll keep in touch.

We'll keep in touch! Oh, no. I felt paralyzed. I started crying. I could not believe they cancelled the tour. I had turned my life upside down and now this. There I was, back in Chicago. I really didn't know what I was going to do. I was just hysterical.

People wonder about what I did next, whether I was being impulsive or even a little crazy. When I look back though, I realize that I had felt such a strong calling to David at that time, even though we had only spent a short time together. I didn't have any doubts about my feelings. I don't know why. Even when I was discussing the plan with my mother about going to find him, I remember saying, "I love him and he loves me. I have to find him. I know he didn't do this on purpose."

But at that time, I pored over the entire message repeatedly, thinking that perhaps I had misread it, but reading it over made everything feel worse.

We're going to reach back out to you but David has a really bad case of the flu.

I really didn't know what to do at first, but then I believed that what happened was fate and after that point, I never wavered. I never thought, *Maybe I shouldn't do this.*

The pull, that calling, was so fierce, that I knew exactly what I had to do, and when I look back, I know I would do it all over again. For love.

10.
BEYOND THE EAST COAST
& ACROSS THE ATLANTIC

I had an idea. In New York, I had met Heinz, this Swiss-German man, who had invited me to come to Monaco for the summer. He was a lot older than me, and I wasn't attracted to him, so I had turned him down at the time of the offer, but after the telegram came, the wheels started turning. I knew I had to switch gears. I thought, *I have got to find David. He really messed things up for me and I have to tell him this.*

Nothing could stop me. I told my momma, "I'm going to go to Monaco. I'm going to go there and spend the summer with Heinz and then find David."

Luckily, Heinz sent me money. I only had $200 in my pocket, not nearly enough to function in such an expensive city, but I was determined. Monaco was my very first introduction to Europe. I held my breath when I first spotted the beautiful landscapes from the compact airplane window; the view was like something out of a dreamy fairy tale. Monaco turned out to be the most incredible place I had ever been with the most beautiful people…

To my astonishment, I even met the charismatic actor Omar Sharif at a party. He was well-known for starring in *Lawrence of Arabia* (1962), *Doctor Zhivago* (1965) and, of course, my favorite movie, *Funny Girl* (1968).

Now, although this principality had a gorgeous setting, Monaco took some getting used to because everybody I encountered was super rich and very snooty. But fortunately, I remained grounded. I had taken David's record with me. I played *Ziggy Stardust* all day long because I was "vibing" on David. In fact, I would go into this trance every time I put that record on. I thought, *If only I could get closer to David by vibrating towards him.*

Of course, when Heinz dropped by he wanted to know why I was playing that record all the time. *What had I gotten myself into now?*

Fortunately, Heinz had a female friend who was always around so I felt comfortable confiding in her. One day, I took her aside. I had to get some sound advice.

I got straight to the point. "Listen, I like Heinz, but I don't feel I can give him what he wants."

Remarkably, she didn't judge. In fact, she understood. "I have an apartment here in Monaco, too," she said. "You can stay there." I exhaled. That response was fine with me.

Heinz still had access to me, though, because he and his friend were really tight. When I told him how I felt, he couldn't contain himself. He was furious. At that point, I was absolutely sure that it wasn't going to work like this.

I explained that I really wanted to find this person, David Bowie. Heinz finally broke down and said, "Just go to Saint Germain. All the celebrities go there." He gave me 500 francs and I immediately made plans to go to Paris.

Visiting Saint Germain du plait and Café de Flore (on 172 boulevard Saint-Germain) turned out to be very sound advice. Café de Flore is one of the oldest coffeehouses in Paris. You can sit there by the hour, nurse your drink and watch the high-profile parade. I was immediately taken with the beautiful, stylish French women.

Then, I checked into the "all-women's" hotel; this kind of accommodation was very common in Paris at that time. I had my model book with me and was ready to face this new city head-on. As it turned out, Heinz had given me good advice when he'd said, "Just go there and meet people," and that's exactly what I intended to do, despite being alone.

So, I made plans to frequent Café de Flore. Now, I had no trouble conversing in French, but I did feel a little overwhelmed, hearing nothing but that language day after day, until finally, I heard a familiar sound.

When I raised my voice over the chatter, I barely expected a reply.

"Does anybody here speak English?" I ventured, nervously.

This gorgeous, beautifully dressed guy answered. I knew he was gay. He excitedly explained that he worked for an exclusive Italian designer, Nino Cerruti, who founded his own house of couture in Place de la

Madeleine in Paris in 1967.

The Cerruti Line was renowned for its collection of wool suits and in the late 1970s the company branched out into the world of fine fragrance. This elite brand had far-reaching effects. Later on, in the 1980s, American cinema stars Al Pacino, Julia Roberts, Jack Nicholson and Sharon Stone would wear Cerruti designs. I couldn't believe my luck!

He formally introduced himself as "Joselyn," looked me over as he spoke and pumped me for details. "What are you doing here?"

"I'm a model," I explained. "I came to Paris to find David Bowie. I heard that sometimes he comes to Paris." Then, I got straight to the point. "I want to work. I need a modeling agency."

Joselyn responded warmly. "I'll help you. You can stay in my house. I'll get you a modeling agency."

Joselyn took care of me for eight solid months. He made sure I ate. During that time, I even made a little money. He and my new colleagues at the agency gave me the nickname "Velvidoe" because I reminded them of a velvet doe with my big, brown eyes and long lashes.

But four months into my living situation, I realized that Joselyn may have had an ulterior motive. See, he had a romantic partner who was an actual baron. He was a classy guy with beautiful curls who lived in the French countryside.

Joselyn forewarned me that he had something on his mind. He'd been waiting for the right moment to ask me a very personal question.

At that time, he chose his words very carefully:

"Ava, we were wondering if you would have a baby for us. We would pay you and take care of you."

So, all along, they were hoping that I'd give them a baby, as if I would sacrifice my figure for that purpose!

Now, that would have been some beautiful baby, but here's what I ended up telling Joselyn:

"I'm not really interested in having a baby. But I don't mean to be disrespectful. You really helped me."

From that point on, Joselyn acted a little bit upset. Our relationship would never be as warm. I was flattered in one sense, that this attractive couple would want me to be the mother of their child, but that wasn't something I wanted to do or be at that time. All I was trying to do was find David Bowie! And I'm thinking, *Honey, I don't got time to have no baby. I got to find David.*

Meanwhile, the agency took hold of my American passport. I started working feverishly in Paris for *French Vogue* and *Paree Match*. I also worked for Jacques Patout, one of the biggest houses in France, and where I wore some of the most expensive clothes, like Versace. And Yves St. Laurent Agency even let me use one of their gowns when I went to a Diana Ross concert in Paris. The press took pictures of me in this beautiful, gold dress. They didn't really know who I was—but I *was* somebody new and I had this fabulous dress on.

Diana and I were standing right next to each other on the carpet. Although I was relatively unknown, shots were taken of both of us. So, yes, before I was even known, that kind of thing happened. Years later, when I was with Luther, Diana would get prime seating at our shows and those precious memories would resurface.

My modeling career was taking off but my heart was still heavy. I was still searching for David Bowie after eight months and the alarming thought occurred that maybe I won't ever find him.

But there is always a part of me that refuses to give up. After all, I had already enjoyed such good karma. One day in a club at the bar, I heard excited murmurs. DAVID BOWIE. DAVID BOWIE. I was sure, I heard his name in these foreign conversations. Again, I raised my voice above the whispers.

"David Bowie? *Oui? Excusez-moi, savez-vous* David Bowie?"
"*Oui*. David Bowie's over at Chez Castel on 15 Rue Princesse."

What? I was dressed nicely, but not nicely enough to be seen in the multi-leveled disco Chez Castel. When I reached my destination, I stood face to face with my reflection on the glass-encased stairway leading down to the dance floor. Nervously peeking down from the top, I spotted David's animated bodyguard, Stuart George, more commonly known as "Stuey," facing forward protectively, definitely blocking David's eyes from mine.

My patience had clearly paid off. I ventured down the stairs. Stuey looked surprised, but was grinning, as he walked toward me and welcomed me as if I were an age-old friend. I could tell that he was happy to see me, but not so sure that David would feel the same way.

"Ava, what are you doing here?"

"I came to find David."

"The guvner's going to be really glad to see you," Stuey said confidently.

"I hope so."

Stuey grabbed me by the hand. And then, David spotted me standing there. My heart lodged in my throat as I waited for a reaction.

"Ava, what are you doing here?" David slowly asked.

I did not stand on ceremony. This was the moment I had dreamed about. Cried about.

"I came to find you," I stammered. "I can't believe you cancelled the tour. I *had* to find you."

David looked astonished. I still couldn't gauge his mood. *Had I come all this way for nothing?* I sucked in my breath. My palms felt clammy; the room radiated heat. *Was my mascara running?*

David's blue eyes sparkled as he took my hand. Then, he grinned playfully and said, "You crazy girl!"

The fact that I had made this pilgrimage half-way around the world just to find David had aroused his curiosity. I was finally able to let my guard down. We got along like a house on fire...

Although I felt once more like we were the only two people in the universe, reality hit. We were still in a crowded club. The diamond-studded woman next to him was freaked out by my sudden appearance. Judging by her outfit, I guessed that she was incredibly rich. She probably thought David was going to go home with her, but lucky for me, he didn't seem too concerned about meeting her expectations. Impulsively, he grabbed my hand. As we headed toward the exit, he murmured "Let's go" without looking back.

We spent the most fantastic night in Paris, trying out gourmet treats from sidewalk cafes, watching the water sparkle on the River Seine, and cozying up in a romantic suite under a vintage chandelier at the Hotel Plaza Athenee on 25 Avenue Montaigne, just a stone's throw from the Eiffel Tower.

Paris, that's the city in which to be in love—yet all the time I kept pinching myself. *I can't believe that this is happening!*

David was drinking red wine, just a split, as it was the pre-drug period, because when you're coming off cocaine, it's an entirely different story. At this point, you really saw the person that he truly was, the pre-celebrity David Jones.

Paris was so much more beautiful, to me, when David and I were in love. He made love to my brain. His personality, then, was very calm and settled. That's what made me fall in love with him.

Now, one of my own strengths was to reel people into my personality—I was street savvy and always nice to people; David could be warm, too, but sometimes he'd recoil in public.

I mean, David loved people, but he was conservative when he was out in public. A couple of times when people started running up to him, he recoiled a little bit. He had a bit of an attitude about people coming up and showing their affection, so I'd be his radar.

I would gently pull him aside and whisper, "They love you, David." They wouldn't always jump out aggressively; sometimes they'd just say, "Oh, David!" And he learned to relax a little bit when that happened.

Once, we got out of a limo and he found himself surrounded by fans. I reminded him, "David, they love you." I made him appeal to his softer side.

Then again, there were so many things that he taught me, too. Once at a party with Andy Warhol, where I was decked out in my favorite Chinese silk outfit, I got drunk so fast on champagne that I started wavering. David quietly pulled me aside; his eyes filled with concern.

"Babe, you're getting pretty high. You don't want to wake up with that photo in the press tomorrow, do you?" he cautioned. "You're with me." I understood his concern. I never drank at a party again.

David's artistic influence on me was also tremendous. He was an intellectual, which I wasn't, at that time. Once, when he introduced me to the film *Metropolis* by Fritz Lang he simply said, "Sit down and learn something."

David definitely helped me broaden my musical horizons. He turned me on to Vivaldi's *Four Seasons*, which I thought was so very beautiful. David was protective of me and always mindful, even when we were onstage, that he could teach me how to be a better performer. He was a progressive thinker.

But then again, he had this old-school side; he'd be playing with dinosaur video equipment. Those days still stick out in my mind.

Despite outside pressures, our relationship deepened. David was always very affectionate toward me. There were moments in public in which he'd be holding my hand, or he'd gently put his arm around me.

I had been brought up to be very tactile, with a lot of touching and with a lot of physical affection. I don't know if that is how David had been brought up, but when I would hang out with him, I'd be very affectionate and he returned it.

Once I started hanging out with him and touring, I was in bed with him every night. After dinner, we had a lot of quality time together. It wasn't like a conventional relationship when we were together—I always had my own place, but I spent most of my time wherever David was.

David had a certain persona in front of his peers, like in front of the Stones, and more specifically with guitarist Ronnie Wood. One time, we went to a party with Bob Dylan and a whole bunch of his peers. That's when David would show his very intellectual side; his very classy English side.

The only person I knew that David would act silly with was Ronnie Wood. That relationship was unique. They'd be joking and laughing. They used to love to watch the British TV program *Monty Python*. I knew every word of the Marilyn Monroe sketch (co-written by Graham Chapman and Douglas Adams).

"Marilyn, did she go down to Malibu?" And then, there was the lobster skit. There were some really funny skits that the actors used to do and we laughed through them all.

So, Ronnie would be that person with whom David would act the silliest—he was David's first link to the Stones. But David had a lot of respect for Mick Jagger, too, and Mick might have felt that same way, that they were doing something that was important in terms of pop culture.

There may have been some boundaries that I didn't know about, but I could see that they all had a healthy respect for each other, and they treated me as someone worthy of being in the coveted, inner circle. Not everyone in the entertainment world would treat me with such kindness. In fact, my resilience would be tested again and again. I would come face-to-face with a series of debilitating circumstances.

11.
CHATEAU: AVA CHERRY
& THE ASTRONETTES

L ater on, when David would be coming down from cocaine, his personality would change. But around this time, he was just regular citizen David Jones, like I imagine he would have been with Iman, his wife of so many years.

Before David went back to London, he turned the topic to business: "I want to record you," he said. His manager would be around in two weeks. We would get to work then.

But at that point, there was a communication problem. I didn't have access to my own phone line. The only phone line David could call me on was my modeling agency phone. A week passed and I didn't hear a word from David or his camp. A couple of weeks turned into a couple of grueling months.

I busied myself with the preparation of the *pret-a-porter* fashion show where I was employed as a runway model. ("*Pret-a porter*" is the French buzz word for factory-made clothing sold in standardized sizes, as opposed to "bespoke" attire which is designed for a specified frame.)

I was getting homesick, too. I had kept in touch with designer Lester Hyatt, and then one day I saw him walking down the street. "My God, my friend," I cried. I screamed and jumped up and down. Lester ended up staying for a week. He was also one of the people I would eventually run to when David and I broke up. He would be there to take care of me.

I still have one of Lester's leopard one-piece outfits from about forty years ago. It's hanging in my closet and it's still like new. Like I said, I never had to buy clothes. I could always fit into the samples.

When I called the studio in Deauville one day to find out about David's whereabouts, I ended up speaking to Mick Ronson. He informed me that David was scheduled to record *Pin Ups* in Deauville, outside of Paris, but was still in London. *When would I see him?* Mick promised he'd let me know, but that's not what happened.

Meanwhile, in the course of my day-to-day work at the agency, I befriended other models. We always looked forward to catching up with each other whenever we had some downtime. There was the typical industry talk, but one conversation really stood out. In fact, this conversation was a life-changer—with my hopes still high, I confided to a new girl I met at a modeling job that I might work with David Bowie.

"Are you serious?" she gasped. "I'm in love with his best friend, Geoff MacCormack."

"What? You're going out with Geoff?"

Her eyes lit up. "Yes. He's going to pick me up."

It was eventually Geoff who lit the way by suggesting, "Let's go to Deauville and surprise David."

My trip to the Chateau in Deauville was serendipity. I ended up there because after Geoff greeted me and asked, "What the heck are you doing here?" he devised that plan of taking the train to Deauville. Of course, we both agreed that "David's going to freak out."

Geoff explained that David was not a big fan of flying; he preferred sharing expensive appetizers with his friends during lengthy train journeys—he'd sun himself on the deck of a cruise liner, rather than take the plane.

When David and I reunited, our conversation began with the familiar question:

"Ava, what are you doing here?"

When he asked, I stood tall. I didn't waver. I had to set things straight.

"You told me in Paris that you were going to call me. I didn't hear from you. You've got to stop doing this to me because I find you every time," I asserted.

"This will never happen again, darling," he promised, squeezing my hand.

And during that time in France at the Chateau, I started doing demos. There might have been one song that we ended up doing with the Astronettes, but I was mostly singing on tape by myself. That's what happened when we recorded *Ava Cherry and The Astronettes*.

This was David's plan. "You could be 'Ava Cherry and the Astronettes.'" The other two-thirds of the vocal trio were Geoff and Jason Guess. We recorded "I Am a Laser," which would ultimately be released by Ava Cherry and The Astronettes in 1995. Later, many critics and fans would consider The Astronettes project a precursor to *Young Americans*.

Singer Ian Hunter (formerly of Mott the Hoople) once described David as "one of the few people who can walk in and there is magic in the room. He has a very inquisitive mind, he's fast, and you feel that the guy knows more than you do so you put yourself in his hands."

My vivid daydreams about show business and romance coming together were finally being actualized. And the songs were taking on a more passionate meaning.

In this case, the raw vocal hook was about "burning." There were crashing cymbals, an infectious beat and this sultry, spoken-word bridge. They all fused together to form an intense narrative.

In the studio, David wanted the tracks to sound very "rocky." On the track "I Am a Laser," he told me exactly how he wanted me to sing. He definitely wanted the rock age to come through loud and clear, and I believe it did. I can't even say I was nervous because I was too much in awe of what was going on. David was intending to add more songs eventually; this studio recording was only meant to be a demo, not a finished project— the rest would be completed in England.

David's manager eventually released it, however, as a finished project, even though the tracks had deliberately been kept in a vault. The material had obviously been tampered with and the contents included that master of *The Astronettes*. A big gap of time would occur before we finally finished up this project.

Still, I learned a lot about David's perspective on making records. As a producer, he was very professional and very nurturing. The whole process was really fun. And all along I was thinking this, I met this guy who I loved and he was helping me with my career. We were together. That made me happy. We were doing things; I wasn't concerned about the future.

When we did an actual recording session at the Electric Lady Studio in New York, Harry Maslin was the chief engineer. It was just like any other day in the studio. We had a goal. We were there to record "Fame" and "Across the Universe"; the final mix was proof that we had rehearsed well.

The bottom line is, I never felt up in the air with David in the studio. I know some producers play games or try to control an artist, but David always explained exactly what he wanted me to do on my vocals. Ultimately, the engineers sped up the tape and created a really original track.

Now, at the time, I wasn't fully aware of David's commitment to the *Pin Ups* album, but I was excited that he had expressed a strong interest in working with me. When he enthusiastically said, "I want to do a track or two with you. We'll let Tony hear it," that was all I needed to hear.

****

Geoff MacCormack aka "Warren Peace" toured with David from 1973-1976, doubling as a backing vocalist and percussionist. During this time period, David's school chum participated in five albums, beginning with Aladdin Sane, *ending with* Station to Station. *Many considered this time period to be David's creative peak.*

Ava soon found herself enchanted by the Chateau d'Herouville aka "The Castle Studio" which David had rented for its serene surroundings and sixteen-track recording capability. When film scorer Michael Magne purchased and restored the property in the 1960s, he attended to his dream of building a studio in the right wing. Future guests would also enjoy the use of ten bedrooms, a tennis court and a swimming pool.

Portuguese folk artists were some of the first visitors to the castle in the early '70s. Around that time, Grateful Dead performed on the lush grounds. By 1973, Elton John had stopped in to record Honky Chateau, Don't Shoot Me I'm Only the Piano Player *and* Goodbye Yellow Brick Road. *After starting up sessions for* The Dark Side of the Moon, *Pink Floyd recorded the overlooked* Obscured by Clouds *during a similar time frame.*

But this 18ᵗʰ century relic has also embraced a passionate, visually-oriented past. Vincent Van Gogh, whose grave can be found nearby in Auvers-sur-Oise, used the chateau and local church as subjects for paintings; Composer Frederic Chopin and paramour/author George Sand enjoyed the environs, too.

When David recorded several tracks for Pin Ups *in 1973, the studio had been facing financial troubles, but he returned three years later with Brian Eno and Iggy Pop to record* Low *and* The Idiot, *and he saw that the equipment had been updated and the decaying walls had been restored to their original splendor. The castle had been through, and would continue to go through, many incarnations, but this one was the only version that mattered.*

We were in love. There really seemed to be an angel on my shoulder. Every place I went, I found myself more and more connected to David. What were the odds? And would my happiness last?

You lived there at the same time that you recorded there. The fireplace alone was as large as the walls of an average study. We met with management and David confirmed that we were going to finish this recording project off in London. But, I waited and waited.

I was young and free-spirited, but I was no groupie. I would just make up my mind to do something and by the time I got to David, I became his girlfriend; I was shielded from that kind of thing.

Now, I'm glad that I made the decision to keep my head on straight; I experimented, but I never got so stoned that I couldn't function. That's why I remember those times and those faces. David introduced me to everybody and I hung out with Mick and Keith and Bianca, Paul McCartney, Jimmy Page and all those people, and I was always able to hold my own.

People sometimes ask whether David and I experienced any prejudice on account of being in an interracial relationship in the 1970s. When I first started working with David, a lot of black people weren't racist, but there was some confusion. They didn't understand about black artists not doing R&B. They'd ask, "Wow. You're dating David Bowie?" But when they finally understood the situation, they'd say, "Oh, okay, he's cool. He's cool."

The thing that cemented David with black people was when we did *Young Americans.* When we took part in a documentary about Sigma Sound at the Tower Theater, I heard from one of the musicians, when we were first doing the project, that they asked a few musicians if they wanted to be involved in the project and that a few of them said no; I don't believe that that was a racist reaction. I think that they didn't understand the music, so they didn't want to participate.

But even after a few of them declined, David didn't say anything negative. He just moved forward, a Capricorn with a solid plan.

"I'll just form my own band," he decided, and that's when he met Carlos Alomar and determined that he and the other musicians would work successfully on the project.

Back in the day, people were open-minded. We were hanging out with Andy Warhol. The crowd was very LGBTQ friendly. I felt very, very at home with all of these people. Yes, very much at home. But that feeling of security, of belonging, being an integral part of the inner circle, would not last.

12.
OAKLEY STREET, LONDON

W hen I first arrived in London, I moved into a hotel room. Then, the plan was that I would live on Oakley Street for about a month. The domicile was spacious enough for David's wife, Angie, son Zowie, a personal assistant, clerical staff and me.

Angie was okay with my being there for the first week and then she freaked out and did not want me around, but there were times prior to that when David and I would be there alone. In fact, I would be there a lot without Angie being home.

Finally, David moved me out to a place called Dasca House on King's Row, which was just down the street. As for David, he lived at 89 Oakley Street from October 1973 to April of 1974, after which time he relocated to the United States.

Fortunately, on Oakley, I had an ally—a cute little girl, Daniela, from South Africa who used to do things for Angie around the house. She used to be my friend when I was there because she also lived in the house and that friendship helped me feel somewhat at home.

Tony Zanetta, former CEO of MainMan Management Company, describes David's hiatus: "After all of these years and in that year of touring and working, David was a superstar and suddenly he's not working. So, he's in London and suddenly Mick Jagger's coming to see him, all the doors are open and he has really accomplished his dream but everything then takes on another dimension. Now, he's experiencing life as the rock star that he always wanted to be."

Things would change drastically after I left. I read about a fur-covered bed that was smack dab in the living room commonly referred to as "the pit" where sexual liaisons randomly occurred but never during my time at the house. And sometime after I left Oakley St., David had walls painted black to express empathy for striking miners. But when I was still there, the walls were still light and the wide corridors were airy.

Sometimes, David would invite Mick Jagger over with a girlfriend or something like that so we could go out and have dinner and be a foursome.

I also met George Harrison one time when we went to his gig, but David never said much about him after we got there. The big reason was that George Harrison tried to hit on me and David turned around and caught him, and that kind of made him mad. I'm sure that's why he never said another word about the former Beatle.

The reason that they called me "Black Barbarella" was because actress Jane Fonda always wore those little space suits in that movie and I was fond of wearing those, too. David had Freddie Burretti make clothes for me and one outfit looked exactly like Jane's.

I became friends with the Stones because my girlfriend was dating Ronnie Wood. One day, during a rough patch with David, we were invited to Montauk Point in New York, so she was there with Ronnie and Mick was there, too, but Mick had no idea that I would be coming. Apparently, he had gone through a glass door; one arm was in a sling. He was shocked to see me.

But later that night, he took my hand and we whisked off together. I was hurting. The reason I felt comfortable talking to him was that we were friends. I wanted to be with someone who would understand—to this day, we are still friends. Mick didn't bring up David, so it was nice. He had given me a chance to be relaxed without answering questions, but when David found out I had been up there, he got mad.

David knew I had been at Montauk. Mick was somebody David admired. That was maybe a no-no for him because he was jealous.

There was a part of David's reaction that made me feel good—just thinking that David would be jealous of Mick Jagger, when he knew I really loved David!

When we hung out together, it was mainly a threesome: Mick, David and me. As I got to know Mick better, we might have dinner or sit around writing songs. We would just play keyboards and guitar and make up stuff.

It was a nice friendship, but we didn't hang out all of the time. I certainly wasn't naïve about their status. I was very aware and impressed that he was Mick Jagger and that the Stones were a great rock super group, yet Mick didn't act like a rock star. He was surprisingly nice, sweet and polite. All the things he should be. I had just started living in David's house in London on Oakley St. when I met him; Mick would often come to visit us.

We did hang out with Bianca a little bit but mostly it was just the three of us. Before I first met Mick, I thought that he was going to be more serious but he was really very funny and he always made me laugh.

Truthfully, I didn't really know about the intricacies of their relationship. I don't think I noticed if they were overly affectionate with each other. The few times that we went out with Mick and Bianca, we were out having dinner or seeing a show. You know how everybody acts, but it wasn't overtly anything. I didn't really comprehend the scope of their relationship—it was very subtle.

I never asked for and wouldn't get any credit for what we were doing, musically. We would mostly be sitting around drinking champagne and having a party. Somehow, David ended up on the guitar one night. Mick ended up on the keyboards and we were playing this song called "Having a Good Time." David did end up doing it, but I don't remember where he put it.

People want to know what it's like living with a rock star, especially when it comes to the question of infidelity. Well, it happened once or twice in the six years or whatever. But I felt like this: If he did stray, with a one-nighter or whatever, it was because he felt he had the privileges of a rock star. I know that before me—and this is one of the problems that people had with me—he had a few different lovers.

But when I came on the scene, everybody was with MainMan, including his wife, Angie. So, I would be around for maybe a couple of weeks or a month and then be gone and then be back with him. When I'm with a man, it's not just for a minute.

They underestimated me in the long run. They'd say, "Why is *she* still here?" after one year and two years. After those years went by, they started resenting me for still being there.

At a party, David might have seen someone who twinkled his eye and was attracted to him, but I was still faithful. I was young and I never cheated on him. That was just the way that I did things, but that doesn't mean that I never got angry.

Once, we were staying at the Sherry-Netherlands Hotel. I had my own apartment on 13th but I used to leave my robe and toiletries there at the hotel. One time, David wanted to be with this other person, somebody who wasn't around for a very long time, but it was a one-nighter. I was still there when David said, "Darling, I'll see you tomorrow."

"What? David, are you trying to rush me? What's going on?" I picked up that he wanted to be with somebody else that night and I got mad. But David and I never had any kind of screaming fights. It was never arguing and fighting. You would feel it more than you heard it. I acted cool even though there was another girl in the mix. I never started screaming, "Who's that bitch?"

No, I was calm. I cooly asked, "Oh, so you're going to see someone else tonight?" I might have even said the girl's name. I don't remember. I just said, "Okay" and started removing my clothes out of the bathroom.

David silently watched my every move. "Wait. Wait a minute. What are you doing?"

"You want to be with some other bitch, then be with her!" I snapped back. I began moving toward the door.

I could tell that he was worried. His voice softened. "Don't move your things. Don't move your clothes away."

So, I knew he really cared when he said, "Don't take your clothes away." He was really saying, *Don't take away that feeling of you being there,* even though somebody else would be there. That's how I handled that night. I didn't take my things away.

I was ultimately there as long as I was. I was there with David. And that kind of thing very seldom happened when I was there.

There were things I inherently understood. If David wasn't comfortable with you, he wouldn't take you around with Mick and all of those people. But I was around with his friends and that is why I'm still friends with those guys today. I was around the people David respected and liked, so I knew I was special. And I was young, so I had to be a real woman to keep this guy. I did pretty good at seventeen.

I mean, I just couldn't be a kid, a body that he was making love to. I had to be a real woman to him, for him to want me to stay around. I had to be someone he could talk to and count on and someone with whom he could have fun and share things.

Now, there were long periods of time in which I'd have nothing to be jealous of, but when there were those moments, I would wonder, *What were these women presenting that made him want to do this?* After all, I'm human...

There was one person in particular that I didn't like at all, Claudia Lennear. She's the girl who the Stones wrote "Brown Sugar" about. She'd befriended Mick and a lot of other rock stars in the business. I remember this particular time on tour when she started coming around for a few days. The problem with her was, she was doing heroin. Even in the short time in which she was coming around, she was a disaster because of her drug overdoses. She would always have to be rushed to the hospital; the ambulances kept coming. Everybody was warning David that she was a bad influence.

David wasn't into that scene, but I'm saying that she was one of these people that was always the same and I thought, *Why does she have to create this drama?*

If I'd thought, here was this bitch and David was really digging on her, I might have felt more threatened, but I felt sorry for her, not in the way like, *Oh, I feel sorry for her,* but I felt better because I knew she had a problem, and that being the case, she just wasn't going to sustain her relationship with David.

Ava and company plan for a high-stakes premiere. `

13.

THE 1980 FLOOR SHOW

W hen I first got to London and I was living in David's house, we were feverishly figuring out what projects we were going to do. We were getting ready to do *The 1980 Floorshow Midnight Special with The Astronettes* (Geoff MacCormack, Jason Guess and myself).

The instrumental players were Mark Pritchett, who served as second guitar to Mick Ronson, bassist Trevor Bolder, pianist Mike Garson and

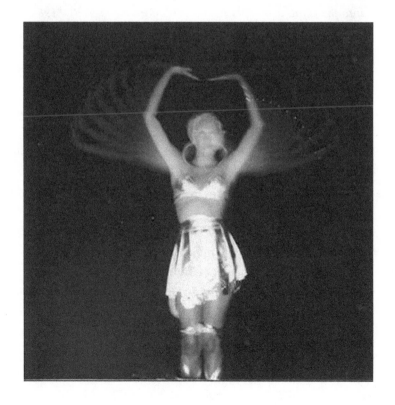

drummer Aynsley Dunbar, so there we were scrambling around, trying to figure out what kind of costumes we were going to wear, what kind of show format it was going to be and what songs we were going to sing.

In addition, we were busy deciding which acts David wanted in the show and what the choreography was going to be. We had a lot on our minds because our performance was going to be televised and emceed by the brassy Burt Sugarman, plus *The Midnight Special* guaranteed excellent exposure. The career stakes were incredibly high.

We held court at London's Marquee Club in the fall of 1973. The show went live on November 16, 1973 and was aired again in 1974.

****

On the actual televised version, dancers spelled out "Bowie, The 1980 Floorshow" with their angular bodies before the vocal excitement commenced. Freddy Burretti's costumes played a significant role in the over-the-top setting. When David first appeared, sporting a glossy multicolored robe, he stared straight into the camera while banging on a tambourine. With "1984/Dodo," however, the showman sprang into action.

Mid-song, Ava and Jason stepped forward and gently disengaged David from his flowing, outer layer, revealing his bare porcelain chest. In contrast, Ava wore a sculpted, black-and-white striped halter with a patent leather belt and a cherry-red, skintight sequined skirt. All the time spent deciding on which outfits to wear had certainly paid off.

For the ballad "Sorrow," David wore a chalk-white tailored suit. But his next costume change featured a billowy purple shirt and tight, canary-yellow trousers. Then, as if the entertainers intuited sensory overload, they shifted gears. "Everything's Alright" brought everything back to an even keel.

David Bowie would not be overshadowed. Sporting a gold lamé suit with a wide lapel and a sci-fi collar, he leaned over his acoustic guitar and launched into the wistful "Space Oddity." Strumming reflective verses, he livened up the pace to show off his head voice.

As if to commemorate the rock royalty that preceded them, the band launched into "1984" and a cover of The Who's Mod anthem, "I Can't Explain." David, a head-turner in his own right, even without the glitz, ceremoniously shook his charcoal-black feathers and then flashed eye-catching sparkles at his bandmates and beyond.

From 1973's pop-flavored Aladdin Sane, *David performed "Time." For this rendition, he sported a sheer toga and sang wistfully to the expressive, submissive dancers, all against Garson's playful, barrelhouse piano and Mick Ronson's often underrated but anthemic electric wails.*

It was on to "The Jean Genie"—a pair of fake, gold hands with shiny nails wrap around either side of David's svelte chest on this outrageous costume. The rest consisted of a sash-like skirt and spiderweb top. At one point, Ronson made a grand, ambiguous gesture; he stopped his visceral shredding long enough to hold the receptive front man in a tight, audience-numbing embrace.

Toward the end of the set, David slipped in a surprising, blues-harp solo. This was essentially an all-star performance allowing plenty of time and space for an instrumental outro where The Spiders applied plenty of axle grease.

"Boy, that David Bowie is fabulous. No wonder he is the superstar he is," barked crusty-voiced American DJ Wolfman Jack after the sonic explosion.

Before circling back to "1984," the ensemble switched gears with an unanticipated cover of Sonny and Cher's "I Got You Babe," a rubato duet in which David crooned to, and along with, singer Marianne Faithfull, whose waif-like interpretation of Jagger/Richard's "As Tears Go by" brought her seemingly overnight success.

Curiously dolled up as a campy, starry-eyed nun, she ogled David, who stood over her, jiggling even more frantically the pitch-black feathers of his flamboyant boa. For the gasp-worthy finale, Ava and company returned. Although the camera angles didn't give the backing singers their due—and David would find fault with the final product—their vibrant voices served as a rejoinder, a welcome reality check that balanced out the somewhat erratic set list.

Pressures mount; identities alter.

14.
STARDUST DISINTEGRATES

Former MainMan executive Tony Zanetta was not in attendance the night David demoted Ziggy Stardust, but he had other pressing issues on his mind.

TONY ZANETTA

I came back to New York to plan what was called Tour 3, which was going to be an enormous, enormous tour. Tony Defries wanted David to play arenas and he had a strict deal which he was trying to do. He tried to do a deal with the promoters that was a 90/10 split with the promoters paying all of their expenses out of the ten percent.

At that point, David was not really a major artist in the U.S., although he was selling a lot of records. He had great press and he had only played about ten cities in the U.S. successfully. No one wanted to take a gamble on him.

By that time, he had been huge in the U.K. He was responsible for about four percent of the music sold in the United Kingdom. He had hit after hit there, but he didn't have any hits in the U.S. That tour never happened but we made a big thing about cancelling that tour so I was not there. Basically, he fired the band from the stage. They had no inkling, except Mick Ronson knew. They had taken him aside separately.

Everything kind of happened for David at the start of RCA in the fall of 1971. That set all this musical stuff in place. Defries got back the records from Mercury and released two of those on RCA. Everybody was busy for the next year-and-a-half. That was when Ziggy's tour started. So, David pretty much worked constantly from January 1972 until that night of the

Hammersmith Odeon, which was July of 1973.

The tour manager gets exhausted, but can you imagine? David had been working towards that moment since he was fifteen-years-old. That goal of being a rock star, he accomplished it.

****

Ava had a strong recollection of the dynamics, too.

AVA

Here's what I remember. When David said no more Ziggy, it was just another one of David's moves. It wasn't something that we talked about. He never actually said, "I'm retiring. This is it." I remember when we did a song from *Young Americans* called "Who Can I Be Now?" Now, *that* spoke volumes. David would go through these things: *Who do I want to be today? Do I want to be Ziggy Stardust? Do I want to be…what?* He was deciding if he wanted to stay with Ziggy Stardust or become a soul persona.

I was there. It wasn't like, "Oh, my God, what are we going to do? What are we going to do?" Everyone kind of knew. Everyone was saying that he was just saying it at the moment and at another point he could probably be somebody else; he would probably change his mind. But when he said he was done with Ziggy Stardust, he was done with Ziggy Stardust. David was a chameleon. He had already started thinking about doing the soul band group. I mean, he was in awe of the album *James Brown at the Apollo*, what does that tell you?

David and I never discussed the Spiders or Mick Ronson. Group politics was not something I was privy to. When he said he was no longer doing Ziggy Stardust, I was just imagining him going to the soul mode. The abrupt change didn't bother me and I didn't hear any of the other band members say anything about it either.

****

Former Spiders from Mars drummer Woody Woodmansey who, with producer/bassist Tony Visconti, plays Bowie-inspired hits with contemporary band Holy Holy, was at the Hammersmith the night David Bowie discarded his Ziggy Stardust persona. In a pennyblackmusic interview from December 2018, Woody relays his reaction:

WOODY WOODMANSEY

We'd gotten used to him doing things just on the spur of the moment. We'd gotten used to that, it was no longer a surprise or a shock, usually. On the last American tour, and the English tour, as well, he was finding it hard to do an hour-and-a half makeup and then get into the Ziggy thing and do the show and get back to being David Bowie or even David Jones.

You got in the limousine with Ziggy Stardust and it had not been like that before. You didn't really know how to talk to Ziggy. It was very alien. You couldn't say, "My favorite football team is on tonight." He would just get that Ziggy look and you would shut your mouth. So, we didn't know.

My immediate thought was it's a publicity stunt. He just decided to do that on the spur of the moment. My second thought was maybe he'd had enough of touring because it was hard on him and maybe he figures, *I'll just be a writer.* It was always a possibility.

The third thing was maybe he's just finishing the Ziggy thing. Or, all of the above, but we didn't know which one it was and it wasn't until a few days later that, okay, it's the Ziggy thing that's finished. And that meant he couldn't really take the Spiders, as a band, into anything else, because with the Spiders, he would always have to be Ziggy, you know. That was my personal take on it, anyway.

****

Guitarist Earl Slick would be asked to replace Mick Ronson for certain future recordings, such as "Fame" and "Across the Universe" as well as other comprehensive assignments. In an excerpt from pennyblackmusic from November 2019, Slick recalled the legacy of David Bowie's early guitarist and how Slick managed his transition.

EARL SLICK

Mick was very much the driving force to sculpting David's sound. He wasn't just a guitar player that was noodling. Mick really stamped that stuff with himself. And he put together a lot more of the arrangements and things than people realized. He wasn't just a guitar player; so, I knew that from listening to everything.

As for his concerns about replacing or replicating Ronson's signature sound:

David seriously let me off the hook. I asked him about it. He said, 'I hired you. I like what you do, so just do what you do.'"

Producer Tony Zanetta recollects the financial woes the ensemble endured:

TONY ZANETTA

We had no money. MainMan spent fortunes of money that it didn't have so we didn't get paid, we had our rent paid, or if we needed a new pair of shoes, the company would buy them. There were people in other situations, like the band.

The band was getting paid, like seventy-five pounds a week, under one-hundred dollars. That was on the first tour in the U.S., but by the second tour they thought there was money and that they should be getting part of this money so they confronted Defries. They went to a lawyer. They wanted money. That was the beginning of the end for them because Defries and Bowie got together and decided, well, that was considered treason and they kind of decided in Japan to get rid of them.

Also, Defries was negotiating David's publishing deals so he didn't want David to do any new music, that was another reason why he retired the act and the next album was *Pin Ups*; Defries didn't want David to deliver any new music until that publishing deal was straightened out.

Sometimes friendly conversations grow too personal...

15.
SPILL THE WINE

AVA

David got along with many rock stars, but as far as guitarist Jimmy Page, of Led Zeppelin fame, that was a whole other matter. At David's place in New York, this is before he left me there, we often crashed in the apartment. David had this sophisticated, sunken living room with all of these silk pillows, like you would imagine in *The Arabian Nights*. The décor was all beautifully done.

One night, a bunch of his friends came over. Now, as you know, Ronnie Wood and David were really good friends already, and this time, David had broadened the circle by inviting guitarist Jimmy Page, too. We were formally introduced. I thought Jimmy was nice enough, until something spilled on David's couch and stained.

David asked me if I did it and I said no. Then, he found out that it was Jimmy that spilled it. And when David found that out, he wasn't happy with the reaction. Jimmy and Ronnie were laughing about the situation and scolding me, and then things got heated.

David finally spoke up and said, "Why'd you let Ava take the blame for spilling the wine?" Then, all hell broke loose. Jimmy and David got into a heated argument.

Then, when they said they were going to go, David completely snapped, "Why don't you take the window?" He was very angry that they tried to let me take the blame.

So, their relationship turned out not to be the most rewarding, even though David had genuinely wanted to meet Jimmy, mostly because he was intrigued by the stories he had heard about the former Led Zeppelin star residing in Aleister Crowley's former home.

David wanted to find out if Jimmy was a warlock or something like that. He had been reading a lot of books about the subject of black magic and was very interested in not only that specific topic, but related topics like metaphysics, but because of the tension, that conversation never ended up happening.

****

Crowley was an English novelist, poet, mountaineer and occultist who founded a religion called Thelema. His writings had garnered a lot of attention from the open-minded, counter-culture movement of the time.

The property currently called the Boleskine House, which Crowley had purchased in 1899 and sold in 1913, has since gone through several owners but is still located in the misty Highlands of Loch Ness. Page bought the manor in the early 1970s because he was intrigued by Crowley's writings and looked forward to composing his own material in the unique setting. Although he ended up spending little time there, he retained ownership until 1992.

Over the years, rumors have surfaced regarding swinging doors, terrifying animal sounds and other paranormal activities related to the manor as well as to Crowley's legacy—he was said to have conducted intensive black magic experiments in the secluded structure.

And just for the record, Ava did not spill one drop of that wine.

16.
TOURING

Ziggy Stardust Tour 1972-73
Diamond Dogs Tour, 1974
First Leg, June July, 1974
Second Leg, September, 1974
Third Leg, Oct. 5 – Dec. 5, 1974

*T*he Diamond Dogs Tour was actualized in three stages. The first leg spanned June and July of 1974. The second leg occurred in September of that same year and the final stage ran from early October to early December.

The lineup during the first leg consisted of Michael Kamen and Mike Garson, who were responsible for keyboards and synth; Earl Slick, on lead guitar and Pablo Rosario on percussion. David Sanborn and Richard Grando handled woodwinds, but a number of changes occurred as the tour progressed. For example, bassist Doug Rauch replaced Herbie Flowers and Greg Errico took over drums. Carlos Alomar became the invaluable rhythm guitarist, leaving in his wake at the Apollo future producer and member of Chic, Nile Rodgers, who would replace Carlos there as house guitarist, but perhaps the most transparent change took place with the legion of backing vocalists. While Gui Andrisano and Warren Peace acted as the two backing vocalists listed in the summer tour, the second leg of the North American Tour showcased Luther Vandross, Diane Sumler, Anthony Hinton, Robin Clark and Ava Cherry. The value of adding these strong voices to the show could not be understated.

On the last leg, the band embarked on "The Soul/Philly Dogs Tour." The rhythm section then boasted bassist Willie Weeks, who had worked with Chaka Khan's early incarnation, "Ask Rufus," and whose playing had been greatly inspired by bassist James Jamerson, one of Motown's greatest, but sadly, mostly uncredited session players. Weeks has cited classically trained, exemplary bassist Ron Carter, also, as an instrumental hero. This A-lister's CV includes sessions with Robert Cray, Randy Newman, Carly Simon, Ron Wood, Rickie Lee Jones and Etta James. The late drummer Dennis Davis, who would become renowned for drumming on a slew of Bowie albums produced between 1975 and 1980, also came aboard.

So, with this new rhythm section established and with Michael Kamen and Richard Grando's support parts slashed, the stakes were extraordinarily high and the pressure was on for the remaining backing vocalists, sans Gus Andrisano (who would stay on as choreographer and emcee) to create that compelling Philly sound.

By and large, the Philly tour was an extension of the Diamond Dogs Tour but there had been a number of other unexpected changes made, too. True to form, on opening night at the LA Universal Ampitheater, and primarily to appease management and press, the elaborate stage set remained. That set, referred to as "Hunger City" and based on George Orwell's eerie 1984 dystopia, came at an exorbitant expense.

In *David Bowie: Starman,* author Paul Trynka describes the conceptualized futuristic set.

PAUL TRYNKA

A decaying future metropolis with thirty-foot-high skyscrapers augmented by a motorized bridge, a remote-control mirrored module, and a cherry picker in which David would descend from the heavens.

But for the next six shows, the band made do with a stripped--down set and a series of new songs.

****

"Space Oddity" and "Panic in Detroit" remained in place, but the set list now expanded to include: "Young Americans," "It's Gonna Be Me," "John, I'm Only Dancing," "Sorrow," "Can You Hear Me," "Somebody Up There Likes Me," and a cover of The Flares' "Foot Stomping."

Another important change was that the Mike Garson Band and backing singers had an opportunity to open the show with fresh, hand-picked material.

Luther Vandross crooned "Funky Music (Is a Part of Me)" and Ava Cherry used her sensual voice to proclaim "I'm in The Mood for Love."

As always, costumes played an essential role in any David Bowie live performance. At this soul-centric show, David's zoot suit dominated. His hair flaunted natural highlights and contour; gone were the spiked locks of blood orange-red.

David had met designer Freddie Burretti on King's Row at the storied El Sombrero in the 1960s. This taste master's vision veered towards the likes of James Dean and Frank Sinatra. The Life on Mars *video illustrates his reverence for classicism. There, Bowie sported a sky-blue, one-button, tailored suit that fit like a glove. The top-notch, underrated designer was accustomed to creating bespoke apparel from an earlier era, and he may have been trying to do justice to the memory of Mr. Cherry's suit with this prototype, but after that show, David would seek stylistic change through the whimsy of designers Kansai Yamamoto, Alexander McQueen and Hedi Slimane; he and the lesser-credited designer would ultimately go their separate ways and Freddy Burretti quietly passed away in Paris in 2001.*

The L.A. concerts created an immediate buzz and drew major stars, including Bette Midler, Diana Ross and a young Michael Jackson, whose jaw dropped toward the photo pit after taking in David's eloquent Lindsay Kemp-inspired mime. After all, both Jackson and Bowie were strong admirers of this mysterious craft, a case in point being Jackson's mesmerizing "moonwalk." With a show offering so much in terms of sensual detail, it was no surprise when The LA Times offered a concise, but favorable review, calling the concert "marvelously entertaining." The L.A. phenomenon appealed to a swirl of new fans, old friends and an endless roster of impressive celebrities.

Ava soaked up the star-studded scene. And of course, she'd been friends with Stevie before she met Luther, and she always remembered how supportive he had been about her relationship with David. And she recalled, "there were so many other white, black, green and blue Hollywood stars, like Liz Taylor."

After a hectic week, the entourage traveled to San Diego, Tucson and Phoenix. Leaving the elaborate stage sets behind meant the vocalists had more visibility, but perhaps more pressure to succeed, and they definitely had to up their game plan, and fast. As the backing vocalists harmonized from their own collective spot, David's own voice echoed from his personal but stately stainless steel platform. Pablo Rosario observed: "David was really wired. He looked like a tiger in a cage going from side to side of the stage."

In December 1974, an appearance from the Radio City Music Hall (where the band engaged in the tour's final week) aired on the Dick Cavett Show. The set included "Young Americans," "1984" and "Foot Stompin'."

Cavett, a highly popular talk show host with a pleasing voice and folksy persona, appeared nonplussed when David clung feverishly to a walking stick. It was clear that the rock star was high, but Cavett took it in stride. David's voice was raw and worn, but his faithful band played on.

David fronts, at first. He's got on a bright, almost-blinding shade of suspenders and a striped necktie. His hair is uncharacteristically slicked-back. Horns blare. Ava's own frame is accentuated with a glittery, tailored jacket, and in a flash, she becomes the surprising star of the televised show. She struts downstage to do "the Shimmy," later declaring that Bowie urged her on at the very last minute. That said, being the professional she was, Ava left the audience with a lasting impression: she could sing, dance on a dime and essentially entertain in front of a TV audience, showing absolutely no signs of duress.

Bowie's voice is tight and guttural. Luther Vandross, Geoff MacCormack and Anthony Hinton echo Bowie's vocal riffs. Carlos Alomar's guitar manufactures a blistering urgency. He first performed "1984" (Diamond Dogs, 1974), followed by "Young Americans" and closed off the set with a virile mashup of The Flares' 1961 classic, "Foot Stompin'" and "I Wish I Could Shimmy Like My Sister Kate," a spirited ballad composed in the '20s and revisited in London during the swinging '60s. Ava's impromptu Shimmy far surpassed the fictional Kate's.

New York vs. Chicago—Ava understood that musical relationships once flourished in Chicago's Regal Theater, as well as in New York's Apollo, and her awareness would greatly impact David Bowie's subsequent career moves.

17.
YES, *THAT* APOLLO THEATER!

*T*he Apollo Theater, originally called Hurtig and Seamon's New
Burlesque Theater, opened in 1914 but would not sponsor an Amateur
Night until two decades later. At the time of the theater's opening,
African-Americans were not only barred from performing, there, but even
from being audience members.

But in the mid-1930s, as burlesque became stigmatized, a new format
was set in place, which would accommodate and embrace an influx of
African-American clients who were making Harlem their new home. The
new "variety show" format featured a combination of big bands and hopeful
newcomers, but although the theater allowed for these fresh faces, new acts
often fielded tough crowd reactions. On one hand, entertainers often got
booed off the stage, but acts could also become overnight stars if the audiences
felt confident that they had perfected their craft.

The mid-1950s underscored Bo Diddley's percussive strums, Chuck
Berry's whimsical lyrics and country-western style twang as well as the slick-
haired "Little Richard," whose growling baritone and seductive falsetto would
bowl over the Beatles and bleed into their early originals.

Several years later, silky-voiced Smokey Robinson would grace the stage.
A youthful Michael Jackson, while fronting the Jackson Five, made his debut
appearance there in 1967. Ronnie Spector, whose mother waitressed at the
nearby King's Donuts, begged her protective parent to let her perform at the
Apollo amateur night. When the distinctive-voiced lead singer of "Be My
Baby" finally got her opportunity, she brought the house down.

The nervous Eleanora Fagan AKA Billie Holiday warmed up the house
years before female vocalists Aretha Franklin and Tina Turner left audiences
speechless, the former with her evocative, Gospel-inspired range and the
latter, whose grinding hips alone, scantily draped by a mini-skirt, rendered

the illusion of the ultimate sex goddess, but coupled with her gift for rendering gut-wrenching ballads, incited fever-pitch emotion.

The Apollo, like many other American theaters, often found itself skating on extraordinarily thin ice, faced with frequent, financial obstacles, especially when competition arose from other prominent venues. In this case, the major culprit would become the centrally located, bustling Madison Square Garden. That being the case, the Apollo closed in 1976, but reopened in 1980, allowing for the influx of new and established acts.

Ava Cherry's early experience with the Regal Theater, a welcoming, community-centered venue which promoted the energy and gifts of black talent, undoubtedly prepared her for the less-forgiving Apollo...

But could David Bowie, a foreigner and outsider, who had merely read about and heard such acts on recordings, put this rich, cultural phenomenon into proper perspective?

Ava was not only there to witness David's early fascination for live, soul music; she also watched him develop a stronger sense of social justice.

AVA

With David, it was never about color. He liked you or loved you. Skin color didn't matter. One reason I loved him so much was that race was never an issue.

But when David felt race *was* an issue, he stood up. In 1983, David spoke to MTV host Mark Goodman. After referring to the station as a "solid enterprise," he adds, "I'm just floored by the fact that there are so few black artists featured on it. Why is that?"

He questioned a further injustice, citing that "the only few black artists that one does see are on about 2:30 a.m. in the morning to around 6." David confronted MTV about Michael Jackson; that conversation had a big effect. I'm so proud of him for saying something; he was one of the only people to come forward at that time. I commended him for that, too.

And as far as our relationship? "You don't like that I'm going out with this black girl, Ava Cherry? Tough."

The Young Americans album would not have happened without me and my influence. David just said, "I want to do a soul band. Who do I see? What do I do?"

"We've got to go to the Apollo," I told him. Tony Sylvester of the Main Ingredient had already extended an invitation and that invitation is what ultimately led to David getting together with Sylvester and Carlos Alomar. It was definitely that night at the Apollo that jump-started David's decision. Tony Sylvester would reappear in my life, but I'll get to that later.

Here's what happened when we got there. The limo door opens. I step out with my blonde hair. David has "Ziggy red hair." I'm standing next to Ziggy Stardust. I could hear the whispers. "Who is that?"

People had never seen anything like us before and David, too, had never seen such excitement. He was so excited about how it all just came alive: The Spinners, The Temps, The Main Ingredient. Comic Richard Pryor was so funny that night, too.

There were five different acts at the Apollo in Harlem and each set was short, only about twenty minutes. David commented most positively on The Spinners and the Temptations. He especially liked the tight harmonies and flashy movements.

But most importantly on the April 26th show that featured stand-up comic Richard Pryor and The Main Ingredient, David formally met guitarist Carlos Alomar, a pillar in the theater's house band. Alomar's imagination (often times with guitarist Earl Slick) would eventually birth the contagious riffs that appear in "Fame," "Golden Years" and "Stay."

Initially, David was going to use in-house players from Philly but remember, they didn't want to do the project or work on the album. That's when David put together Carlos Alomar and the rest of the band. A sea-change was in the air.

A musical revolution was taking place; only nobody yet knew it...Ava, producer Tony Visconti and two still-committed fans reflect back on the recording of Young Americans and more.

18.
SIGMA SOUND AND SIGMA KIDS

*I*n July, David completed recording David Live. On August 8 of 1974, Ava joined guitarist Carlos Alomar and a brand-new lineup of players in Philadelphia's Sigma Sound Studio to record the majority of the material which would land on Young Americans. (On the subsequent fall tour and in celebration of the "plastic soul" phenomenon, David would appear in Antonio Cherry's 1940's "gouster" suit.)

Sigma Sound was then owned by a member of the duo Kenneth Gamble and Leon Huff, co-founders of Philadelphia International Records as well as a prolific songwriting force.

The entire Young Americans entourage included saxophonist David Sanborn, pianist Mike Garson, guitarist Earl Slick, Sly and the Family Stone drummer Andy Newmark and bassist Willie Weeks. However, Newmark and Weeks did not perform on "Across the Universe" and "Fame"; these tracks were recorded at Electric Lady Studios in New York in January of 1975.

There, John Lennon sang and played acoustic guitar on "Across the Universe" and co-wrote, "Fame"; also presiding was percussionist Pablo Rosario. Dennis Davis and Emir Kassan contributed drum and bass sections—Davis would continue to play on Station to Station and through to Scary Monsters. Jean Millington and Jean Fineberg added vocals to those of Luther Vandross, Ava Cherry and Robin Clark.

Executive Tony Defries, of MainMan, would retain ownership of David Bowie's master tapes until October 1982, the same year in which Bowie collaborated with producer Nile Rodgers on "Let's Dance."

Ashley Naftule, for consequenceofsound.net on March 6, 2020 recalled:
(David Bowie Fell to Earth and Found His Plastic Soul on Young
Americans): "The title track is a marvelous display of limber, ecstatic voices
twisting around Bowie's lead; Vandross, Cherry and Clark's voices, combined
with that irresistible saxophone squeal, create the perfect sandbox for Bowie's
evocative lyrics."

****

AVA

In all of the pictures, we looked like we were having fun, whether the captions read, "Philadelphia, Philly Sounds" or "Sigma Sounds." The sound of the times circled back to those classic Philly acts, like the O'Jays and Teddy Pendergrass.

Sigma Sound was ultra-hip. The studio was modern, in that you could get the kind of sound you wanted to get out of it, although it was an old studio, but it was well-kept. Some of the finest voices that ever graced rock came out of that studio. I loved it. I didn't know ahead of time that we were going to record there. I suppose, when David was talking to Carlos about where we should record, it was an easy choice. "Sigma, oh, okay!" It was definitely a wonderful place to record. It had an incredible sound and had great engineers.

We attracted our share of fans and groupies and they're still around right now, I think, they call themselves, "the Bowie Kids." If I was around seventeen, they were our age or younger and totally devoted to us. Every concert we went to, they were there. They followed us around the country. We'd be going to the hotel and they would be there standing and waiting for us. I've got to admit, David's fans were very, very loyal. They were very sweet, very kind, young people. I got to know them really well because sometimes when David would walk right in, I would stop and talk with them and so we became friends with the fans that followed us from city to city.

****

Two of "the Bowie kids" or "Sigma Kids" that followed the entourage "from
city to city" speak from the heart about their wild strategizing and how their
devotion paid off in ultimately unimaginable ways.

THE SIGMA KIDS, August-November 1974, Sigma Sound reflections. December 14, 2018

One of the legendary "Sigma Kids," Patti Brett remembers this special period of her life with an incredible fondness. In her recollection, she reflects back on the unique times in which she and her partners-in-crime witnessed the birthday of the Young Americans album. Before beginning her recollection, however, Patti references the friendly South Philly tavern, Doobies.

PATTI BRETT

I've worked there forty-one years but it's been in my family for forty. We just celebrated our forty-year anniversary in October. I can do whatever I want. People come in and say, "Oh, is this a Bowie bar?" I say, "Yeah, kind of." I don't know if I would necessarily call it "Bowie-themed," but there's an awful lot of Bowie stuff in it…

Once we got into the studio to listen to *Young Americans*; there were ten of us and we did all know each other because we had been hanging out in front of the studio for two weeks. Technically, here's what one of our days was like: David would come out of the Barclay Hotel in the afternoon and sign autographs and chat with everyone and take pictures and then head to the studio, so there would always be people at the hotel, there would always be people at the studio, and then in some cases, there'd be a car, so we could drive to the studio. We would jump in the car and run every red light so we could beat them to the studio. We would wait until they got out. That went on for two weeks, the whole time that they were there.

Because David told us on the Diamond Dogs Tour, when he was at the Tower Theater, where he recorded *David Live* in July, that he was going to be in town in about a month recording a new album at Sigma and that we should look for him, so that's exactly what we did.

Patti was incredibly excited to be asked to chime in with her opinion on this new album.

Oh God, yes. We couldn't believe it. The night that David told us about it, I don't believe anybody actually believed that he said that to us.

As for the album, we loved it. We actually had gotten very friendly with Carlos (Alomar) and Robin (Clark) and Carlos would always have a cassette of things that they'd done in the studio on that day. I guess he would listen to it to work out what they were doing and he would invite us up into their hotel room and we wouldn't get home until the morning. He and Robin would play it for us so we actually were hearing things before we got into the studio. And we're also talking about our idol and we were all teenagers. So, I'm not sure if it mattered but we did really love it.

Young Americans was one of my favorites and not just because I got into the studio. It's really one of the best songs that is on that album. In retrospect it really reminds me of my youth. I was eighteen-years-old at the time. I had just gotten out of high school and I had just started my first job. It was a much easier time to be living before I became an actual adult because it wasn't that hard then.

In terms of the studio? Honestly, I had a completely different vision in my head or memory in my head of what the studio looked like and then I saw the photographs from Dagmar (Krajnc) of all of us in the studio together and I don't remember it looking like that. My memories of it are: it was very dark, they had the lights dimmed when we went up to listen to the album and it was probably a medium-sized room, it wasn't too large and it wasn't too small. We were comfortable in it and they had chairs out for us.

David was behind the sound board, so he was behind the glass. He told us what was going to happen and then he came out and sat down and I think everybody was just in shock being in there. Everybody was incredibly nervous and after he played it through the first time Lenny McFadden jumped up and said, "Play it again!" David had the cutest smile on his face and he said, "Really?" And everybody screamed, "Yes!"

Then a party broke out and David came out and danced with everybody and took pictures. For me, David went from being my idol to my friend.

I lost track of Ava many years ago and I've been seeing things that she's been doing recently because of the Internet. I know she had reached out to a friend of ours and we asked if she could put us in touch with Ava. I don't recall when the last time I saw her was, but during that period when they were recording everybody got really friendly with everybody. We took Ava's bodyguard shopping. We convinced David's chauffeur, when David would go into the studio, to let us into the back of the car so we could get cigarette butts and cups and pull hair off the seats.

But there are a lot of musicians on that album and everyone could not have been nicer to us. The place where the studio was back then, it was Skid Row then and it was a very unsavory area and people thought we were insane for hanging out on the streets in this horrible neighborhood, but everybody had a band, and everyone, even David, looked out for us. They made sure that we had a way home, they made sure we weren't hungry: 'Anyone hungry? Want a sandwich?' I remember Chinese food one night. They were very nurturing—very nurturing.

I wasn't inside the studio while they were working but Ava was always with David. They always left the hotel together, they went into the studio together and always left the studio together. And everyone else sort of came on their own.

So, during that period, we got incredibly friendly with everybody. As for Carlos and Robin, I'm still friends with them. I see them on a somewhat regular basis; some of the people from the studio I'm still friends with. I stayed in Philadelphia and everyone else went their way. We lost track of a lot of people that were on the album but when we have an opportunity to get together, and it isn't often, it's always enjoyable. We have fun reminiscing.

We're all adults now. I think probably for most of us, like I said earlier, David was our idol and we didn't know the band when they arrived and we just got to be friendly with them not knowing really anything about them.

Now, I certainly did know Ava from the 1980 Floor Show but none of us knew who any of those other people were. I hadn't heard of Luther Vandross, Carlos Alomar or Robin Clark. So, we got to be friendly with them on a different level than we did with David because David was already our idol. So, I think our relationship with them was always very different through the years.

Some of the people that were in the studio, some of the kids, still had that 'He's my idol' kind of relationship, where even though I felt we were friends, I think some couldn't break down that wall and be comfortable around him. A lot of people were always really anxious.

We had a reunion many years later after a show in Philadelphia that Carlos arranged. We went backstage. David greeted us at the door and gave flowers to everyone. He came into the room, looked around and said, 'You guys all got old.' He had this little tiny goatee and I said, "You look a little grey there." And there were people that were shocked that I would say something like that to him. I'd circle back, "Oh, come on. He's a person."

Once Sigma happened, it became something beyond us. I didn't have a long-lasting relationship with him. I saw him on tour and that was it. I still felt like we could talk to each other, person to person, even though he always will be my favorite artist.

As for Ava, she was absolutely a fashionista. Probably the guys, too, but several of the girls were in awe of her because of how she looked, with the really short hair and it was bleached. She always had on the most fabulous clothes. And she was always fabulous and if I could think of one word that summed Ava up, it would be "fabulous."

We're talking about the '70s, so fashion was sort of all over the place then. You had people that were in jeans and T-shirts and you had people that were doing retro-looks. What I admired about Ava was that she had just an incredible fashion sense. I can remember this one jacket she had that was very short-waisted and a long skirt that went down just a little below her knee and I remember thinking that that was just such a lovely outfit.

I don't know if it was possible in the '70s, but she certainly could have modeled. I don't know with height restrictions if that could have happened—she was stunning, but approachable. Now, David was usually in casual clothes. He always had that hat on though; the fedora that he wore back then.

The song that stood out the most for me was, "Somebody Up There Likes Me." I remember in the studio thinking that that's such a beautiful song and it still to this day will make me teary. Some of the other things I can't say because of the internet. Things have been released and I can't say, "Oh, I really liked this in the studio because..." but I do remember when the album came out, when it was finally released, calling Carlos and Robin and talking to them about it and trying to sort out who was singing all of the parts. The background vocals are incredible on that album. So, I'd play something on my record player and say, "Okay, who's singing this part, who's singing that part?"

Patti explains the back story behind the Sigma Kids becoming an actual phenomenon.

So, at the studio when we were up there, we listened to the album for a second time and took pictures and chatted and they said it was time to go but before they left David wanted Coco to get everyone's names and addresses because he wanted to make sure that we had tickets for the next show when they came back. David came true to his word; we got tickets for the show at the Spectrum, but they weren't in the front and we weren't having that. So, I still have my ticket that he gave me in its entirety. No one sat in that seat; well, somebody could have, and I could have used it because I was in the front row…That was in November and three months after they recorded the album.

Luther, Ava, Carlos, Robin, Diane Sumler, Anthony Hinton, all of those guys who were singing background for David's portion of the show came out ahead of time and did several songs on their own.

There we were all in the front row and they were looking down at us and smiling and waving and David did the same thing when he came out. And beyond that, he would look out into the audience and say, "Where are my Sigma kids?" And he'd look and he'd say, "There you are." For years and years and years he would look out into the audience and he'd say, "I know you. I know you. I know all of you," and he would point to us. So, it was David that started it.

After performing at The Spectrum, David came back and played a week later and actually did some more recording at Sigma. That's also when he recorded the first Springsteen songs, "In the City" and "Growing Up." We were hanging out at the studio then and actually got to listen to those songs, but at an after party after that second Spectrum show at a place called Club Artemis. If you've even seen that intimate picture of David coming slowly down the steps, that's the party that got raided, but we got to listen to it again there.

It's very odd that it became what it became because it's such a big deal with Bowie fans. And I think it's a really big deal for other people. I mean, nobody does this anymore. Who invites teenage kids into a studio and gets feedback on a new album? I don't think anyone has ever done it since.

So, until the Internet came along, it was just sort of our story. Nobody knew about it except for those who had been involved. Because of the Internet, the word got out. I can remember years ago being on some website and seeing threads about that and thinking, "Wow, what is this?"

I'm not sure how it happened. Dagmar Krajnc was there to photograph the event and I don't know how those photographs leaked but I'm certainly happy that they did. And yes, I spent a long time on that Sigma Sound sidewalk…

MARLA KANEVSKY

Marla had just turned sixteen on the week at which the following Sigma Sound session occurred. To that end, she exclaims, "I could not have wished for a more perfect week!"

But several years after the Sigma Kids enjoyed their coveted session, Marla's world turned upside down when she lost her parents who were both in their fifties. Marla recalls, "David signed an autograph for them the night of Sigma. They also saw him in concert in 1976." She is grateful for the experience she enjoyed as a fan because, "David's music and the people I met because of him helped me through some of the most difficult times of my life."

Marla's son, Zane, who was named after a David Bowie song, met David "several times over the years, once even at Sigma Sound in 1997, when David was in Philly and did a fundraiser for a local radio station at Sigma." Such is the miraculous circle of life. Marla currently resides in New Jersey but says, "My heart will always be in The City of Brotherly Love and I want so badly to be able to live there again."

Being a Bowie fan back in the '70s was a magical time! I first learned of David Bowie when I was just fourteen. A friend lent me the album *Ziggy Stardust and the Spiders from Mars*. I was mesmerized.

My first Bowie concert was in 1973 at the Tower Theater in Upper Darby, Philadelphia. At one point during that show, I locked eyes with David, and my life was never the same. I wrote a pretty in-depth fan letter to MainMan that year and to my surprise I was contacted and told that David read my letter, thought it was very sweet and wanted to send his thanks.

Throughout the years, I have had countless experiences regarding David and it has been such a magnificent ride. I have met some of the most amazing people over the years and have made and maintained lifelong friendships, all because of our mutual love, respect and admiration for David.

When David came back to The Tower in July of 1974 for a week-long run for his Diamond Dogs show, an incredible sequence of events began to unfold. I, along with several friends, attended every show and always in the front! We would not settle for anything less!

Over the course of that week, we also would hang out at his hotel to wait for him in the hopes of meeting and chatting with him. Keep in mind, finding out where he was staying was a hit or miss undertaking. Sometimes it was as easy as calling a hotel and asking if David Bowie was a guest and surprisingly on several occasions we would get a simple, "Yes."

Other times when he was expected to be in the city, it would take dozens of phone calls and A LOT of foot work. REAL foot work, like walking all over the city to see if there were any clues that he was in town.

During his stay in Philly while on The Diamond Dogs Tour, he was staying at The Bellevue Stratford Hotel on Broad Street in Center City. We spent our days before the show, and evenings after the show in the area waiting, hoping, to catch a glimpse of him. One night after one of the shows, we were having a late-night snack at a deli up the street from the hotel.

Suddenly in rushed Earl Slick, a member of the band, who seemed to be looking for us. He came over and told us that David would be coming outside shortly if we wanted to meet him. Well, of course we jumped up from our table and rushed out the door. It may have been a dine and dash…

We raced down the street to the hotel, and sure enough, David came outside and sat on the steps of the hotel for quite a while to chat with us. He shared with us that he would be returning to Sigma Sound Studios and that we should "keep an eye out for him." It was thrilling to know that he, David Bowie, was sharing information with us that in fact not too many people knew.

A few weeks passed and we started our search for him. Again, no Internet, no social media, no cell phones, none of that. We relied solely on footwork, patience, perseverance, excellent timing and perhaps a bit of luck. We scoured the city daily for any hint of his presence. Finally, one day, I saw his blue limo parked in front of Sigma Sound Studios. We waited and waited and waited when at last Jimmy, David's chauffeur, came out of the studio with Zowie, David's adorable three-year-old son. They got into the limo and we followed suit, jumping into our cars to follow, hoping they would pull up in front of a hotel and that is exactly what happened.

The hotel was the beautiful Barclay Hotel along Rittenhouse Square in the heart of the city. We staked out our spots in front of the hotel. During this time, we began to meet members of his band who were recording with him, and also staying at the hotel. All of the musicians and singers, including Ava Cherry, were very kind, but none so much as Carlos Alomar and Robin Clark. They seemed to take us under their wings and they went over and beyond what I could ever imagine. Each day, we would be at the entrance of the hotel and wait for hours and usually close to 5 or 6 p.m., David would emerge from the hotel and stop and chat with us. It was the beginning of the workday for him and he was anxious, I'm sure, to get to the studio but usually took the time to acknowledge us and that was beyond cool!

While David was settling into his limo, we would hightail it to our car, pile in and drive like hell for the little over-a-mile ride to ensure that we would get to Sigma Sound Studios before his limo pulled up. We would stop and jump out of the car, even with it still running if there was a chance of missing his arrival. I believe that David was astonished by our actions the first few times, when he saw us waiting for him at the entrance to the studio, just moments after he saw us at his hotel.

I am certain that David, as well as the other members of his entourage, were both amused and bemused by our actions of dedication for David. Not only were we there when he entered the studio in the early evening at the start of the sessions, we would be there early the next morning at 3:00, 4:00 and 5:00 a.m. at the end of their "workday." After the third or fourth day, it became our well-known routine. We would greet David as he emerged from the hotel in the late afternoon, briefly chat, take pictures, etc. and then we would jump into our cars, race to Sigma and be there at the entrance to the studio before he got there. This happened every day for almost two weeks.

We hung out on the sidewalk of Sigma for hours each night, sometimes being able to hear David and the others singing and playing. It was so exciting, knowing that a David Bowie album was being made just on the other side of a wall, so close, yet so far away.

Members of the band and singers would often come out to spend time with us. They would give us messages from David, telling us "David sends his love" or "he cannot believe you are still here, so devoted…" After hours into the night, David would come out. We knew he was tired--so many times we stood back and just watched as he left. We would rush home for a few hours of sleep/rest, a shower, a change of clothes and some food and then head back only a few hours later to do it all again!

Over the course of this time, we met so many wonderful people connected with David. Ava Cherry, who at the time was a background singer with David and his oh-so-lucky girlfriend, was only a few years older than us and what a fortunate lady! She chatted with us on several occasions and was kind and also surprised at our perseverance and tenacity.

One night, David told us he had a surprise for us. He would not divulge what it was and had us promise that we tell no one else. It would be only for the handful of us who he was speaking with. Our lips were sealed. We were told to be at Sigma on the evening of, I believe, the 23rd of August. Of course, we would have been there anyway, but knowing something special may be happening, a few of us dressed up and we were waiting patiently outside the studio, not knowing what to expect. It was raining and we were invited inside to wait, still unsure of what was about to happen.

After a while, Stu, David's bodyguard, came to tell us to prepare to enter the studio, my heart beating faster with excitement. What was happening? We formed a line and we were escorted upstairs to the recording studio. I was in some sort of daze, not believing what was going on. We all sat on folding chairs waiting with anticipation for the evening to unfold. Then, suddenly, there he was! David, standing behind the control room glass, also dressed in a pale, blue suit. How sweet, he, too, thought to dress up for this special occasion.

We then were told that we would be hearing the album in its entirety: the music, the songs that had been recorded over the past twelve days. We were going to hear that! And it seemed as though David truly cared about what we thought of it. He really wanted to see our reaction and to know our opinions of what we thought of his venture into the soulfulness of the Philly sound. We sat quietly and magically the studio was filled with music, the entire *Young Americans* album was being played for us. I believe, right from the reel to reel. It was incredible, David Bowie hosting a listening party for a group of devoted teenage fans inside Sigma Sound Studios. We were hearing music that had been recorded just over the past couple of weeks, new to us and not yet heard by any other fans anywhere!

Once the album played through, we all sat. David was looking at us, seeming shy and a bit nervous as to what our reactions would be. Then we said, "Play it again" and yes, it was played again. We had loosened up by then. We danced, talked, took pictures and I was quite aware that this was a once-in-a lifetime event. We were treated to champagne and, I believe, corned beef sandwiches and the night was truly a dream I had never even imagined would happen. After several hours, it was time to wrap it up. We hugged, cried and I think almost every emotion I could feel was felt that night in that room.

I went home on a cloud. Knowing David and his group were leaving Philadelphia the very next day, we continued on with our routine. We went home, tried to catch a few hours of sleep, showered and changed, and yes, still went back only hours later to bid farewell to our idol who had showed us a truly human side of himself. Treating fans to such an amazing experience, something that had never been done before, and I don't believe any other artist has done anything like it since.

We returned to The Barclay Hotel on the day of David's departure with bouquets of flowers and endless words of gratitude and appreciation for what he had done for us. We were told that additional recording would be taking place again that November so they would be back, and of course, so would we, now fondly dubbed "The Sigma Kids" by David and the others

After all these years over four decades, I still realize what an incredible and unique experience this was and I am so very fortunate to have been a part of it all.

****

American Producer Tony Visconti worked intermittently with David Bowie from 1969 until 2016's Blackstar. In this excerpt from an interview published in www.pennyblackmusic.co.uk. February 2019, Visconti recalls working with Ava Cherry, Robin Clark, Carlos Alomar and Luther Vandross, as well as multiple instrumentalists, on the Young Americans album at Sigma Sound and his initial impression of the Sigma Kids.

TONY VISCONTI

Young Americans was a most enjoyable record to make. We had all new musicians with the exception of Mike Garson on piano. The rest of the musicians were crazy good and that included Andy Newmark on drums, Willy Weeks on bass (my idol) and Dave Sanborn on alto sax. Carlos Alomar was a fresh-faced kid from the Bronx and brought a style of guitar playing that was definitely one of the strong building blocks of that album. But Luther, he was a blessing. He was a friend of Carlos and Robin Clark, they were school days friends. Luther was the choirmaster. When it came time to do backing vocals, Luther would sing everyone's parts until they learned them confidently. It was all done off the cuff, spontaneously. There is a tape floating around of Luther, Robin, Ava and Carlos learning their parts for "Can You Hear Me". It is extremely enlightening. David and I can be heard talking from the control room cheering them on and suggesting ideas. Nothing really took long to record, everyone was so talented and professional.

The Sigma Kids started out to be annoying fans but then it kicked in that they were beautiful kids, great fans, great people to chat with. We got to know each other very well and I know many of them now! Of course, we had to invite them into the studio to hear the album when it was nearly finished. They knew all the songs anyway because they listened at the back door of the studio the whole time we were there and the soundproofing was terrible.

19.
THE UNIVERSAL AMPHITHEATRE, LOS ANGELES

Setlist (setlist.fm), The Universal Amphitheatre, Universal City, California, Diamond Dogs Tour, September 2, 1974.

1984

Rebel Rebel

Moonage Daydream

Sweet Thing

Candidate

Sweet Thing (Reprise)

Changes

Suffragette City

Aladdin Sane

All the Young Dudes

Cracked Actor

Rock 'n' Roll with Me

Knock on Wood

(Eddie Floyd cover)

Young Americans

(Live debut)

It's Gonna Be Me

Big Brother

Chant of the Ever-Circling Skeletal Family

Time

The Jean Genie

Rock 'n' Roll Suicide

John, I'm Only Dancing

*D*avid longed to crack America; he had already conquered the U.K., but perhaps he was needlessly concerned about audience reaction. Animated fans, streaming through the aisles, seemed just as prepared to roll out the red carpet as their across-the-pond counterparts.

Serious contenders, they were not to be undone by their overseas peers—

they had done their homework, too, and to prove it, they arrived with hair suitably coiffed, made-up eyes that humbled the stars, glam-inspired threads and attitudes shifted into high-gear.

Veterans Ava Cherry and Geoff McCormack stood at the ready, voices warmed. Vocalists Diane Sumler, Anthony Hinton, Robin Clark and newly-anointed arranger, Luther Vandross, tingled with anticipation.

There was a lot to take in, not just the fact that celebs like Elizabeth Taylor and Diana Ross occupied coveted front row seats: there were other concerns, such as the hot lights, the fast lyrics, the synchronized moves.

Title song "Young Americans" was multi-purpose: the pointed, political references qualifying it as a social think-piece, but there was enough back beat, riffing and repetition to satisfy everyone else.

AVA

One of my favorite arrangements on *Young Americans* is "Somebody Up There Likes Me" because it is so soulful. That was a very emotional song for us onstage. But when we performed live, "Young Americans" was the most requested.

Initially, Luther faced waves of stage fright when he was onstage with David and the entourage. David constantly encouraged him. I battled my own fears about playing to a huge crowd; David also persuaded me to break free.

One time on the first Young Americans tour, we were playing at the Universal Amphitheatre in L.A. to a crowd of about 20,000. The stage was huge. David says, "You go there, Ava. You stand there, Luther, Robin."

"Huh?"

"I'm going to come over to your mic and sing with you," David announced.

Now I'm already nervous about singing on this big stage.

David reassured me. "You'll be alright. It's a beautiful night." I took a deep breath, but then, "Liz Taylor is in one of the front rows."

"Liz Taylor?"

David's standing there singing under the spotlight. The light is following him and all of a sudden, he's coming toward me. Finally, he comes right over to my mic and I just kept singing. It was cool. All the time

I'm thinking, *I'm here, nothing's going to happen and I'm going to just do it.*

The whole experience was fantastic and I thought, *I'm never going to sing in front of a small audience again.*

That wasn't the end of Liz, though. She showed up at a rehearsal at the Universal Amphitheatre in Los Angeles during that *Young Americans* Tour. I was kind of jealous of her but in a nice way, because although Liz was very beautiful, I wasn't threatened by her in that way, except that David wanted to sleep with her because he admired her so much. He thought of Liz as a beauty queen. Now, it was never about ego or color. David didn't care about things like that if it was somebody that he liked.

So yeah, I was a little bit jealous. Nevertheless, I was very polite to her, although somewhat disappointed, because on that particular night, I would have done something with David, but he went and did something with Liz instead.

David wanted Luther to do a song with me for a show so Luther and I got together a couple of times in his hotel room to write. "Maybe It's the Love" is a song that I sang a little bit of at the Universal Amphitheatre show, but at that time, it wasn't yet finished.

Since then, though, I've added some lyrics and recorded it. This new version has not been released yet, but because we had it on tape and it was for me that Luther had started it, I decided over the last couple of years to reclaim it. The whole process involved channeling Luther. It involved asking, *what would Luther do here? How would he phrase this?*

I think the fun thing about Luther is that whenever he did write, he was always wanting to write about love. The first line of the song had to do with the wonderment and closeness of love.

It wasn't my idea, starting out the song that way, but when Luther started to come up with those lyrics, I thought to myself that since I felt that way about David, that lyric was appropriate. It was definitely a love song written for somebody that you care about. All I did was follow where Luther was going with it.

When Luther came up with those lyrics, it smacked me in the face. It was a song written for someone you would care about. Luther used to write when he played the acoustic piano a long time ago, but he stopped playing when we began working together. It was kind of like Aretha, who started her career sitting down at the church piano under the guise of her minister father; I think Aretha could play better than Luther ever did.

I worked professionally on the recording of *Young Americans* with vocalist Robin Clark, Carlos Alomar's wife, when not hanging out socially with David.

When not working, I spent free time, too, with Luther. We mostly hung out around the hotel in every city we were performing in or we would just go out to dinner, as I didn't choose to go out to clubs.

Carlos Alomar ultimately worked with David Bowie from around 1975 to the early millennium. He was an attractive Puerto Rican man. He was a little bit stocky, but he had a nice physique. In those early days, he never dressed like a rock star. In fact, he mostly wore jeans and a T-shirt and never dressed formally.

Toni Shimek recalls events leading up to and the Diamond Dogs performance at the Arie Crown Theater on October 22nd and 23rd, 1974.

TONI SHIMEK

When I met David Bowie, I was awed. He and Ava drove up to our house in a limo and my mom made us dinner. It was surreal. Ava had always been exposed to a lot of celebrities and having talent, I guess, David saw that talent.

We went to their concert at Arie Crown and afterwards, we went back to my mom's, but we got back kind of late. She wasn't even sure if we were going to show up and then we all had this beautiful dinner my mom had made. It was incredible.

From that point on, whenever we went to a concert, we always had backstage passes. We got to know the band and everyone on a first-name basis. It was fun. Backstage there was a beautiful buffet. I couldn't believe that I was part of it.

During one of the shows, Ava did a solo and I was so moved. I knew Ava had talent, but to see her onstage for the first time professionally was amazing. I was so proud. I was screaming. I wanted to stand up and shout, "That's my sister!" We had wonderful, front row seats.

I was elated and this is something that I'll remind her of until this day. The song was so beautiful and so moving. She was so relaxed and just drew the audience in. I would have been terrified. At the end, everyone was applauding. It was wonderful and it's been that way ever since. Ava's music is her bliss.

She had this beautiful, white dress on and during that time her hair was bleached white. You know, David Bowie had the same look, Ava adopted that androgynous look, too.

Setlist (setlist.fm), Arie Crown Theater, Chicago, Illinois, October 23, 1974, second show of two nights: Diamond Dogs Tour

Rebel Rebel

John, I'm Only Dancing
(Again)

Sorrow
(The McCoys cover)

Changes

Space Oddity

Moonage Daydream

Rock 'n' Roll with Me

Love Me Do
(The Beatles cover0

The Jean Genie

Future Legend

Diamond Dogs

Young Americans

Can You Hear Me?

It's Gonna Be Me

Somebody Up There Likes Me

Suffragette City

Rock 'n' Roll Suicide
Encores:
Knock on Wood (Eddie Floyd cover)

Panic in Detroit

It was an album that changed David Bowie's trajectory and baffled some fans, but its legacy would be long-lasting.

20.
YOUNG AMERICANS

D*avid Bowie's ninth studio album, Young Americans, which was released on March 7, 1975, included the following personnel: David Bowie, vocals, guitar and keys; vocalists Robin Clark, Luther Vandross, Ava Cherry; conga player Larry Washington; Carlos Alomar and Earl Slick, guitars; Mike Garson, piano; David Sanborn, saxophone; bassist Herbie Flowers; drummer Tony Newman; bassist Willie Weeks and drummer Andy Newmark, who performed throughout except on "Across the Universe" and "Fame"—drummer Dennis Davis and bassist Emir Kassan (The Main Ingredient) contributed to these tracks.*

The trio consisting of drummer Dennis Davis, guitarist Carlos Alomar and bassist George Murray AKA "The D.A.M. Trio" would thereafter perform on Station to Station (1976), Low (1977), Heroes (1977), Lodger (1979), the Live Isolar II Tour-Stage (1978) and Scary Monsters (Super Creeps) in 1980. Carlos Alomar would continue to perform with David until the Outside tour in 1993 and then play on Heathen in 2002 and Reality in 2003.

Greatly inspired by the dance music scene, David began this recording project during the Diamond Dogs tour, first at Philadelphia's Sigma Sound Studio in August and November of 1974, then at New York's Record Plant in December and finally at the Jimi Hendrix-construct, Electric Lady Studios, New York in early January of 1975. Co-produced by Tony Visconti and David Bowie and engineered by Harry Maslin, Young Americans was the first David Bowie recording to feature powerhouse Carlos Alomar, who would also serve as David's musical director for more than a decade.

AVA

David enlisted Luther to take charge of the vocal arrangements, but Luther never explained the arrangements of the parts for *Young Americans* prior to entering the studio. He would come up with ideas as the tracks would go by.

"Ava, take this note."

Now, this might have sounded random, but Luther did this methodically. He had fantastic tone, vocal ability and control of his voice. As a performer, he would bring people right to him. Maybe that's why when we were getting ready to tour, David would ask, "Should we take Luther?" Initially, Luther had been part of David's image, but he always had so much of everything. He would be dancing by his big self...

****

David Bowie deliberately shifted genre gears for this project which featured raw vocals and an extended outro. on Beatles' cover "Across the Universe." Lennon added original guitar parts and sang background vocals in addition to co-writing "Fame" with Bowie and Alomar.

Ava was in the studio to witness John Lennon's contributions to "Across the Universe" and "Fame"; the latter quickly became a number one hit in the U.S. Alomar's funky guitar riff was duly noted by King of Soul, James Brown, who unashamedly laced it through his own recordings.

AVA

Meeting John Lennon was such a sweet experience. "Today I introduced Ava to a Beatle," is what appeared in a diary excerpt displayed at the *David Bowie Is* exhibit held in Chicago. (The exhibit ran September 2014-January 2015 at the Museum of Contemporary Art and was organized by the curators of the Victoria and Albert Museum, London.) It obviously meant a lot to David to meet his idol and then to introduce John Lennon to his partner!

David was so excited to meet John at the Electric Lady Studios in Greenwich Village. I had never seen him get as excited about meeting anyone else before. John was wearing those famous wire-rimmed "granny" glasses which were so popular at the time. That was the first thing that

David noticed as his idol walked through the door. He and David hugged each other as though they had always been old friends.

Yoko Ono came, too. She brought us this huge tray of sushi, but after she brought us lunch, she just said goodbye and left. I finally understood why the Beatles didn't like her; it was because she was a feminist. In fact, I'll explain an incident that proves my point. But first, I'll tell you what happened during the actual recording session at the Electric Lady Land Studio, where Harry Maslin was the chief engineer.

John was playing around on his 12-string before he and David actually got down to work. He was in a lighthearted mood and was mumbling positive things: "I'm really enjoying myself," and "this is really nice."

It was like any other day at the studio; we had a goal. The agenda was set. David had asked John to play acoustic guitar on "Across the Universe" and sing on "Fame." The final mix would prove that we'd rehearsed well.

And even though there were these two superstars in the room, there were no ego issues; it was just two talented guys having a great time recording.

"Fame" may have only taken one day to record, but it had taken effort to become a viable product. The recording required major focus and even some improvisation. Carlos Alomar recycled the infectious riff he'd dreamed up for the band's cover of "Footstompin"; John crooned the word "aim" over that rhythm track and David brainstormed the word "fame."

My job was to sing the vocal line "fame" in the background. David showed me how to use my voice to achieve the right effect, in other words, how to keep going down in stepwise motion. Later, the engineers sped that part up and created a really original track.

I always enjoyed and looked forward to working with David in the studio. I never felt up in the air. I know some producers play games or try to control an artist, but David always explained exactly what he wanted me to do on my vocals.

So, "Fame" was co-written by Carlos Alomar, John Lennon and David, and I contributed as a singer, but initially, I was not credited as a vocalist on the recording. Because of that omission, I was not able to receive proper royalties when "Fame" was featured on a television commercial for Cadillac.

Later, my attorney and I notified David's estate so that I could receive royalties and now my name is credited on all versions of "Fame."

But back to the recording...David came into the studio agitated, probably because of the endless and ongoing managerial issues he was facing, and maybe his voice reflected that anxiety; in fact, maybe that's what gave his vocals that compelling edge, but anyway, the arrangement came magically together and garnered a lot of critical acclaim. "Fame" would even get included in The Rock and Roll Hall of Fame's "500 Songs that Shaped Rock and Roll."

That night, we went to dinner at the Dakota, the cooperative apartment on 72nd Street and Central Park West in Manhattan, where John and Yoko lived on the seventh floor. The Dakota is an exclusive property. John and Yoko had bought their unit from the actor Robert Ryan after getting a green light from the prickly board. The apartments in this massive stone building were built like individual mansions. One apartment consisted of four or five huge rooms.

There we all were, sitting on this big couch in the living room facing each other. Yoko kept leaning over and stroking John's head, as if he were a cat. David looked over and whispered to me, "What the fuck. Why is she stroking his head?"

I whispered back, "Because he loves her." I understood how much John loved Yoko. He put her on a pedestal, but he also treated her as an equal, which I thought was strange behavior for a British man.

This all happened when we were doing cocaine. David and I had been up all night long, enjoying John and Yoko's company, but suddenly the sun was peeking through the window. We had completely lost track of time. In fact, it was going on 6 am.

David asked, matter-of-factly, "Ava, can you make us some breakfast?"

Yoko narrowed her eyes and immediately shot back. "Why should *she* have to make us breakfast? *She's* been up all night, too."

John was curled up on the floor, laughing until his eyes filled with tears. "Ava doesn't have to make breakfast," he blurted out.

So, David and Yoko had a little tiff about that; Yoko had stood her ground. That's when I realized why the Beatles didn't like her when they first met; yet she was so sweet and John was so polite and friendly.

Now, at the time that we did those sessions, I didn't have any sense of where those records would go. I didn't know the scope of it. I didn't realize what David didn't do in terms of shaping my career.

David didn't educate me about the business part of the music industry. I didn't know my name should be credited. I was in love and that's all I knew. I did not take things seriously on the business level.

When we finally got to work on the Astronettes album, Tony Sylvester wanted to produce it. Tony had been partly responsible for making things come to light at the Apollo. So, it really wasn't a surprise when Tony came right out and asked David, "Can I produce Ava?"

And I wanted an answer, too. *Why can't I just do a couple of tracks so I have R&B stuff under my belt*? I thought. The explanation would have been that Tony had an attraction for me and maybe David was worried that I would cheat on him. Little did David know that that never would have happened. That's when I thought, though, *What will happen when we're not together anymore?*

Despite my concerns, David still told me no. I didn't argue with him, but I kept thinking about the situation. And in regards to Tony, I knew this was about him being a man. This was clearly a conflict.

We had some heavy conversations about this situation. I told David that I didn't want to be ostracized by my own people. Tony would have been an ally. I was constantly battling this issue, which is why I wanted a black producer to produce me. I would eventually find such allies in the black community, people like the DJ Frankie Crocker, but the road would still be paved with shattered glass.

If I could create an instant replay, I would have become much more aware of the business side of my career. So many black female artists fall into what I fell into. You just want to work with *that* person. If I had to do it all again, I would say, "I'm going to work with somebody else besides you." I would have said that.

Ava reflects back on her partying days...

21.
AFTER HOURS

*P*art of Ava's after-hours life has traditionally included going to clubs, *sometimes with David, sometimes without. With Toni, she frequented Chicago's now defunct Coconuts Record Store, where her sister recalls pushing open the door to find a huge poster of Ava stretched across a wall...*

AVA

David and I went to Studio 54 after he presented Aretha Franklin with a Grammy Award, although we went there other times, as well. Studio 54 was a fantastic place. People partied; there was a big drug scene. All the top artists of the day would go and hang out in the VIP section. Even though I don't party like this now, I won't lie. I had fun.

A couple of times, I went there with my friend Lester Hyatt, that top designer, who headed his own company. There would be a million people outside the door of Studio 54, trying to get in, all dressed crazily or beautifully. You wouldn't get in if you dressed too crazily. You had to be high-fashion.

Now, I would be dressed to kill and the security people didn't even know who I was. One night, I was wearing a sexy black, lace catsuit, a diamond-studded turban, black ostrich feathers and high-heeled shoes. The guy just looked at me and opened the gate. He didn't know if I worked with David Bowie or if I worked with anybody. He didn't even ask me my name! The whole idea was that if you looked fabulous, you were just going to get in there.

Max's Kansas City was where the musicians used to go to jam. It was kind of a dive, but we'd go to places like that in London, too, like Sombrero's.

All of us from MainMan used to go down there to drink magnums of champagne. One night in 1972, I was there with Leee Childers, who was one of the chief photographers from MainMan. I ended up sitting on his shoulders in a booth. People were cheering—I don't know why, but I do know that I was really lit after drinking a bottle of champagne all by myself. I used to love to drink champagne. We had some good times.

Once, we spent an evening there with the New York Doll's flamboyant lead singer David Johansen. David loved the Doll's high-heeled shoes, and he also loved that they painted their fingernails bright colors.

In fact, David loved anybody who was different and presented themselves the way they felt they wanted to present themselves. The LGBTQ community loved him because they could just be themselves in his presence.

As far as the club scene, it was all about who you knew; who was going to go there when, rather than the physical club environment. The scene had to do with your friends, your clique.

Like in Chicago, some of the places that Muddy Waters used to frequent, like Kingston Mines. You used to find Mick Jagger and the Stones there. They would go into these booze dives just to jam. They didn't care if it was a dive, as long as Albert King or Muddy Waters would be there. Once, Keith Richards took over as bartender at a Chicago club when he turned up for a surprise set with his heroes.

Speaking of which, I saw Muddy Waters and B.B. King a couple of times and met B.B., too, in New Zealand, when I'd been sent there on a promotion for Warner Brothers, and he was performing one night. The vice-president of the company took me to see him and we went backstage.

As for Max's, I performed there myself around the time of the *RIPE* album. It was a dive; I'll never forget the smell of spilled beer and sweat, and the graffiti in the bathrooms, but it was always full of life.

Another great club was the exclusive Tramps in London's Mayfair area, which has been around since 1969. You had to be a member to get in, and like Studio 54, the management expected clients to set the fashion bar high.

This was the expectation: "Please dress to impress, the club reserves the right to refuse entry on this basis." All of the superstars went there:

Michael Caine, Rod Stewart...the cast of Monty Python and the Stones were frequent visitors. People from all around the world would go to Tramps. Inside, this club really radiated British elegance. I mean, Tramps was very posh.

Typically, we got dressed up and drank gallons of champagne. One night, when we went there with Mick and Bianca, we had the best time because everyone was loving each other. I really enjoyed being with Bianca. Everyone was taking our pictures since we were all together, sharing such a good time. We walked around from table to table, greeting other celebrities.

Because David treated me so beautifully, I felt that I was an integral part of his life. He took me out to dinner with his close friends. I was part of his family. I really was. I was really his woman. I'm still friends with the Stones because David introduced me to everyone.

Then, there was this exhilarating "Prince Moment." I'm in this New York club with my friends, really looking hot. Prince came in and sat down in the middle of the room. Meanwhile, I'm sitting at my table, talking to my old friend, Lester Hyatt.

A stranger appears. I hear, "Excuse me, Prince wants to know if you want to have a bottle of champagne with him." I look over and there he is, waving. "What?"

I go over, giddy with excitement. He kisses my hand, widens his bright eyes. "Please sit down. Have some champagne." He didn't talk much to me at first, but I kept on talking to him. I think he and his band were performing on the same night that we were.

I started up by telling him how I loved his work, but then our conversation shifted and took a more in-depth turn. I'll always remember the way Prince put me at ease.

"It's really funny how they treat artists in this business," I said. He agreed. Prince had made some intelligent choices. He had limited the usage of his music masters for a period of six months. After that time, he made sure that the rights would bounce back to him.

We talked about how the industry cheats artists to the point where they don't receive their just desserts. We continued this deep conversation, which I liked and valued. He added that it was important to do something about this lack of fairness. Now, this was right before he began to call himself "the artist formerly known as Prince…" I was so impressed when he said that he was going to do something about this injustice. And he did.

I always wanted to look and act my best. David and Luther taught me so many things about being an artist and being in the public eye. I did everything along the years the way I remembered it. It's all lasted on me, whatever my professional training was in this business, learning it from the bottom up all the way up to producing myself.

I listened to the people who were really successful. I took chances. I was brave. I was never afraid. Those feelings have lingered. I've been able to do things that I'd never done before, learn something that I didn't know before. Perhaps it all harkens back to the beginning of my career. My hunger to succeed. My inner drive.

I had to keep in mind the reality of the times as I moved forward. Here's what one insightful writer said about backup vocalists, and this is a thought that really resounded with me over the years:

"These women have had a major impact on the way lead singers (usually white men) sang their songs, wrote their songs…"

Being one of those women, those words hit me hard, but they also helped me reaffirm my years of hard work and dedication.

Nothing lasts forever...

22.
BREAKING UP WITH BOWIE

I was hoping we'd be together forever. I would be there as long as David wanted me to be. *You belong to me right now and not to anybody else.* I was there longer than anybody else and that was creating some conflicts, too, because David's secretary Coco (Corinne Schwab) wanted to get rid of me. In the beginning, though, when we were on pretty good terms, and she would ask me to wake David up. I felt like part of the team.

"Ava, there's the coffee."

At the same time, they were all used to seeing David move on to other women. Eventually he did.

I knew Iman on a social level before she and David started dating. I didn't know when David actually started dating her, but I was invited to their Midtown engagement party by one of our mutual friends in the early 1990s. I was standing there looking fabulous when Iman walked up to me, waving her fingers in my face.

"Ava, look at the ring David gave me."

I still wasn't over him yet. I didn't feel mad, but I wondered, *why did she feel that she had to get my okay?* It was as though she was shouting, "He's mine now." It kind of hurt, because I was still in love with him.

When our relationship finally ended in L.A., David was staying in Marilyn Monroe's former apartment in West Hollywood. We hadn't seen each other in months. I was burning inside for him still, but didn't exactly know what he was thinking. Looking back, the whole story is fairy-tale like.

When I first met David, he only smoked a spliff and had a glass of wine. More drugs happened when he hung out with the super groups. Towards the end, I was afraid for him. He said, himself, after I was gone, that he did more drugs. He peaked himself out and decided not to do drugs anymore when he met Iman. Drugs kept him from having those deep, emotional feelings. Drugs made you cold, indifferent.

I used to hide the drugs from him so he wouldn't do too much. When he wanted them, he was like a child stomping his feet on the ground. I think he saw that I was a nurturer. I was a communicator to him from all the people. He would see the fans and recoil. He would calm down if I reminded him…

"It's alright. They love you, David."

But it was not just the drugs—show business caused David to feel tense. When David handed Aretha Franklin a Grammy® Award in 1975, a fan grabbed his tie. David started choking. A quick-thinking security guard cut the tie off. I'll always remember the look on his face: David was gasping for air. It was as if he had discovered that being super successful could have its pitfalls, even with the fans.

We were all so shocked when that happened. "It's rather like living in a goldfish bowl, isn't it?" David had asked me. And that is why he wandered around New York by himself. He was trying to prove that he wasn't in that goldfish bowl anymore.

David was so in love with Aretha. When he first started dating me, we went through this crazy "I just met you and I'm really feeling you" phase and there were songs of hers that linked me back to that primal feeling.

I still have Aretha Franklin's record, "Until You Come Back to Me" (That's What I'm Gonna Do) and I keep playing it, and that's because this heartfelt ballad speaks to the earth-shattering changes a lover goes through after a long-standing relationship ends. It's about the phone that no longer rings.

I used to play that song over and over and I couldn't stop thinking about it. David would call me when I was playing that song; the phone would ring and it would be him. He'd say, "Isn't that the song you were playing the last time I called?" The lyrics spoke to me and still do.

What led to our breakup? First of all, there were a lot of people around David who were trying to push us away from each other because I had been there for a long time. They were sick of me being there. They wanted

© Bob Gruen

to change up to somebody else. There was pressure around me, there were people that I felt wanted to see me gone—that's one thing.

I was very naïve, because at the time, I didn't see people in a mean way; I've only acknowledged this now, that they were there. There were knives in my back that I didn't know were in there.

The conditions that led to me leaving felt terrible. I was always friendly to everyone. People even come up to me now and say that I was so nice, "You were the nicest person," because I was so very innocent. I really just wanted to love David and be supportive to him. I never interfered with business or anything like that.

But they felt intimidated because they all wanted to be with him. They either wanted to be his girlfriend or confidante. I never made waves with those people so when I started to feel the knives in my back, I didn't understand why. I knew that I never did anything to anyone.

For a while, I didn't feel it from Corinne, who was his personal secretary, but then I started feeling it from her, too. She'd been in love with David forever, from the whole time she'd been there and she'd been there for forty years.

I really started feeling it after I was there for a number of years, that Corinne was thinking, *I'll be glad when she goes*, that kind of thing…I didn't know who it was exactly, but I felt that people were trying to get rid of me. As time went on, I noticed that she was starting to become cold to me. I put two and two together. It was time for me to go.

I just kind of internalized it and acknowledged, *Oh, they're trying to get rid of me now.* I kept trying to hold on but I felt this sense of impending doom concerning what was going on with MainMan. I was hearing that there was a lot being spent out of David's money, that people were flying all over the world and staying in the best hotels and that his money was dwindling.

When David and I were living together in New York, I had been trying to warn him. I told him that I'd heard that people who were working in the company, MainMan, were trying to spend his money, like on those first-class trips and five-star hotels and magnums of champagne, and that all that money was his. I had heard that from somebody and I told David about it, but he didn't believe me. Or maybe he did, but he just didn't discuss it with me.

Still, I tried. "David, I don't know exactly where it's coming from, but I heard this and you should look into this…"

At first, David was dismissive. He said, "Oh no, everything's okay. Everything's fine," but about six months later, all hell broke loose when he found out that someone was stealing his money and that he was broke.

Of course, he was beside himself. Shocked. I remember the fear in his eyes. "How can I be broke?"

When it happened, he completely shut down and was so depressed about the situation. You would be, too, if you heard that people were taking all of your money.

So, that's really when I started to feel these knives in my back and I really started to feel it from Corinne. Sometimes, when I'd be trying to get David on the phone, she would say he wasn't available and I knew, after that happened, that that was the beginning of the end.

And then when he found out that his money was stolen from his own people, he just broke down and cried and said, "Ava, I care about you but right now I have to worry about how to deal with this problem. I have to get a lawyer and I'm really upset."

I'm not going to say that some of the drugs weren't starting to take their toll, in terms of David not getting enough rest and sleep and not eating right. After a while, when you're doing drugs so much, your body takes a while to function. Normally you'd be feeling relaxed and not tensing.

You're up when you should be relaxed. David wasn't sleeping a lot. Most of the time he was making me stay up with him, too. But sometimes I had to fall asleep. I was tired.

I remember one day we were talking and he started to cry. "They're taking everything that I built up. They're stealing my money from me. He's my manager and I can't believe my manager did that to me."

By the time he started to talk to me about his concerns, he had obviously talked to someone else who knew more about the situation, and who confirmed that it was true, and he was already freaking out about it.

By then, he was really thinking. I could sense the wheels turning in his brain, as he was thinking. "What can I do? They're taking my money. How am I going to get my money? How am I going to stop it?"

But David, what about us?

"I care about you. I love you, but I have to fix my problem. Right now, my money is tied up!"

I was heartbroken about David's situation, but wondered: *Was I still part of the equation?*

"What do we do?'" I stammered. "You mean, you want me to go?"

He explained, "I've got to go to L.A. and I've got to get lawyers. I just can't take anyone along with me. I've got to just do this."

"But darling, maybe I can help. I love you..."

By the time he said something to me about the situation, it was already too far gone, it was too late to go into action. David was really sorry. He had to do this on his own--fight this thing about the money.

Of course, I was crying. I loved him so much. I didn't do anything wrong and he wasn't accusing me of doing anything wrong, but the circumstance was at its peak.

So, to set the record straight, we didn't break up because of something that happened between us. *That* was the reason. Of course, I was freaked out because I was still so in love with him.

Secondly, I didn't know what I was going to do. MainMan said they were going to get me an apartment, which they did, but I was going to be on my own and I didn't know what I was going to do. I was really worried about it and I did a whole lot of crying myself. I cried, cried, cried, too.

But fortunately, someone from my past would be watching over me. The next morning, my girlfriend, Claudia, called me up out of the blue, as if nothing had gone down. How could she have known?

"Hey, girl," said my old friend, Claudia Jennings. It was so comforting to hear a familiar, friendly voice.

It was so weird. I knew Claudia from Playboy. She'd been on the cover as a playmate. Hefner loved her and we were close friends, but I hadn't talked to her for a long time, and now for some strange reason, on the day before David started talking to me about all of these troubling things, she had decided to call me up.

"Hey, Ava. It's Claudia. I'm coming in from L.A. to New York tomorrow. Are you around? We can hang out and have lunch."

As I answered the phone, I tried to keep my voice steady. I managed a weak "hello," but Claudia didn't buy it. She must have detected the sadness in my voice.

"What's wrong? Are you okay?"

I couldn't hold back any longer. I started to cry. "I guess I'm breaking up with David. I don't really know what's happening but I'm freaked out. He said he's going to leave for L.A. and he can't take me with him."

She said, "What? Oh, my God. Look. You just stay there until I get there." I said okay, although I didn't know what she was planning to do. I wasn't mad. I was sad and upset, but I was so glad that she would be coming to my rescue. I immediately felt protected and loved and knew she wasn't going to let me down. And I also knew that I just didn't want to be in New York all by myself.

As soon as Claudia came over, I introduced her to David. He looked at her face as though he'd seen her before, he looked at her face as if he already knew her, and yet, David had never met Claudia before. Still, he was on a mission.

"What's going on?" She started right out like that, the minute they met. David immediately tensed up but Claudia didn't flinch. She was committed to getting the facts.

"Ava told me that she had to leave here and that you two were breaking up."

David started to explain that he had to go to L.A. It sounded like he was reading from a script.

Claudia stood her ground. She wasn't buying it. "What about Ava? What are you going to do with Ava?"

"She'll have to take care of herself for a while, make her own way," David shot back.

David was already sending out flares. Claudia shook her head and redirected her focus to me.

"No, no, no. Pack your stuff. You're going with me. I'm going to Jamaica to see Chris Blackwell. He owns Island Records. Pack your bags. You come with me."

When she said that, David looked back at her in disbelief. She was getting ready to take care of me. It was girl power.

All I know is, it was like a dream—all of a sudden, this woman had become my knight. David was thrown off base. He had rented an apartment for me and paid the rent for three months, but I didn't have any furniture in it. So, I didn't even tell the people involved what I was going to do; I just didn't move in.

"Just pack. Let's get going." Claudia's authority was a comfort.

With those words, Claudia was giving me hope, saving my life. My friend, Claudia, was shaking me out of the darkness. Saving me.

But it was a scary feeling, not knowing what would happen next, which I tried to process, and tried to explain. She just happened to show up in New York! What was going on? But I got everything packed up and next thing I know, I was saying goodbye to David.

David seemed very upset about Claudia showing up and whisking me away. He said he didn't think it was right that Claudia was doing this, yet he didn't want to actually get involved.

Claudia whisked me away and all of a sudden, I was on the plane to Jamaica. I felt protected and heard. I knew that she wasn't going to let me down. She was one of those people who, once she took you under her wing, you weren't going to fall. She wasn't ever going to let that happen.

There were other celebrities who consoled me. Iggy Pop, whenever he was around, was always fun and always nice. When David and I broke up and I was in L.A, I ran into him and we hung out for a couple of evenings.

He was totally sympathetic. He knew that I was really in love with David, and that David was trying to control me through my emotions a little bit, and that this was a difficult process. He was telling me to take one day at a time. He talked about David going through this terrible time, of being ripped off, and that even if I took it personally, David didn't mean to hurt me. Iggy Pop was very, very compassionate.

Bette Midler could be outspoken in public, but knew I was really fragile. She's a woman and she understood how I felt. She helped me tremendously in a time of great need.

But Claudia was the one who stopped the chaos, whisked me away and gave me the courage to move on.

Whisked away by an old friend, Ava reboots.

23.
BOB MARLEY

S o, there we were in sunny Jamaica. We hung out with Chris Blackwell of Island Records, who was managing Bob Marley, and even spent some cool time with the reggae star. Our plan was to stay a week and then go to Barbados and finally to Florida for another week.

I admired Bob Marley because he had always been receptive to new ideas. He was inspired by everyone from producer Curtis Mayfield to the Beatles.

Marley had been raised primarily by his single mother, Cedella "Ciddy" Malcolm; his grandfather, Omeriah Malcom; and maternal great-grandmother, Katherine "Yaya" Malcolm in the district of Nine Mile in Jamaica.

With the Wailers, Bob cut his first tune, "Simmer Down" in 1964. Lineup changes two years later resulted in Bunny Wailer, Peter Tosh and Marley working as a trio. Their reggae style was driven by electric guitar and a slowed-down beat. The cool genre began to gather steam and garner admirers back in 1969.

We were there in Kingston, Jamaica in early December of 1976, which turned out to be an intense time. The elections that year had triggered political upheaval. And although the reggae star had declared himself neutral, he was accused by a group of siding with one specific party.

So, during the time of our stay, seven armed men raided the Marley home and brutally attacked Bob and his wife, Rita, two days before his group, Bob Marley and the Wailers, were set to perform at the Smile Jamaica Peace Concert, at National Heroes Park, on December 5. Ironically, the band had planned that concert to ward off any threats of violence.

Despite this traumatic event, Bob Marley kept his word. The band performed a 90-minute concert for 80,000 fans. I admired his courage and held him in high esteem.

And there I was with Claudia, who was a successful actress. She was a truly loyal friend, but I was wondering how she viewed our relationship—was she sacrificing her professional life for me? All I knew was, she took care of me. I don't know what I would have done without her intervention. She was a lifesaver. It was like God was over my shoulder. The situation happened and boom.

Claudia and I were staying near 56 Hope Road. Bob would often be playing in the back of his house. One day, mesmerized, we listened to him rehearse. That was really something.

I should also mention that I had seen Bob Marley live earlier that year at the Santa Monica Civic Center on May 27, 1976. When I put this performance neck to neck with other incredible acts, Bob Marley always comes out on top.

That L.A. concert was sold out, so Chris told me that I'd have to stand on the side of the stage if I wanted to catch his act. Of course, I would have stood anywhere to see Bob Marley. That night, I witnessed the most incredible movements during that performance. It was sexual, but spiritual. Bob's dreads were swinging back and forth. He was very sensual, but it was the spirituality that spoke to me. He played the expected hits, "War" and "Everything's Gonna to Be Alright." I don't know exactly what it was about him, but I was very aware that Bob was a sexy man.

This was Bob Marley's first American tour in support of his new album, *Rastaman Vibration* which had already raised a ruckus in the U.S. Critic Robert Hilburn wrote a review in the LA Times on May 29, 1976 about that same concert ("Bob Marley Has Arrived"): "His moves and music were absolutely riveting. At times there was a magic in the hall Thursday that reminded one of the days of the old Fillmore when rock music, more than simply entertainment, was a meaningful and communal experience."

Claudia and I hung out for a while. Wow. It was a sexy encounter. I had never been a groupie and I had met lots of superstars, but I do admit that I was tantalized by Bob Marley and how sexy I thought he was. This is what I told my L.A. roommate Michael the day of that concert, as I dashed out of our apartment:

"I'm in love with Bob Marley. I'm going to make love to him tonight."
Smirking, he responded, "Oh, sure, right."

Yes, I'm going to make love to Bob Marley...

I was longing for love, wanting to taste it. Once I set my mind on it,
I knew I had to put my arms around him, like a tigress stalking her prey.
Wonder what his lips are like? I whispered to myself, scheming.

And then, when I saw him on stage, I repeated to myself, *I have to
make love to him.* I wasn't surprised that there were huge clouds of smoke
that afternoon backstage or that it was really crowded.

I walked into this room and there were two seats which were higher
than everyone else's. Bob was sitting on one of them. The wheels were
turning.

All these people were around him so I leaped on to the top of that
one empty step stool so that we could both be of equal height. The other
people there, surrounding him, were all of the same height. All of a sudden,
he noticed me sitting there at the very same level. Wasn't he thinking, *She
wants me to notice her?*

Bob smiled at me. I had finally gotten his attention. But I still wondered,
How am I going to do this? I waited patiently until everyone left the room.
He waited, too, and then looked at me, as though for the first time. It was
up to me to make the next move.

"Uh, Bob," I began, inching forward, "I really admire you so much and
I'd love to talk to you about your music."

"Oh, yeah." He moved closer, too. "You want to talk to me about my
music?"

He laughed and handed me a hotel room key. That was it?

By the time I got to the hotel room, it was full of people, including
members of his family, and his wife, Rita. I didn't know Bob was married
until I got to the room.

At first, everyone was socializing, but then the crowd slowly began
to trickle out. His wife saw me and said, "Have a good time," and then she
left, too...

In those days, people were easier on their mates. They did whatever
they wanted to do. Bob's wife was used to him sleeping with other women.

They left the room with us still in there. It was very romantic. When I left, he said he really enjoyed my company.

Then we both laughed. So, I did see Bob Marley again after that night, later in December, but never again at that level. But I had done what I had told my roommate I was going to do.

That was the only time that I did that with a superstar. The reason we didn't meet anymore is because Bob was married. This wasn't something his wife wanted to see as a daily habit.

But it was an experience I'll never forget. He even teased me about getting pregnant. Bob would ultimately father more than eleven children. He had a knack for that kind of thing. In fact, here's how that conversation went...

"You have a baby?"

I said no.

"You want a baby?"

I said no.

I didn't argue with him. I knew he hadn't given me a baby. I had protected myself from that—I do treasure my little one-off with him, though. He was such an attractive, sexy man.

He was wearing his usual outfit, jeans with a cool-looking shirt and jacket, but the dreads were the most magnificent part of how Bob came across, not that jean jacket. When I came home and told my roommate the story, he was just hysterical.

I learned more about Bob Marley when I attended a rehearsal. He was very serious about the pacing, where he wanted the song to pause, where he wanted it to slow down. He was very direct but nice, not demanding or anything when working with other musicians.

I had so much admiration just for Bob Marley's songs. But when I saw him perform live, it was just so powerful. He was the most incredible, powerful, who-could-make-you-feel-something artist. Besides David's, his show was really incredible. He was sexy as hell, oh my God, the way he would move on stage and the way his dreads would swing in rhythm to the beat.

Of course, I was already comfortable being with producers in the studio by that time. David also had that knack, he knew how to work with musicians. He knew if you don't do things right at the right time, you ruin the entire process.

But back to my days with Claudia. After our jaunt to Barbados, we were off to L.A. Claudia had been living there with Bobby Hart, who managed the Monkees. She was already making additional plans for me.

"We're going to go back to my house in Laurel Canyon," Claudia announced. When I got there, I knew what I had to do. I made a phone call to Michael Lippman, David's lawyer. I had known Michael from before, so when I called his office, he immediately took my call.

"I know I haven't seen you in a long time. I just want to talk to David. I heard things are going on with his management."

"We got a lot of things fixed," he shot back.

"Can you please ask David to call me?"

"I'll ask him."

The next day, the phone rings and I rush to pick it up. I was grateful to hear David's voice.

"How are you?" he mumbled. He was clearly not himself.

"We just came back from Barbados," I explained.

"Where are you now?" His tone was urgent.

"Laurel Canyon."

"I'm going to come and see you."

"You are?"

After I gave David the address, he assured me that he would come down immediately. As soon as I heard the bell, I ran to the door, breathless. We embraced.

"I was worried about you," I admitted. Then I did a double-take. David was standing there, sullenly, gripping his suitcase. When Claudia came to the door and joined us, she did not stand on ceremony.

"David, why did you bring a suitcase?" she bristled.

"I'm going to hang out with you," he returned.

I sucked in my breath. David was not in a good way.

Claudia, always sensitive to my feelings, sensed my concern. She nodded. "It's okay, Ava."

Fortunately, Claudia was extremely well-connected. She was friends with actors Natalie Wood and Robert Wagner. They had a place in Century

Center. She asked them if she could stay in their two-bedroom apartment.

So that was it. She swiftly announced, 'We're going to go to Century City."

Now, Capricorn is a masculine sign. Claudia was that powerful. David's a Capricorn, too.

She takes us to this apartment. We get on the elevator. David hates elevators. We walk into the apartment. David never even said thank you.

We get a place for a month. Claudia had her own room. There were things going on that David didn't talk about to me. He stuck pretty close to us the whole time, but he was going through these radical, emotional changes and he wanted to dissect my relationship with Claudia. He was trying hard to get into her head.

David was very possessive. He didn't want me to work with anyone else. He was probably wondering how much influence Claudia had over me. It was clear: Claudia was protecting me because she felt that I was so fragile, but this bothered David.

She wasn't the only woman who came to my aid during this devastating time. Singer Bette Midler visited Claudia's place the night before David showed up. I was crying and she was very sympathetic. I'll always be grateful for her soothing words. But all the while, David wanted to know what made Claudia tick. I could see the anguish in his eyes. Was he losing control over me?

He still wasn't together. He was staying with us until he decided what his next move would be. Claudia paid all of the bills. I believe she justified this by thinking, *I'm helping a superstar*, but she never discussed the money with me. In fact, she seemed okay with taking care of the finances until she found out that David had run up about a thousand dollars of long-distance bills. When she saw that phone bill, she paid it but things would never be the same, she was very upset after that point.

Still, we had fun. We went to a bunch of parties during that time. Then, Michael found David a place and he left us. I felt the weight and loneliness of the void, but Claudia took it in stride

"Get used to it, Ava. It's over," she said, matter-of-factly. Claudia refused to languish over the situation. She still had her home and she didn't want her boyfriend to know everything that was going on. She didn't want to bombard him with other peoples' problems so she got herself another place. I treasure the time we spent together; eventually, Claudia would die on the Pacific Coast Highway in the pouring rain.

David and I saw each other after that but those encounters were one-offs. One night, he invited me over to Marilyn Monroe's former house. It was a nice house and I felt comfortable being there with him until he told me that it was haunted.

We were still super connected. I still wanted him to touch me. He was still so sweet to me but I didn't get the impression that we were going to get back together.

After I left David, Ronnie Wood asked Claudia and I to come and visit. So that was when we went to Montauk Point and hung out with the Stones. I guess Ronnie hadn't told Mick. With his arm still in a sling after walking through a glass door, Mick came into the room and smiled.

"Ava, what are you doing here?"

I didn't tell him right away. He was trying to go to sleep. They were in rehearsal during that time for the Steel Drums Tour.

It was like a private concert with people I respected and I dug being around. Keith Richards and I stayed up talking all night long. He was so down-to-earth and we soon found ourselves talking deeply about life. He had such a sweetness about him. Keith always made me feel comfortable, and just like Claudia, he recognized that I was really fragile. Even now, he gets mad when he thinks about David breaking up with me.

They did old classics, like "Satisfaction," which they've been doing since day one. But each time they played those same songs, they came up with an entirely different sound.

Over the last ten years, whenever the Stones would put on a show, I would be there. It would be the most incredible show: the brightest lights, the most vivid screen, the biggest stage. They really spent a lot of money. I loved watching Mick run to one side of the stage and then the other.

Their fans amazed me. Everybody, young and old, the droves of people in front and behind you, they knew so much about the music. They knew all the lyrics and if you were coming backstage, you were treated so wonderfully. I never saw anything like this before. They used to put on the dog.

Lobster, filet mignon. There were tables lined with bottles of vitamins. You could take those vitamins and make smoothies. We never had that, not even later on with Luther but after leaving David, I could always turn to those memories for consolation.

Where Ava's brief brush with royalty was upstaged by an unusual sandwich.

24.
THE QUEEN MOTHER

A short time after meeting Bob Marley, I ended up rubbing shoulders with posh royalty. It all started when I met Michael Butler, the original producer of the counterculture, sixties-themed musical, *Hair*. Michael enjoyed being around the British elite. He struck me immediately as a very intelligent and creative man who liked to live well.

Michael owned an estate with polo grounds where top American polo teams would play. We were in the midst of doing a play about the reggae culture, which is why he sent me to Jamaica to meet with some people and conduct research. I went to rehearsals but the project fell by the wayside. Now, they may have put the show together on a small scale at some point; I don't know, we never completed the project together, but our friendship yielded some incredible experiences.

First off, I got to meet the entire British polo team, which was really cool. I found polo to be such a fascinating equestrian sport. Because I became really friendly with the team, they invited me to the Queen's Jubilee, where they were planning a polo match with Prince Charles.

In London, I stayed just outside of Windsor in the house of one of the team players, which was really upper-crust. I discovered that with the British elite, everything is about protocol, including the way the table is set and everything else.

So, here I am, this little Chicago girl with short, blonde hair. The team was convening right behind Windsor Castle and they invited me up for the week. They had set up this great big tent right by the place where the match was being held.

I walk in the tent and the Queen Mother is sitting there. The polo player wives were going up one-by-one to greet her. The guests were dressed the way they dressed, very formally, and there I was in my shorts and T-shirt. Nobody seemed shocked. I looked nice, but I suddenly felt out-of-place; it's just that everybody there was conservatively dressed.

I said hello to the Queen Mother and bowed. She was very sweet. On the other side of the tent, there was a big table where tea was being served with sterling silver flatware. And there were a lot of cut sandwiches on the table.

So, I go over to the table to make myself some tea and get a sandwich and I see all these sandwiches with no crust on them. So I said really loud, "Where are the crusts on the bread?" They roared with laughter. Turns out they always cut the crusts off the bread, but I didn't know that.

The Queen Mother laughed and then calmly explained, "Oh, darling, here we take the crusts off the bread." That was the extraordinary day that little old me got to meet the Queen Mother.

Ava learned much from Luther Vandross…

25.
LESSONS OF LUTHER VANDROSS

Multi-Grammy® winner Luther Vandross, Jr., whose sonorous background vocals appeared in recordings by Judy Collins, Bette Midler, Todd Rundgren, Ben E. King, Diana Ross and Donna Summer, also produced records for Dionne Warwick, Diana Ross and Whitney Houston and too many other artists to list.

Ava had sung in tandem with Robin Clark and Luther Vandross during the leaner David Bowie years. Rising to the occasion, she fulfilled Vandross's precise demands after Bowie designated him vocal arranger extraordinaire.

Later with Vandross, she punctuated album projects such as Give Me the Reason (1986).

Although during Luther's lengthy solo career the instrumental lineup would predictably undergo changes, the following artists figured prominently: arranger/pianist Nat Adderley, Jr. (Who doesn't know "The Work Song"?), bassist/co-writer Marcus Miller, bassist Byron Miller, percussionist Steve Croon, jazz guitarist Doc Powell and bassist Tinker Barfield. Over the years, background vocalists included Alfa Anderson, Lisa Fischer, Cissy Houston, Pat Lacey, Paulette McWilliams, Cindy Mizelle, Kevin Owen, Alfonso "Fonzi" Thornton, Brenda White and of course, Ava Cherry.

Luther always had ambition. In fact, he reportedly once even snuck backstage and pretended to be a fashion designer so he could meet Patti LaBelle and the Blue Belles. The charade paid off—Luther ended up becoming president of Patti's fan club and a selective buyer for the vocalist's extraordinary wardrobe.

A phenomenal mentor, Luther's background singers became an integral part of every performance. On a circular stage, as Luther's silky voice rang out, his angels made sweeping gestures or emphasized cadences with tight, empowered fists. Perhaps "Any Love" prompted the most dramatic overtures. "Searching" sometimes invited undulating gestures that were far more subdued. Years later, YouTube fans, still stunned by key live performances, referred to Luther's singers as "beautiful, handsome and statuesque."

AVA

Of course, I already knew Luther Vandross well when he was part of David's band, when he wasn't big yet. He was just a really talented artist who was trying to get work. When I first met him, funny enough, I was making a thousand dollars a week, and I think, he was making less than that. He called me and told me that he had asked David for a raise. I think David gave him that raise, but begrudgingly.

So, when I first met Luther, it wasn't like I was meeting anybody with superstar status or anything like that. But we'd spent professional time apart, with both of us growing professionally in different, but meaningful ways.

Here is how we reconnected. I hadn't worked with Luther since we had both worked for David. I was sitting in this restaurant having lunch on Sunset Strip in L.A. There was a dinner going on in the other room and the door swung wide open. I looked over in the doorway and I saw Luther sitting there at the big table.

Now, all I could see from that angle were the people sitting there on Luther's side—I couldn't see the whole room. In those days, I was full of energy, so I go running into the room. There were all of these stars: Aretha, Gladys Knight & the Pips and a bunch of other superstars sitting at the same table, deep in conversation.

I got down on the floor; I got down on my knees to speak to Luther. But then, I suddenly realized that I'd just run in there and didn't really know what was going on.

Luther must have sensed my embarrassment. Nevertheless, he acted very sweet. I started whispering, "I didn't know what was going on..."

He says, "That's okay, Ava. How are you doing?" He asked me for my phone number. I wrote it down and nervously handed it to him. Then, I stooped down and crept out of the room so that I wouldn't be interfering with anything else.

Shep Gordon was Luther's manager at the time. The next thing I know, I get a call from Shep. He said, "Luther's getting ready to do a tour and he needs a second alto. He asked me to give you a call and see if you might be interested in doing it."

Yeah, I'm getting excited. Shep gave me all the details. I'd have to fly to New York to audition with the other singers. Now Shep, he was a great manager, but it's a tough business. He and Luther fell out as managers, as sometimes artists do when they count their money and they don't think they've got everything coming to them; sometimes they fall out.

But I was very excited. I flew to New York and auditioned with Lisa Fischer and Alfa Anderson; Kevin Owen wasn't there yet. This audition was for the international Bad Boy Tour. I remember Luther asking me to speak French when we did that leg of the tour. I had learned a little French in school but became fluent when I lived in Paris in my early modeling days, back when I worked at French Vogue and Paree Match and my agency sent me to Spain and all of those other European places.

I learned early on that Luther was a very generous man. He would always buy things for the girls—Cindy, Lisa, Paulette and me...One particular year, I came on tour and I had a mink coat. All the girls loved that coat. It was a black, diamond mink. So, for Christmas, Luther bought everyone a mink, including me. So, at that point, I had two mink coats.

There were other times when Luther spared no expense. Once in London, he took Lisa and me to Versace. I eyed an original Versace jacket in a boutique. Now, this was when the designer was still alive.

 "Ava, do you like that jacket?" Luther's tone came across as nonchalant and friendly.

"Mm hm," I said, not predicting any particular outcome.

"Go try it on."

Now, this was a five-thousand-pound Versace jacket which I still have. Luther bought it for me and I never wore it, but I still have it. I wanted to keep it nice. And he bought Lisa a jacket, too. Then there was that Louis Vuitton handbag that cost about four thousand dollars. As for the expensive, hand-beaded gowns? Each of us female singers had three, and Luther bought us shoes, hats and purses. He spent about ten grand at Versace.

****

The vocalists treasured their gorgeous performance gowns, but the onstage logistics often posed challenges. Working with Luther Vandross meant enduring ten-hour rehearsals with choreography always coming first. Practicing a set routine in a leotard is one thing, but what about singing and dancing in view of thousands of people in a floor-length Tony Chase gown and heels?

A native New Yorker with a naturally good eye, Chase developed his first product line in 1982. His clients included Bette Midler, Dolly Parton and Cher. Espousing the philosophy that he serves "all women," not just runway types, Tony was never intimidated by a generous pair of hips or ample cleavage. Still, what was it like for a member of Luther's entourage to sing and dance in a dress that deserves to be delivered in a Brinks truck?

AVA

When I first met Luther, he didn't have the money for fashion, but when he started making money, he became more and more interested in the suits designed by Versace and the Armani gowns that we wore.

It was an experience because the first ones we had, the black ones with the sequins and the trains, well, we had to learn how to walk and move around with those long trains and all those gowns weighed about forty or fifty pounds. They were all hand-beaded, all the way down to those trains. Now that was funny because sometimes I would pick up my train and pull it up to my heart. Most of the time, Luther wanted to have the trains move with us, so that when we moved around, you could see the train move, too. I would do that, except for every now and then...

Lisa's train was heavier than mine and she couldn't always pick it up. It was a fun experience. I loved wearing those glamorous gowns. Now, by the time we got to wearing those green ones, we'd have to put those skeletons on underneath, which were the same, round size as the dress. They would first put the skeleton on us and then put the dress on over that so that it would look round and full. That was a different experience, too, learning how to walk like that. There was a different balance. The trains were pulling you. Your legs would have to stay strong as you were walking. You had to walk so that the skeleton wouldn't tip over. They were fun, though. They were so much fun, those dresses, but they were heavy.

Now, when we wore gowns, we'd wear shoes made from scratch from beads that would match the gowns. Sometimes those shoes hurt. I had a charley horse once. You're flexing your foot in a way when you're doing certain dance moves. I was in pain. I was doing a routine with Luther and I told him that I had such a bad pain in my foot.

He consoled me. "On the next song, you come offstage." So, I was able to get offstage for about ten minutes. I was going to fall and I could feel that I was about to have a spasm. These are all the things that you have to worry about onstage.

Of course, Luther always entered the stage dressed to kill, too, with his jacket fabric echoing the gowns or a silk bow-tie and vest tucked snugly underneath. I admired his consistent sense of style.

Luther admired me for my natural sense of style, too. He would invite me to dinner and say, "Ava, you have good genes. From head to toe you're perfect." I'd be wearing the same clothes that I'd worn in my much younger days. And Luther had no problem giving it up. He'd casually tell me, "Diana

Ross told me how professional she thought you looked tonight."

To Luther, performance was an art. The stage had to look absolutely perfect. Luther would pore over those 1000-page, hardcover Erte books and pull out staging design ideas. Luther was fascinated by those Erte-designed fashions from the 1930s. When you were dealing with Luther, you knew that the audience would be seeing the best presentation of every show, from the beaded gowns with those long trains to every drop of makeup and, of course, the lighting.

Russian-born Romain de Tirtoff (Erte) was considered "the father of Art Deco." After relocating to Paris, he designed everything from programs to costumes and stage sets, with his work featured in the Ziegfeld Follies in 1923. He ultimately designed 240 covers for *Harper's Bazaar.*

Now, Luther and I had our moments, but he would try to keep his entourage happy. If we talked about leaving the show, he'd pipe up: "Just when I was ready to give you a one-thousand dollar raise?"

Luther also wanted us to wear these long lashes so our eyes could be seen from the top of the stadium. We called them "sweepers" because they were so big. We didn't like wearing them, though, because they were so heavy on our eyelids. I didn't really like them, but Luther did. He was insistent: "I want sweepers on their eyes, every night. Every night!"

One night, Jeff Jones was doing our makeup and he said, "Oh, my God, there's no more sweepers!" We were laughing. "There's not?" We knew that Luther was going to freak out or blow a gasket. Because I thought we could get away with it, we put two together to make them bigger.

I took a deep breath. I had a routine with Luther where he said, "She won't talk to me" and I walked up to face him, and the look on his face when he saw that those weren't sweepers! He just kind of looked at me and mumbled under his breath, "Where are the sweepers? What did you do with the sweepers?"

Now, there we were in the middle of the routine, but I wanted to burst out laughing. I finally whispered back, "There aren't any more." Luther kept on looking at me, as if to say, *Why, why, why, aren't those sweepers on your eyelids?*

When he came backstage after the concert, he started back up. "Why didn't they have the sweepers backstage?" We explained that there weren't anymore. Luther shot back, "I want you to buy cases of them. I never want to look at Ava and not see those sweepers on her face."

I'll say this, Luther wanted us to look beautiful and we did look beautiful. He wanted everything to look perfect when we went onstage with our dresses. Our attentiveness did not go unnoticed. In fact, *Chicago Tribune* entertainment columnist Greg Kot ("Vandross in Control," October 13, 1993) wrote this about our performance at the Rosemont Horizon during the 1993-1994 Never Let Me Go World Tour: "Resplendent in emerald glitter."

Denise L. McIver wrote in Variety (January 10, 1994) about Luther crooning, "Never Too Much" and how the then-trio added just the right flourish before a star-studded audience: "Then, backup vocalists Lisa Fischer and Ava Cherry —wearing breathtaking gowns—and Kevin Owens, arrived onstage, and led them for more than two hours through his extensive repertoire of Grammy®- winning, platinum-selling songs."

But sometimes we had a problem with those hand-beaded dresses that went all the way down to the bottom of the train. We would lose those beads, sometimes. For instance, maybe Lisa would step on mine or I would step on hers. Sometimes, the threads of the beading would come off and we would have beads all over the stage. Luther would see them and go, "Oh, Lord."

I'd hear him telling the little old wardrobe lady, "I want every bead back on there tomorrow when we do the next show." Sure enough, this patient hero had the dress beaded perfectly by the next day.

And Luther would always remind us, "I'm not playing the lottery." He'd be paying everybody top salary for the tour and he wanted everything to be perfect.

In every arena, we'd be grossing around twenty-five thousand unless we were performing with another artist. We'd go into the stadium and I'd be friendly to everyone. I'd be looking glamorous and I'd say hi to the sound guy. We had extra sound and lighting people every day. We had our own crew that we would travel with—like fifty of us—but we also had extra, and I would go in every day and say hi to everybody.

They'd say, "Hi. You're coming in here to say hello to us?" And I'd say, "Yeah, you guys are helping us to make the show great." The people in every town we went loved me. I was so nice to them.

Sometimes, things backfired. On one particular night, we're onstage with the lighting guy. Lisa and I are getting ready to go upfront. Luther's talking and, all of a sudden, the lighting guy puts an extra special light on me. Luther, all of a sudden, looks over at me, like, *What the heck is going on?*

The lighting guy had blinked the light on and off to let me know that it was him. I was getting all this light every night. Light, light, light. I didn't know it because I couldn't tell where the lights were hitting the stage until Luther came to the stage and I heard him say to somebody, "Why is all that extra light on Ava?"

And then the sound guy would make my mic a little louder, too. All these beautiful people were just wonderful people. But one day I said, "You guys almost got me in trouble." And they said, "Oh, we didn't mean to, but you're so beautiful and so nice. We just wanted to give you a little extra..." It was sweet, very sweet.

When I was working with Luther, I would wear something different every day. I went to this rehearsal one day, wearing this pink, beautiful suit.

Ava with Lisa Fischer and a friend after Luther Vandross's passing

He followed me onto the stage.

"Ava, you look impeccable from head to toe. Everything you are wearing, I love. You have such style." I got a lot of compliments like that from Luther.

But as far as performance… "Ava, I know you're used to being a lead singer but it has to sound like one voice, so pull back." But by the time we finished out that year, we could blend like butter.

Luther really taught me something else, too. If you make a date to make a session, you show up. I will always remember how Luther pulled me over to the side to explain this to me. He would never make these judgments in front of the group. This happened during the recording of "Original Sin" and I'll always remember those words.

One time, when I first started working with Luther, I came to the session and Lisa Fischer was already there. We were asked to sing our parts. All of a sudden, I realized that I didn't remember my part. I tried, but I kept missing it.

Luther comes up to me after the rehearsal. He sang the part into my Dictaphone. He faced me and said, "You have to get the part by tomorrow. That's so important if you want to be on this tour."

I kept turning that Dictaphone part on and off so I could memorize my part over and over again. I kept on practicing and practicing and when it came time for Luther to hear me, I sang it exactly right.

Another time, I was singing really hard. I'm a second alto so my voice is very strong. Luther came right over. He was gentle, but firm. He said, "This has to sound like one voice, Ava. Pull back a little bit. You're sticking out."

Even after all of these years, Luther's voice still echoes in my mind. *Why are you saying that to me? What did I do wrong?* When I first heard those words, I felt self-conscious. I was still learning my craft. I could only sing if I was facing the singers directly, but after a while, I developed more confidence. After a while, I could turn around and sing the same note that they were singing. I could hear the different harmonies and how the arrangement had become so finessed. Luther helped me become a better singer. We were feeling each other's intensity. We just sounded like angels. Like butter.

Once I arrived at a session at 3:00. But by 2:30, Luther had already finished working out the vocals. He said, "If you ever ask me to do a session with you and you show up late, I'll never work with you again."

"But I didn't mean for YOU to be there at 2:30," I countered.

"I don't care. If you call a session at that time, YOU BE THERE." Luther really did leave an impression on me.

The goal was this: Singing—where we blended together, sounding like one voice. We had six hours a day of this. We had Paula Abdul and Lester Wilson. Luther would get a chair and watch. We'd be doing different things.

He'd say, "Ava, extend your fingers. Extend your arms." He was watching you.

There was nothing but rehearsal, rehearsal and more rehearsal. All that rehearsing will make sure you were tight. Rehearsal. Rehearsal. Rehearsal. That's the only reason.

Sometimes, there'd be smoke on stage, oil-based smoke, and we'd get bronchitis. I told Luther that we were getting sick from the oil-based smoke and he changed it to steam but then during a dance routine, Lisa fell because the stage got wet. You always had to worry about hazards.

Another performance challenge we faced had to do with the everyday, onstage mechanics. During the second stage of my working with Luther, we had cordless mikes for about seven years. When I first started working with him, we had cords. Those gowns sometimes weighed forty pounds and we had to learn how to walk erect with them on.

At times, we would be playing places where the temperature would be about ninety degrees and Luther would tell the staff to turn the air-conditioning off. You'd see the audience fanning themselves and each other. A lot of the pictures of us onstage show that we were really working up a sweat. It was dripping from us. I would constantly be wiping sweat from my brow. My chest was also dripping wet. We were all aware that temperature affects the sound of the voice. The voice gets cold and that's why Luther didn't want the crew to turn on the air-conditioning, because it's terrible for your voice.

It really didn't bother me too much, even though the lights were hot up there. It bothered the people in the audience more, I think. They'd shout, "Turn the air on." But yes, Luther was a stickler for that. No air-conditioning.

In terms of the *Give Me The Reason* album, Kevin Owen, Lisa Fischer and I did the background vocals on the "Give Me The Reason" title song. I remember one night on the road, Luther said, "Ava, Lisa and Kevin, I want you to record 'Give Me The Reason' with me. You guys are going to go along with me and the rest are going to go to the next gig."

We had been on the road for a long time. We were completely wiped but Luther had already made plans for us to go into the studio. It was early, about one or two in the morning. Now, and I'm still surprised as I tell you this, that recording came out so beautifully, but there we were, so tired, slumped down on chairs. We'd get up to the mike, but every time we finished, we'd slump back down into a chair. Overall, though, it was so much fun and wonderful working with Luther in the studio.

What a master. Luther got so much out of you and knew exactly what he wanted. We just had a ball. Now, he had his standards. You couldn't garble your words. You had to enunciate crisply those background parts. Luther had the most beautiful tone. He made you feel.

When I record, you always hear the words that I'm saying. A lot of times these singers, you hear them and think, "What did they say?" but Luther was a stickler for enunciation and a stickler for catching sharp notes, too. Sometimes we'd be on stage, and if there were a sharp note, Luther would whip his head around, as if to say, *Who was that who sang that sharp note?*

Once, there was a discrepancy with a note onstage that Paulette McWilliams and I were singing. Luther thought it was me. Now, Paulette was a really fine singer but she makes mistakes and we were singing on the same note but I think Luther thought it was me. He turned around afterwards and asked, "Ava, was that you singing that sharp note?"

"No," I said. "It wasn't me." Now Paulette sang pretty much perfect every time but everybody makes mistakes and I made some, too, but at that particular time I didn't make that mistake. And he'd remind us, "Just be careful about those notes!"

As far as performing live with Luther, "For You to Love" is one of my favorites. It was so beautifully arranged and so elegant in terms of the choreography and all of that. I loved "Any Love" but the choreography was really hard on that one.

Now, I was on top of the stage with Lisa and Kevin but there were other singers in the pit: Paulette McWilliams, Cindy Mizelle, Patricia Lacey and Tawatha Agee was there sometimes; in fact, there were generally three additional singers at a given time. There were other people whose gifts Luther enjoyed, but they were not on stage with us: Fonzi Thornton, who was Luther's best friend and Marcus Miller, the bass player who co-wrote many of Luther's best-selling songs.

Yogi Horton was an incredible drummer who had played with the Rolling Stones. He was an incredibly funny guy who could do impressions of Sammy Davis Jr. and all of that. He could make you laugh and I loved him.

Yogi was from Atlanta. Every time we went there, we enjoyed his family garden, from which they grew everything that they cooked: tomatoes and onions and greens and peppers. Every time we'd go, his family would cook these magnificent meals for us. We couldn't wait to go to his parents' house because they would really lay it out for us.

Now, I got sick at one point in the tour and had to leave for a couple of weeks. During the time I went to L.A. to recuperate, a tragedy took place. Yogi and his wife were in the hotel room getting ready to play at Madison Square Garden (ironically his wife's name was Ava, too, and a lot of people thought that any reference to "Ava" was about me.)

Looking back, Yogi had had some problems with drugs at that time but no one could have anticipated the trauma that finally transpired—Yogi jumped out of the window and killed himself.

When Yogi died, his family was so hurt and traumatized by his passing and, of course, I felt really bad because we loved Yogi and his family so much.

On January 12, 1986, when Luther had relocated to the West Coast, another tragic incident shook up the entourage. This time, it involved fifteen-year-old singer Jimmy Salvemini and his brother/manager, Larry.

Luther had taken a strong interest in Jimmy's promising career and had just finished producing the vocalist's debut album. The bond had deepened considerably since they met. Luther loved introducing the brothers to his favorite spots and was always anxious to show them off to his colleagues.

He even took them along when Stevie Wonder asked Luther to add some background parts to a new track. The boys were excited and couldn't wait to hear the final studio mix...

On that morning, the three men were riding in Luther's Mercedes-Benz down L.A.'s Laurel Canyon Boulevard. Luther cautiously approached the swerving Mulholland Drive; Jimmy was seated next to Luther and Larry was in the back seat. Luther was coming up on the left, as cars flew up from both directions. When Luther approximated his destination, a vehicle veered into his blind spot and broadsided Jimmy's side of the car. Luther was devastated. There had been a three-car collision; other passengers came away with broken bones.

At Cedar-Sinai Hospital, Jimmy, Larry and Luther were rushed to the emergency room. Luther was treated for cuts, bruises and broken ribs, but Jimmy was diagnosed with a collapsed lung; fortunately, they would survive, but Larry's fate, that was lethal. After a harrowing two-hour operation, Larry was pronounced dead.

We didn't know if the tour was going to continue. We didn't know if, or how quickly, Luther was going to recover, mentally or physically, because he was really traumatized by the accident as well.

Now, Luther was a very strong person. He bounced back, but the band helped him to bounce back. We had booked all of these dates, and sometimes, even when tragedy hits, you have to move on anyway because people had paid for their tickets. I think his family thought working would be good therapy for him, rather than thinking about this tragedy all of the time and feeling so sad about it. But the cost for all of us was great.

So first of all, you were hurt, and then one of your best friends, who is sitting right next to you, gets killed. How do you rebound from that?

Finally, Luther decided that we would go ahead and tour. I remember being surprised. I wanted us to continue the tour. I needed to be working, but we all decided that we would give Luther a lot of love and moral support, which is what he needed most of all at the time.

Luther pulled through. He was very, very professional and I believe our support was healing for him; just the fact that he could talk about it with us. When we were all on the same bus, we could interact, but after a while, Luther made another decision. He got his own bus.

Cissy Houston was one of the Sweet Inspirations. She sang background on a lot of the Luther Vandross records. Apparently when she did "You Give Good Love," she wasn't really noticed. The way to achieve that degree of visibility was to open for a major act, like for Luther. That being the case, Cissy asked Luther if her daughter, Whitney, could open for us.

Luther wanted to help, but this was a big ask. "Well, let's listen to what this record is and we'll see what we can do."

One day when Lisa, Kevin and I on our way to a gig at Madison Square Garden, Luther filled us in.

"Cissy wants her daughter, Whitney, to open for us, so let's listen to the record." He put on "You Give Good Love" as we were riding in the limo. By the end of it, we agreed that the record was really great and Luther decided to give Whitney the spot.

Whitney was very sweet and innocent and only about eighteen when we met. She was not very knowledgeable about makeup and clothes. She wore dresses that went below her knees, and at any given time, her hair was hastily pulled up in a braid. She would often come into the dressing room as Lisa and I were getting our hair and makeup done. Wide-eyed, she'd exclaim, "Wow, this is how you guys put on your makeup and how you do your hair?" So, Whitney learned from me and Lisa how to do her makeup and hair. Of course, I had been in fashion for years before that, at this point in my career, I mean, this was second nature.

And after that, people would always say, "You look like Whitney Houston," and I'd say, "Wow, if you really knew the story, because she really looked like me and Lisa. She learned how to do her hair and makeup by coming into our dressing room before the show."

Luther would often peek out into the audience when Whitney was doing her show to see how it was going and notice that it was emptier at Whitney's show; people didn't yet know who she was. She picked up speed after being out there with us for a while. Ultimately, the arena was packed by the time we walked on.

Whitney's vocal tone was totally different than her mom's. Cissy was old-school and Whitney was more new-school. Like her mom, Whitney was a team player, not like some of our other opening acts.

I'm going to tell you about one of the greatest, highest-grossing tours financially for Luther. It involved Anita Baker. She had a No. 1 album at the time, and Luther did, too. Luther wanted Anita to open for him for that reason.

The situation began to heat up after Luther's accident on Mulholland Drive. After that incident, Luther considered himself lucky to be alive—there had been talk about cancelling the tour, but he decided to forge ahead. Of course, he needed people around him to encourage him and support him, so cancelling the tour would not have been a good decision. We were surrounding him with love in order to help him heal. He did, and it was a brilliant tour.

You have to consider what our tours were all about. They were like Broadway musicals. We had skits and lots of costume changes. No expense was spared.

At first, things were cool on the three-month, Any Love World Tour (1988-89) which began in September. Luther was busy celebrating *Any Love*, a top ten album which had reached Platinum, but the first major, terrible thing that happened was this: our other act, Anita Baker, who joined us in October and was enjoying the success of her only No. 1 U.S. pop album, *Giving You the Best That I Got*, decided to put "Stop to Love" in her show, while we had it in our own show. The acts were being promoted as The Heat: Luther & Anita Live.

We were getting ready for a show one night when one of our people tipped us off, "You're not going to believe this…"

When Luther heard that Anita was going to sing "Stop to Love" in the show, his jaw dropped. "What?" He was so pissed off and I definitely didn't blame him.

"She's not going to do this. She's not going to be singing this song."

So, as Anita came up to the stage, Luther confronted her. "Anita, why are you singing 'Stop to Love' in your show?"

She snapped back, "I can sing any song that I want to in *my* show."

Luther shook his head, "No, no, no, you're not going to do that song." They argued back and forth. Luther threatened to sue her. I don't know if anything happened legally, but she stopped.

And after that, the dynamics changed. Luther started disliking Anita a lot. Every night when we went into the dressing room, he'd be talking about her. Her behavior bugged him, and he had something to say about it every single night.

But that wasn't the only issue. Now, our dressing rooms were pretty much on one side of the arena. When we were tending to makeup or wardrobe, as we did about twenty minutes before we went onstage, we'd be startled because all of a sudden, the doors would slam shut. There we were locked in our dressing rooms. You'd have to have a key to open up.

So. more than a couple of times, Anita's people would lock us in our rooms before she went onstage. To make it worse, when our friend Teddy Pendergrass came to visit, he even got locked in the room with all of the furs and couldn't get out.

Luther didn't know this was happening and we had to act fast. When we told him what Anita was doing, he was shocked. "What? Why would she do that?"

Luther didn't really get where Anita was coming from and we didn't either, but he made it clear that he was going to do something about her antics right away. Now, there was usually nobody in the hallway at all before the show—Luther changed all that. He put a big chair in the hallway and sat there all by himself. Anita was beside herself. "Luther, why are you sitting out here disrupting me before I go onstage?"

Understandably, he roared, "This is my show, not your show. I can sit anywhere I want to sit. And why are you keeping people from leaving their rooms? Why are you locking the doors? My people are professionals. They would never disrupt or change anything while you do what you do. There is no reason for it. And we are also getting ready for a show. You cannot do this."

Anita, in a huff, responded. "I don't want anybody on the stage when I'm getting ready. I need my meditation."

Luther came back, "You're going to have to get over it. You're not going to be pushing my people around."

Anita then threated to quit the show. "Alright," Luther fumed. "You're the opening act. You don't want to make the money? Then you stop. We'll let somebody else take your place."

Anita did her act, but Luther was still livid and made this announcement. "For now on, they are to be on the other side of the arena.

We don't want to see them." So, that's how we ended up doing the whole tour.

After some time off and after Anita had finished touring with us, Luther went looking for another opening act. He chose En Vogue, an American R&B act consisting of Dawn Robinson, Terry Ellis, Cindy Herron and Maxine Jones for the *Never Let Me Go Tour* of 1993, which included England, Germany, France and the Netherlands as major stops.

Lisa and I had mostly played in arenas like the United Center, mostly large places that held about 25,000 seats, but En Vogue had never played arenas before coming aboard our show. Nevertheless, when Luther decided that they were going to be on the tour, Lisa and I were cool with that. We had class.

But as we were rehearsing and getting ready for the show, we started hearing rumors that these young women were saying, "We're going to blow Ava Cherry and Lisa Fischer off the stage." And of course, that wouldn't have happened. After all, these girls had never even played arenas. We had such a classy, beautiful show and here they were, trying to knock us down. In fact, the press at every show backed us up when they compared our performance to theirs.

Yet En Vogue had the nerve to let it leak that they were saying stuff like that…Still, we just did what we did. And remember, we had twenty-thousand-dollar gowns on, all handmade, but they had knock-off dresses.

On the very first day of the show, we performed brilliantly. I didn't see En Vogue open, but we saw the next day that *USA Today* had written a complimentary piece about how Luther Vandross came out in all of his splendor, and there were several nice comments about Lisa and I. As for En Vogue, the reviewer simply said that their performance was okay.

When we passed by their dressing room, the girls were crying. They basically had to have their tails between their legs because they had said all of these things, while Lisa and I had never said anything about them at all. We always made it a point to be professional and polite, the way we should have been.

But there was war after that. They would come out with the same kind of hair style and the same color gowns that we were wearing. So, Luther had no choice but to make this edict in the dressing room.

When Luther spoke, his voice was trembling. "You can't wear the same hair that Lisa and Ava wear. You cannot wear the same kind of dresses or dresses of the same color. Nothing. You can't do it."

But they would still be doing it. I guess they were trying to look like us. I don't really know. Their motivation was not to do their show; it was about us. Things started to get worse and worse; tensions started to really escalate.

At that point, Lisa and I would go before our own show and take a look at theirs. When En Vogue started to disobey Luther about hair and clothes, Luther started taking things away because they were not only disobeying him, they were using our stuff. Now, their stage was on top of our stage. Our sound was helping them, and our lights, too. And here we were, letting them use all of our stuff.

So, one night, Luther went out there and demanded that En Vogue start breaking down their own stage sets. But still, they kept on and kept on and kept on. And one night, we went up to the high section, where the audience can only see the performers from the screen; they appear very small once you're sitting on top of the arena. Luther took the screen out so that people could not see En Vogue, or in order to see them, the audience would have to squint to see the stage.

They still didn't stop, so Luther took their sound away. He warned En Vogue that they would have to provide their own sound people. This led to fighting and people calling each other names. So, all of that developed because of their initiative, because of what they did, not because of what we did. Luther ended up firing En Vogue before the tour was over. But vocalist Oleta Adams took their place and she was brilliant.

Luther taught us many things, such as where your voice will sound the best onstage. A lot of times we didn't have monitors on the floor, we had them overhead because having them on the floor didn't make the stage look great but it wasn't great for a singer's hearing. You had to hear up above you. So, I learned my stagecraft, how to work a stage.

The choreography was crucial. Now, Lisa and I were singers; Paula Abdul choreographed some songs on one tour, but Lester Wilson did most of the choreography. It was hard and sometimes we cried or said, "Oh, God…" There were ten-hour days, six days a week.

You learned how to work with a band and how to feel them while you're singing. You learned how to blend with the other singers. Now, I had been a lead singer on my own and Luther acknowledged that. "Ava, I know you've been a lead singer, but now you've got to blend with five or six other singers..."

Without looking at them, you have to feel them and that's hard. There's an art to being a background singer. It's different than being a lead singer. You could be a great background singer and not be making records. But he encouraged us to do both, so I actually learned how to sing lead and how to do my own background parts from Luther.

Luther would often pair us on stage together. As for Kevin Owen, he was my brother. He was actually kind of a buffer for me when I was frustrated. He'd say, "Come on, Ava. You can do it." We did a lot of dance routines together. Kevin had been a choreographer so his steps on stage were always superb. He knew how to walk with us, with the trains of our dresses and everything. He was the perfect match for that trio onstage. Kevin was extremely professional and an extremely talented vocalist.

Luther knew he wanted two females on stage and a guy. But he must have changed his mind—after we left, Luther had Cindy and Brenda White King, and another girl that I didn't know well, up there with them.

One of the highlights of touring with Luther was performing at Wembley Stadium in London. When I was with David, I'd been in London a lot and had released a couple of records there. I was always doing promotion out of that city so when Luther told me where we were going to tour, I was so happy because I already had so many friends there. Life was different in the U.K. When I lived with David, I lived on Oakley Street, which was right off of King's Road, but I also lived in Kensington and Queen's Gate Terrace—I lived in some posh areas.

Luther loved Wembley as well. He loved being there or anywhere in London. We had a chef who would follow us around and cook incredible meals for us every day. We'd look forward to those meals. I remember thinking, *when we get to London, we'll get to eat all of that great food...*

Not that we didn't have great food here in the U.S., but the chefs across the pond really did it right. I felt very at home in London all of the time. Even after we finished touring, I took an apartment there and stayed for about eight months. After each tour, I would stay in London and just hang out because I had so many friends.

In places like Tennessee and Chicago, Luther was king. I think people all over the country appreciated him, but they really loved him in England. They would scream through the whole show. Luther would say, "I can't wait until we get to London," because we wouldn't really have to work as hard there. They would watch us come onstage, the music would start and the audience would go, "Ah…"

Wembley was an electrifying experience and we also played Albert Hall which was great, although a little bit posh, but we had so many wonderful gigs in London.

Backstage I had crème de la crème people coming. A lot of stars came backstage. Luther would ask, "How do you know all of these people?" By living there, London became my second home.

Now, in contrast, there were definite drawbacks on our American tours. Up until about two years prior to Luther's death, he'd complain: "If you were a black artist doing pop, you'd have a hard time."

You had to be pop in order to be number one. Michael Jackson finally made it there; everybody else was trying to get to where he was, but the system wouldn't allow everybody in.

When I played with Luther in Detroit, we'd often end up at the 15,000-seat Joe Louis Arena. Luther quickly got tired of playing that arena. It wasn't about the money; Luther understood that only playing the Joe Louis Arena meant you weren't accepted as a pop artist at that time.

Diana Ross was with the Supremes for all those years, and after she dropped them, she became the "Queen of Pop" in her time. The same thing happened with Lionel Ritchie when he embarked on a solo career.

But I noticed that when they became pop artists, they lost some of their black audience. I'd go to their concerts and mainly see white faces.

During the time that I worked with Luther, we generally had a loving relationship. I know he loved me and I loved him, but sometimes there were some powers that be that didn't like me—they would get petty or sometimes we would get into little arguments about things. But then again, Luther would ultimately attempt to make things right. So, sometimes Luther would praise me, and other times, he would call me out and ask me if I was singing a sharp note. He would often get moody because, I think, sometimes the diabetes would make him moody. It wouldn't be just me; it would be other people, too, sometimes, more so the people who were there at the end. When I came aboard, Paulette McWilliams and Lisa Fischer were already there. Kevin Owen was the only one who came later and then Cindy Mizelle.

I loved payday when I was with Luther, mostly because of the ritual— there was this guy who was tall, light-skinned and lanky whom we used to call "Count the Money" who became the man in charge. He had his arm handcuffed to the suitcase containing the cash with which everyone would be paid. When we saw him walking, we'd chant in unison, "Count the money, count the money..."

Now, Luther always asked for his money before he went onstage because some of these promoters were shady and they tried to avoid paying people. Meanwhile, we'd be waiting for "Count the Money" to get an advance. Yes, the minute we saw "Count the Money," we knew it was payday.

But outside the collective, like brothers and sisters do, we all had our personal commitments. When I was with Luther, I maintained a solo career; I was always doing something solo. Even when I was working with him, I would always be working on a record or something like that.

During the last few years of my time with Luther, we had some amazing moments. In honor of Inauguration Week, we attended Bill Clinton's Presidential Gala, more specifically, "The Call for Reunion" at Lincoln Memorial. The A-listers kept on coming: Michael Bolton, Bobby McFerrin, Smokey Robinson, Tony Bennett, Melissa Etheridge, Trisha Yearwood, Harry Belafonte, Sidney Poitier...

On Sunday, January 17, 1993, Luther sang "The Impossible Dream" and received a huge standing ovation. He was very proud to perform at that function and we all did a beautiful show. Canadian entertainer Celine Dion also did a wonderful job. That was also around the time that I finally came face-to-face with my mother's idol.

As I mentioned, Frank Sinatra had been my mother's all-time favorite singer and after he died—when she was recovering from an operation— she sank into a deep depression because she loved him so much.

When I heard that Frank Sinatra would be on the bill with us, I screamed "Oh, my God, Frank Sinatra!" He was in the dressing room right down the hall. I noticed his son, Frank, Jr., standing outside. He looked just like his dad and it was clear from his demeanor that he was very sweet.

Breathless, I approached him. "Excuse me, Frank, Jr., could I get your dad's autograph for my mom?" I explained that my mom idolized his father and that I did, too, and that I would love to meet him.

Frank, Jr. came back with, "Oh, my dad's not feeling too well today, but he'll give you an autograph." When I told him my name, he went, "Oh, my God! Ava!" because his dad had been married to the actress Ava Gardner. He didn't have to coax me to go on in.

Frank, Sr. was so sweet, too. There he was, impeccably dressed in a tuxedo. I confided, "Mr. Sinatra, I'm such a fan and my mother worships the ground you walk on. I grew up on all of your songs. I know every lyric, every line."

"Oh, that's so nice," he shot back. Then, he asked me my name. Just like his son, he reacted strongly with, "Ava, oh, my goodness, that brings back some memories," and "Old Blue Eyes" then gave me a hug.

I told him that I was on tour with Luther Vandross. Frank and Luther had been planning on doing a duet, but unfortunately, Frank had to cancel before they got onstage, as he had the flu or something. Yet he was still very gracious to me. I tried not to laugh when he reacted to my name. And when I showed him my mother's picture, he smiled and acknowledged that she was very beautiful. Because my mother had played his records all my life, I felt like I knew him. It was a very wonderful connection for me. That was my Frank Sinatra moment.

Around that time that we did the President's Gala with Bill Clinton, Luther and I had had a little tiff and I didn't come back. Well, we got over that and I went on to do another project, but that was the end of our touring together.

Luther would call me back every once in a while, for special shows. For instance, I was in New Zealand and his road manager, Taft, called me for a show and then once in Marseilles, he asked me to work on a show, there, too.

Taft was a killer road manager, the best you could find. He was the number one exceptional road manager. He made sure everyone got their money and everyone was picked up and everything was correct.

Being on the road created health challenges, but I was on it. I started trying homeopathy and using herbs to heal. Luther and friends would call me Dr. Cherry. One time we had bronchitis. The crew was putting smoke on stage and Luther told them to stop; every time we cleaned out our lungs, they started up again, but I had my juice and blender backstage. I was determined to stay healthy on the road.

We had every tour catered with Luther and David. That's the thing about working with a large tour, those things get catered every time.

At home, I go to the gym every other day. I eat vegetables and fruits and goji berries, almonds and walnuts. I also maintain a steady diet of protein, especially in the form of chicken and fish. No dairy, but I drink almond milk.

Taking care of the voice, now that's a constant. It's such an essential part of the body. It likes warm more than it likes cold. Warm tea is better than ice cold milk. Oregano oil keeps germs away from the respiratory tract. I also drink peppermint and ginseng tea. With the voice thing, when I cut diary out of my diet, this is what helped me the most. The most important thing is the discipline. When I see something works, if I see it keeps me healthy, I do it.

A person doesn't get a million chances. When it came to drugs, for example, I thought, *I'm not going to do it,* and I didn't. There are so many things that I still want to do. I'm definitely into taking herbs and vitamins. If I had to, though—go ahead, nip me and tuck me.

Luther always suffered from low-grade diabetes and was taking pills at the time for that. He had weight issues, too, and sometimes he would go on a very strict diet where he would only eat some protein and vegetables once a day and so sometimes we would run into him when he was especially moody.

Sadly, Luther struggled with food issues for a good portion of his life, but stayed away from liquor, cigarettes and drugs. He often worried about the effects of extreme temperature on his voice and that of his singers.

Luther always had two sets of clothes. He would want to look his best while on tour so he would diet. For me, all the talk about Luther's weight was difficult. I never dealt with weight. I always ate whatever I wanted to eat. I could always wear the same clothes and he'd notice and comment, "You wore those same clothes ten years ago. You've got really good genes."

When I first met Luther, he was probably the biggest and when we were touring, he'd get a little bigger, but I personally kind of liked Luther meaty. I thought it was sexy. Once he got very, very thin but that wasn't my favorite weight. My favorite weight was when your bones tell you that you're supposed to be a certain weight. When you're trying to be thinner, it makes your bones look different so I personally liked him when he was meaty. I did. But he could move around that stage, baby. He could dance around that stage.

The reason that Luther became ill was because of the stroke. His mom, Mary Ida, told me that the week before he had the stroke, he told her that he was eating more, and she told him, "Son, don't eat that much today."

He started complaining a week before the stroke that he was having headaches in the back of his head. Of course, his mother was a little bit concerned about that. This was a week before the stroke and she had talked to him every night and every morning. One night, when she called, she became really worried when her son didn't answer.

At first, she thought that maybe he was with a friend, but she called him in the morning and he didn't answer either and she started really getting worried at that point. Finally, his assistant, Max Szadek, went over to his apartment and forced down the door. Luther had been lying on the floor for many hours, suffering internal bleeding from the serious effects of the stroke.

It was very sad because they had to try and connect those dots. It was very sad and touched me in a personal way, as my dad had had a stroke, too. His whole left side was paralyzed and he never came back; some people never do.

They have to try to connect those dots with you at the hospital within three or four hours afterwards, otherwise there is some brain damage. I don't think they got to him until after he'd been laying there for about ten hours.

There was always hope. His business manager, Carmen Romano, had thrown Luther a big birthday party. When I got to the party, Luther still hadn't arrived. Mrs. Vandross and I started talking. We were standing in the kitchen when Luther came in; he was seated in a wheelchair. Mrs. Vandross had tears in her eyes. She loved Luther so much and he loved her so much. The whole thing was so sad but we made the best out of the situation. We all just partied and honored Luther's birthday.

Of course, we were all so sad and upset and didn't know what was going to happen. They managed to save him, but then he was in therapy for about another two years before he passed. And I did see him a couple of months before he did pass.

Luther Vandross died July 1, 2005, at 54 due to complications of a stroke. The stroke occurred after he was adding the finishing touches to his collaboration with Richard Marx, "Dance with My Father," which was ultimately awarded four Grammys. Earlier in his career, he had signed with producer Clive Davis's label, J. In 1981, "Never Too Much" sold a million-plus copies. Between 1981-1984 he scored a major R&B hit annually.

"There are no sad faces here. It's not a mournful service. I'm celebrating because Luther would want us to," said Patti LaBelle, speaking at Luther's well-attended memorial service. "God gave him a mighty voice to sing you a song."

The three-hour service took place July 8, 2005 at Harlem's Riverside Church, where the beloved singer's open casket stood side by side with a white-robed choir. Luther, too, was dressed in pure white.

At Luther's funeral, every type of delicious food and pastry was served. His repast was incredible. Everybody showed up. I went to the gravesite with Stevie and saw Freddy Jackson, Peabo Bryson, Wallace Simson, Alicia Keys and Patti LaBelle. Everybody who was anybody was there to pay their respects. People sang and eulogized Luther. Everyone who ever toured with him was invited to come onstage and we all sang "Power of Love."

Songwriters Ashford & Simpson, as well as Usher, Aretha Franklin, Stevie Wonder and Dionne Warwick were in attendance. Aretha's passion flowed forth in the spiritual "Amazing Grace." Patti LaBelle sincerely sang "No Ways Tired" and Stevie Wonder delivered the plaintive "I Can't

Complain." Cissy Houston's "Deep River" brought fans, friends and family members together in another contemplative moment.

Fans flocked to view the procession in pouring rain, as vehicles slowly drove through Harlem, pausing respectfully at the renowned Apollo, where Vandross had been awarded second place a couple of times...

Luther's legacy was achieved through tireless determination. In the beginning, he was mentored as a young vocalist with Listen My Brother. He also celebrated life on the steps of Sesame Street. In those early days, he forged a friendship with the then-aspiring Chicago "House" icon Frankie Knuckles in the Bronx, all before finding fame.

I saw Luther face life's toughest challenges head-on. You might say that Luther and I were cut from a similar and very durable cloth.

Ava recalls a heartfelt conversation with her father...

26.

ANTONIO CHERRY

AVA

When my dad died, it was such an emotional time. I was living in L.A. doing studio work and singing gigs. My mom called to tell me that my dad only had a couple of months to live.

I can still hear the weariness in her voice. "No use in you coming home, A, there's nothing you can do. They took Dad in. He has cancer."

But I told my momma that I wanted to come home. I hadn't seen Dad in a year-and-a half. I ended up spending a month with him, and it was a wonderful month, too. My father never complained, but he talked openly to me. He used to say, "I wonder when God's going to take me."

I would ask, "Dad, are you in pain?"

He'd say, "Just a little."

If he had lived longer, he would have been in excruciating pain. He was 6'3" and weighed 175 pounds and when I saw him, he couldn't stand. I was powdering his diaper when I saw that he had tears in his eyes.

"I'm sorry you have to do this."

"Dad, I love you so much."

My dad had so much dignity. He was waiting patiently "for God to take me." It was my intuition that told me that I had to go home, that I had to see him.

"Ava, this is a hard business. Don't ever give up on your brain. Keep doing it."

We shared such quality time. In the month that I spent at home, I got to change my dad's diapers and feed him. I got to ask him questions and tell him things that I never got to say to him before.

Those final days brought forth a flood of bittersweet memories. One day, my momma started getting mad at my dad. My dad had been a tennis pro. If he hadn't been a black man, he would have been successful. He let all of that go and got two regular jobs.

One day, I spoke up. "Dad, you never followed your dreams. You could have been a tennis pro."

As soon as those memories came back to haunt me, I knew I had to readdress that sensitive subject.

"Dad, can I ask you something? Remember when I was 13 and I asked you why didn't you become a tennis pro?"

He remained silent.

"I'm so sorry I said that to you."

"No, A, you were just 13."

"It was so wrong for me to say..."

My dad would only open his eyes when my mom would say something to him. I tried my best to offer support.

"Listen, Dad, when you feel dispirited, just let go. When you feel like you have to let go, let go."

When that happened, he opened his eyes and said okay. He held off a while and I went back to L.A. About two weeks later, the phone rang. As soon as I said hello, I could see my dad standing there in this white robe. I kept my eyes closed. I knew it was him. I saw him in Glory. I was so glad he didn't suffer in pain.

Even now, I talk to his picture. He's been gone more than twenty years and it seems like it was yesterday.

"One Less Bell to Answer..." That song, which was recorded by the Fifth Dimension in 1967, always sticks in my mind. That's a band that stayed healthy and worked healthy. They're still together, but that specific lyric reminds me more and more of my father.

Why didn't they ask me?

27.
20 FEET FROM STARDOM

20 Feet from Stardom *is a 2013 documentary directed by Morgan Neville that premiered at the Sundance Festival on January 17th. The film received an Academy Award® for Best Documentary Feature at the 86th Academy Awards Ceremony. Through this film, producers Gil Friesen, Caitrin Rogers and Michael K. Ross shed light on the challenges faced by unsung singers of the touring and recording industry via extensive interviews and related footage, which included shots of Ava Cherry. Also included were Darlene Love, Judith Hill, Merry Clayton, Lisa Fischer, Tata Vega and Jo Lawry.*

After a Chicago screening in July 2013, Ava was invited as a featured guest to participate in a Q&A. Because she appeared in the film and had so much experience in the industry, she was the perfect choice to host post-film discussions in her hometown.

AVA

Truthfully, I was not involved in that documentary as far as them photographing me for the actual show. They already had so much footage of me with different artists that they had to put my name in there, but they never interviewed me. I asked why and I was told that they didn't know how to get ahold of me. But truthfully, if you really want to get ahold of somebody, you can. Nobody made the effort to actually get ahold of me so that they could speak to me in person so they ended up using a lot of footage of me with different artists instead.

It was an excellent documentary, but I wish they would have asked for my personal point of view. I did a Q&A in Chicago around the time of the documentary's release in which I feel I gave a more accurate picture of the industry than some of the other singers did.

Of course, at the time, it made sense for Lisa Fischer to be in it, because she was with the Rolling Stones and Luther. So, they thought of that as a double way of getting a testimony about the Rolling Stones and Luther and whomever else she had worked with.

I remember reading an article about Merry Clayton. She'd been asked to sing backup on Lynyrd Skynyrd's "Sweet Home Alabama." Now, keep in mind that, even though this song has a catchy backbeat, Merry probably had to grit her teeth to get through that session. See, black people were still facing segregation and rampant racism in that state and all across the South.

The singers they actually pulled in to do the documentary were Judith Hill, who sang with Michael Jackson, Darlene Love ("He's a Rebel"), Merry Clayton and Lisa Fischer. But there are so many more, especially black singers, that contributed to rock stars and people in the business and the filmmakers just picked those four. There were a couple of other people shown on the documentary, but it was mainly about those four.

They went out of their way to find every image of me with Luther and David. Now, Merry Clayton, I can understand giving her what she got. I mean, if it hadn't been for Merry Clayton…"Gimme Shelter" was one of the most powerful songs ever recorded with a singer, especially a black singer. The Stones were already a super-successful band but when Merry did that vocal, it kind of changed the face of it. Her appearance made the sound deeper and so much more intense.

Every singer's situation would be different. If we hadn't been associated with a specific act, things would have been different. If I had done that documentary, I would have asked, "How do you think you contributed to this rock band's success? What do you think you brought to the table?

The film developers studied the inequities of this business and the singers broke it down in a meaningful way. Still, I had a lot to say. I wish they would have asked me.

With David, my contribution to pop culture there, was when he decided to leave his glam rock era and create a soul band, which he discussed at length with me. He asked me, "How could we do it? How could we go about it?" So, I helped him with that and with what he was envisioning.

What I started moving was about David's thought of even hiring a man of color, and after hiring him initially, performing soul music. After I was gone, Carlos, who was a full-fledged guitarist, could also move on to play on other projects, and he could do that with David as well. I'm sure David liked Carlos Alomar's work ethic.

So, as far as getting the party started—"Hey, you're almost there and you should be there," is a common phrase, but something else has to happen. When I was doing the Q&A, I explained that a lot of other things happened. They don't all make it. They don't all think, "Hey, you're almost there."

People got caught up in drugs. They started out well but then they got caught up in that situation or they didn't work for a while. They didn't really push themselves. They never reinvented themselves. They didn't continue to pursue their craft and pursue their goals like they did in the beginning.

One audience member asked about singers who had dropped out. It really depends on you, how you conduct your life. A lot of people in the industry who got caught up in other things, alcohol or drugs, took it to a degree where they couldn't come back.

But other people like me are never going to give up. They're going to be throwing dirt in my face, but it's about your *chutzpah* and what kind of drive you have. In this business, if you don't know it well, it can really bring you down. *"Wow, I've worked so hard. Why am I still here? Why am I not there?"*

It's really potluck. You were there at the right place and the right time or you didn't carry on when you should have. There were some groups that would ask you to tour for three or four years and then they wouldn't ask you to tour again, but every single singer's situation would be different. They should have asked me.

Back home, Ava knows what she has to do. In her own words, and through those of production experts, Bobby Colomby and Bob Esty, the team looks back and analyzes the key factors that positively and negatively affected the making of Streetcar Named Desire. Additional past and current projects are also highlighted.

28.
BACK HOME AND SOLO

1980 *RIPE!!!* RSO, You Never Loved Me

1983 *Streetcar Named Desire*, Capitol

1986 with Luther Vandross, did *Any Love* album and more.

1987 *Picture Me*, Capitol

1995 *People from Bad Homes*, Griffin

1997 *Spend The Night*, J-Bird Records, 6-track EP, 1997

Mayfield, a native Chicagoan, began his career as a teen vocalist with The Impressions. His songwriting canon would go on to include 1965's "People Get Ready" which fused soul and political consciousness-raising. He went on to compose the soundtrack for 1972's Super Fly. In the mid-90s, he was awarded a Grammy Legend Award and a Grammy Lifetime Achievement Award.

AVA

I did not go off the deep end. I saw the folly of it. So many people lost everything they had. When I left David, I came home and Curtis Mayfield signed me to his label, Curtom. Life threw me into something else. Curtis Mayfield gave me the opportunity when nobody else did. His actions changed the trajectory of my life.

Working with Curtis Mayfield was wonderful. "Okay, now, babe, sing that part like this." He was a very nurturing producer. If a director/producer knows how, they can get so much out of a performer.

I also worked with Motown producer Gil Askey. Now, this was soul music. It was a completely different kind of singing and it required different kinds of producers. R & B and soul producers are so different. Curtis could sing the song exactly how he wanted it to sound and he made it easy.

I have to emphasize that they were two different genres: rock and soul, and not everyone got it, but then there were vocalists like Tina Turner who did. She was able to mix the rock sound with soulfulness. Aretha and Gladys Knight were my favorite vocalists, but when I sang, I sang an octave lower than Aretha.

RIPE

Recently, *Ripe* got reissued. The experience I had with my first recorded album in 1980 was mostly about me learning to work with different producers. Of course, I had worked with David, but that was more about the rock music side of what I was doing. When I did *Ripe*, that experience was about my education with R & B producers, specifically, working with people like Curtis Mayfield and it was a great experience. I even had a chance to showcase my material at Max's Kansas City.

Before that, I had been doing rock stuff with David. This was a great experience because I didn't do that much writing before the first album. I let other people write for me because I was more concerned about singing the songs than writing them.

And I had some help. One of the guys who produced one or two tracks on that album was the musical director for Motown and Diana Ross for many years. His name was Gil Askey. His hit song was with a girl named Linda Clifford who's from here. "Run Away Love" was a huge, huge hit.

But I had problems with Gil in the studio because even though he was a really good producer, he didn't really like David so every time we'd sing a song he'd say, "Oh, you're going to sing it like David Bowie wants you to sing it."

We would get into tiffs about the fact that I had worked with David Bowie. It kind of bothered me because these tiffs kept me from doing my best. And we kept getting into confrontations about it.

I finally went to my manager at the time, his name was Mark Stuart, who was Curtis's manager, too, and I told him that I couldn't work with Gil because he seems to have some kind of animosity about my working with David Bowie. I explained that his negative attitude really comes out when I'm trying to perform, you know—he gets into arguments with me.

Mark immediately set to work, trying to mediate the conflict. I breathed a sigh of relief when he replied, "I'll ask Curtis if he can produce you." But I wasn't out of the woods yet...

He asked Curtis and fortunately Curtis responded with "Yes, of course." So, he did. He produced two successful tracks.

Curtis was so patient, but he didn't need to have a lot of patience with me because of his bedside manner. He relaxed me with his tone. He was soft-spoken. He never got excited or shouted, so he made me feel relaxed. Every singer, their first time around in the studio, should have a producer like Curtis Mayfield. He would sit patiently with me and simply ask, "What about *this* song?"

The first song we did was an upbeat ballad, "Love is Good News" for which Curtis had already written the music, and as he got to know me, he added the lyrics. He wrote that song for me. After we recorded it, I went out to do it live and everybody loved it.

Maybe what was so exciting was that it wasn't finished music. It started out with bass, drums and keyboard and Curtis added on more instruments as I sang.

"You Never Loved Me"

"You Never Loved Me" is one of the best disco songs ever. It's a 1980s classic that everyone wants me to redo. They're getting ready to re-release it on a compilation actually. It was a huge dance hit for me. Frankie Knuckles, who was a very big Chicago DJ, "the Godfather of House," rerecorded my song but everybody still liked the original version best. Before he died, he talked to me about redoing the record. At that time, I told him that I also liked his version a lot...

Picture Me (Pasha)

I felt as though I was more experienced in the studio during the time of this recording. I was so much more comfortable as a singer and I felt confident that I could write my own songs. I also began to experiment with different vocal styles.

I worked with Glen Ballard (Michael Jackson, Paula Abdul) who was with singer/songwriter Chris Jones. He has a song, "Picture Me," that showcased my voice in cool ways. He was easy to work with, too. He would ask me, "How do you feel about this line?" And if I said, "That's great," he would double and triple the background parts that I would do by myself and make them go in and out.

Luther is on "Intimate Sin" with David Laskey and a couple of other singers. In those days, producers usually put other background singers on with me. But on "Picture Me," I did all of the background vocals.

I liked when I heard my own background vocals on the final mix. There were some songs that I liked where the other singers sang background, but I liked the way I sounded singing my own parts.

Luther reinforced this. He would always tell me to sing my own background parts. A lot of the other singers were doing that and I eventually preferred singing my own background parts, too.

Becoming a solo artist was a big deal; *Ripe* was my record. Oh, and seeing my picture on the cover…I was very happy being a solo artist during that *Ripe* period, because truthfully, it was right after that whole scene of leaving David Bowie happened and I really needed to be doing what I was doing. I needed to engulf myself in my own work with my own songs because I was still pretty fragile.

Ava's sophomore solo album, Streetcar Named Desire *(Capitol) was released in 1982 and produced by Bob Esty, with tracks composed by Mark Isham and covers by bassist/vocalist Glenn Hughes (Deep Purple, Black Sabbath). The album was reissued as a CD in 2013 by the Gold Legion Label. Christian Wikane wrote the accompanying booklet. The album was exploratory in that it featured electronic, funk and soul influences. (Ref: The Second Disc, September 6, 2013, Joe Marchese)*

AVA

Perhaps one of the most powerful songs on the album was "Love to Be Touched," which oozed with sensuality. It was all very natural. I was very young and feeling very sexual about myself. I was able to visualize my feeling about what I wanted. During those times, it was about making love, telling the other person what you felt and what you wanted.

Every time I turned the radio on, I heard this song played on pop stations and I got so excited. Then, the label asked for pictures. After that point, they stopped playing the record.

It hurt. But then, I saw that radio was really prejudiced in those days. There was "payola." You could get played, but you had to pay through the nose. The DJs played my first album to death, specifically these tracks: "Single Woman, Married Man" and "Love is Good News." But later, now, that was a different story.

The record labels created a situation, where if you weren't in the pop column, you wouldn't have the biggest hits. You would not be considered a superstar.

But I digress. "Protection" was enhanced by Mark Isham's flugelhorn solo; the theme was somewhat risqué for the era. I've never been spanked by any guy. I probably said that just for the shock of it. It was more to be cute.

On "Awkward Situation," I enjoyed the background vocals of Arnold McCuller, who was noted for singing with singer/guitarist James Taylor and vocalist/guitarist Bonnie Raitt, Charlotte Crossley, who was one of Bette Midler's Harlettes and Leslie Smith. The co-write was penned by McCuller, Jan Michael Alejandro and myself.

The theme was about my going into a club with a guy I was dating. A girl comes up to me because supposedly she is dating him, too. It's a song about normal jealously. The things I said were meant for the times we were living in.

"This Time Around" (Glenn Hughes, Deep Purple) features multi-instrumentalist Mark Isham's expressive trumpet.

Glenn Hughes wrote that one and I had seen him perform it. The weird part about it was that I heard him singing it once and I was so taken by it that I wanted to redo it. Glenn has a beautiful voice. So, I asked him if

I could record it because I wanted to redo the song and he said yes.

When we did, Mark Isham redid the whale sounds on his trumpet and made it such a beautiful track. I enjoyed every moment of making this record. But I was also glad that we got that serious song in there. I really wanted people to see that we were having fun overall but that that one was a serious song about the world and people and how we interact. It really enveloped me and made me feel happy and it also said something about what was going on at the time.

I enjoyed every moment of making that record. Producer Bob Esty was just a really super person to work with. He made it all feel easier. At that moment, I was starting to write my own lyrics and melodies to these songs.

We worked on the *Streetcar* album for a long time. We were immersed in the process and trying to see if things worked on top of the track, especially seeing if the new material worked along with the other tracks. It was a new and different experience working with Bob as a producer/pianist.

Bob was a sweet, soft-spoken guy who was even-tempered. As he started to organize the tracks, he would do whatever was necessary. For example, he'd sing a background part or he would write lyrics. He'd say, "Sing it with me," or "Let's do it that way." He was very creative and wanted the best quality he could possibly achieve. It was really cool.

He had also worked with Paul Jibara, who wrote Donna Summer's "Last Dance" (*Thank God It's Friday*, 1978) and on Barbra Streisand's "The Main Event/Fight" (*The Main Event*, 1979) as well as with Cher.

Our goal was to create a World Music band sound. Zoo Drive, the band that played with me, consisted of all white guys: keyboardist Paul Delph, guitarist John Goodsall, bassist Doug Lunn and drummer Ric Parnell. They were all great musicians. We were trying to create something in the market with a multi-racial situation.

Unfortunately, Paul Delph died. He was such a cool guy and did a lot of singing for Zoo Drive. He wrote material with me, too, and was an integral part of the album. He was in charge of the band and led them with the basic sound. After he died, Bob Esty took over the arrangements.

Composer Mark Isham played flugelhorn, keys and synth. But a lot of power and ingenuity definitely came courtesy of the Zoo Drive members.

As for visual image? I don't always design the album covers based on what the music is. My image on that cover was not about the album being up-tempo. When I was thinking about "Techno Love," I came up with that image. I don't choose an album cover because of a sad song or an up-tempo song. Whatever picture came out best is what I'd use. It wasn't something that I thought about for a long time before I made a decision.

The theme was something that I thought about for a long time, though. It was meant to be about fun, simple encounters with a man and feelings about my power as a woman. Women were more aggressive in how they felt about sex, drugs and rock 'n' roll during this time, and around me, there were a lot of strong women—I'm talking about iconic women like Grace Jones, Aretha Franklin and Donna Summer.

So, as far as the cover shot, it was meant to illustrate an aggressively fun project. That attitude was meant to show "aggressively fun Ava" because we were experimenting with different looks.

Aretha was older than all of us, but as far as her lyrics, she could get hung up on a man and get caught up on that. That happens to everyone, but most of the other women I mentioned were all about their female independence; how they could control their bodies and control how a man dealt with them. Most of the other women in that era were more about asserting their female independence.

I don't know if I would have called myself a "woman's libber," but I was definitely a free spirit and about carrying on as a woman the way I felt I should be. I was not about being dictated to by a man.

"I Guess It's Love"

I liked it a lot when I recorded that song. I don't remember why it got on the Gold Legion, but not on the original. I might have been talking about my former relationship with David.

"Techno Love"

Melody and synth by Isham, co-written by McCuller and Esty. "Techno Love" is about connecting on the dance floor and feeling the vibes and the electricity of all the people.

"Having Been Far" (Mark Isham)

We wanted it to be the kind of album where it started out with an instrumental vibe that would set up the actual music on the album, so Bob and Mark wanted to include a prelude and then wrap it up at the end. It was great because we had something very beautiful at the beginning and then we ended it with the same beauty. I love how they arranged that with the whale sounds and everything because Mark Isham's composition started and ended with such a beautiful instrumental.

Since the 1970s, the award-winning Bob Esty acted as producer, arranger, instrumentalist and vocalist on recording projects with the following artists: Jon Anderson, The Beach Boys, Cher, Gloria Loring, Les McCann, The Pointer Sisters, Dusty Springfield, Barbra Streisand, Donna Summer, The Weather Girls and more.

In June of 2019, Bob Esty responded to a series of interview questions about Streetcar Named Desire. *Sadly, the acclaimed producer died in Los Angeles in September of 2019.*

BOB ESTY: INTERVIEW

Can you comment about the production of the title song?

The band did the track in one take. Ava did three or four takes. Ava wanted to convey a sense of fun to the audience. I loved that she chose the material. She did a very bright and funny vocal. The record label people loved it.

Regarding the textually rich and sensual "Love to Be Touched," can you elaborate about the process of balancing instrumental and vocal tracks?

The instrumental track was done by five friends of mine. It was engineered to feature Ava's magnificent vocals. When she talked, it was so funny. I mixed down the music to feature her vocals.

On "Techno Love," Ava performed spoken word against a strong bass line and percussion. Was "spoken word" still a new technique in the early 80s?

I don't know if this technique had been done before.

When Streetcar was re-released with Gold Legion, a 2013 reviewer (soultracks.com) wrote that the album "seemed channeled from the future." Was the album ahead of its time?

It was a departure from the sounds of the late 70s and early 80s. It was done with four pieces, a lot less instrumentation than was used then.

Besides producing Streetcar, you co-wrote, sang backup and played keyboards. What are your memories of working with composer Mark Isham and the other musicians?

I loved working with Mark and the other musicians. They are so talented.

What qualities do you look for in an artist with whom you agree to produce a record?

I look for anything special for the recording. It is essential to bring out what is unique in each performer. Ava was so funny; she brought a lot of joy to her work.

Regarding Ava's greatest strengths as a performer?

Ava is a great singer. She is great when she sings/talks. Ava has a brilliant sense of humor. I loved working with her.

****

AVA

Ageism and racism. In the article "The Final Word on Tina Turner" by Hannah Giorgis, the author talks frankly about her subject's recording career.

"She wonders aloud how listeners would have responded to her music if it had been released without her face, without any indication of the artist's race on the marketing materials."

I related to Tina Turner's statement, because I'm still haunted by what happened with my own recording projects, although I always look toward the future.

Author James Dickerson, in *Women on Top: The Quiet Revolution That's Rocking the American Music Industry*, spelled out Turner's legacy: "Turner became successful by overcoming every barrier put before her: age, sex and race."

In *Respect: Women and Popular Music*, author Dorothy Marcic said this about Turner: "At age sixty-one, she ended up firing the first group of tour dancers because they couldn't keep up with her." In that same book, Marcic recalls Turner's promise: "I will never give in to old age until I become old. And I'm not old yet!"

In 1997, Chaka Kahn decried racism in the music industry in a conversation with author/journalist Lisa Robinson for *Nobody Ever Asked Me About the Girls: Women, Music and Fame.*

"Because of the color of my skin, they expect me to be a certain type of artist; I'm actually much more versatile than they think."

Rihanna's insight also appears in the book when she recalls "a big discussion with the Def Jam Marketing department" about her brand.

"Was I urban (the industry's term for black music and hip-hop) or pop?" she asked when facing this conundrum. When artists are typecast, revenues and opportunities are often affected.

Drummer/producer Bobby Colomby (formerly of Capitol Records and original member of the group Blood, Sweat and Tears) was the person who felt that *Streetcar Named Desire* was really a unique record in terms of the way we did it and the kind of people that we used in the studio. He felt that the album should have become a huge success. Bobby definitely befriended us and helped us in every way to get *Streetcar Named Desire* recorded and he tried to make everyone understand why we did it.

Not everybody understood the concept of what we were trying to do. It was not just about making the album, it was also about black artists doing music, period, black artists doing what would be considered rock or pop. It wasn't about what color we were or anything like that, which was kind of proven when we put out "Love to Be Touched" as a single.

When we first sent "Love to be Touched" to radio stations, my picture hadn't been put on the cover and *White Pop Review* was playing it to death. They were playing it all the time and then they asked me to send them a picture and when they saw that I was black, they slowed way down on playing the record after that.

In one record review, a critic remarked that if the record was not a success it was because of poor promotion; that it was a really good record and that I reminded them of Donna Summer. That's the kind of record it was.

Another factor was that we were considered "New Wave." Like I said, on the record you couldn't tell if I was black or white. At that time, white radio was not playing a lot of black music. That's the truth. You had to be super pop. Even artists like Michael Jackson had to fight for airplay, too. They even admitted that fact on MTV.

David once asked an MTV host why the channel only played black artists at odd times. In fact, David addressed this issue specifically when he was interviewed by MTV. *"Why wasn't Michael Jackson's video played as much as the white artists?"*

One of the things that I really loved about David was that he liked everybody. It was never about race. It didn't matter what color. If he didn't like you, it had to be for some other reason. I never saw him be racist in any way. If David liked you or loved you, he liked you or loved you, period. One of the reasons I loved him so much is that I knew that race was never an issue and was never going to be.

****

Jon Pareles, for the *New York Times,* underscored the concept of "crossover" in the music industry:

"A crossover hit is a song that gains popularity in one format, then "crosses over" to others, gathering sales momentum to break into the pop Top 40" (nytimes.com, May 17, 1987). In his article "Pop View: Who Decides the Color of Music?" Pareles talks about the success of Tina Turner, Michael Jackson, Prince and Whitney Houston and how they "crossed an implicit color line." He brought up the possibility of a "hidden double standard."

Pareles said, "Because if black musicians want to reach white listeners and record buyers, they're told they must 'cross over.'"

Chante Joseph wrote about race in "Back to Black: How the Music Industry Reckoned with Race This Year" (guardian.com, December 28, 2020). He discussed the use of the term "urban" to describe black music: "It has been a contested label since the 1980s, used to sell black music to white audiences and radio stations, pigeonholing black artists with little regard for the music they make."

BOBBY COLOMBY (Blood, Sweat and Tears drummer, record producer) on *Streetcar Named Desire:*

I was an A&R executive at Capitol Records. They gave me a bunch of music from artists that were signed to a label that they were going to either buy outright or distribute. I'm not sure what the deal was and I went through whatever it was that they gave me and it was all really over the place but Ava really emerged from that as a serious artist, someone that I thought could really sing; I thought her imagery was great and I thought there was something about her, that for me, was a lot more interesting than anything else in that group. And then when she was assigned to that label, or, I don't know, either indirectly to that other label or directly, hopefully, I got involved in trying to help her get an album out.

I am a musician. I had had a career before that moment in time. And I have a saying about not wanting to go the standard route. In other words, most of the A&R people that I'd worked with over the course of my career weren't really musicians and would simply sign someone because other labels were interested. They'd be at the showcase and then they'd outbid other labels because they were with larger labels and then they would do something like look at who is on top of the charts and ask who produced those records and then just pair them with whomever they signed. As inappropriate as it might be, that was their way of saying, *"It's not my fault, because everyone else wanted them,"* or *"That's not my fault, that was the number one producer at the time,"* not understanding any of the nuance of what artists go through and how they create music or anything else.

So, not that I'm all that special, it's just that I come from a different education and I think I understood the process a little better than most of these people. As a result, and I'm not saying that all of them were terrible, but a lot were, but there were promotions guys or sales guys or sons or daughters of other executives who thought that they had an eye and an ear.

And I didn't want to say, "Well, she's African American, so let's get African American producers and let's do a Motown record." Nothing about what Ava was doing resembled that style. And I always appreciate an artist that is telling their own story, which actually means someone who writes their own songs, or at least lyrically, so that if you're going to market them, and you, as a journalist, put a microphone under their chin, and say, "So tell me something about the song," the answer isn't, "Oh, I don't' know, it was written by Diane Warren" or "Someone gave it to me." That doesn't inspire you to want to write anything else about them and their association with that song.

But when the artist writes the song, there's a story behind it and sometimes it's not on the nose and there are other parts to a story that they're not saying in the lyric and it kind of makes it more interesting.

Ava, being a more interesting person, I thought about that part of what made her special. I wanted her to be involved in the creative process, much more than, unfortunately, a lot of artists were at the time. So, that meant that it shouldn't sound like everyone else's record. Nothing should be standard because she's not standard, so somehow, and I don't even remember how this person came up, there was a producer who played piano, wrote songs, wrote arrangements, named Bob Esty…

Bob was a really interesting guy, and more importantly, he had skills. He loved Ava. He thought she was out of this world. So that combination, and of course, you don't just say, *"Here's a huge budget, go crazy."* You do a couple of things, or, you know how it is, I show up at the studio and have a listen or they send me some of the stuff in progress so I know that it's going in the right direction.

I thought that what they were doing from every standpoint, and certainly they had enough that I could hear, with a very good promotion team (which Capitol did not have at that time), that could go into it, but unfortunately, the whole notion of crossover...Capitol just had no clue at all.

Let me give you an example of that. This has nothing to do with Ava, although it does, sort of...

When I was leaving the label, I heard a singer, Robbie Nevil. He was really good and could write but it was a songwriting demo for a publishing company. We weren't trying to pitch the artist, we were just trying to pitch the song to someone, but I thought the person was terrific. And the content rhythmically had a great R&B sort of thing, It was great. So, I tried to sign him. I was leaving the label anyway, but the guy who was running the division said, "Oh, no." He passed.

So, I signed the artist to a new label that I was helping get started at the time, Manhattan Records. My friend who was running it was Bruce Lundvall, who was my product manager in my band when I was a kid. I called him and said that I think you should sign this guy. He signed him. I think Robbie's record was No. 2 in the country. The song was called "C'est La Vie."

At a meeting, a lawyer at Capitol Records, who was my friend and was trying to poke the hornet's nest, said, "I don't know why you're signing an act on the label." I said, "Because that person can't hear and doesn't understand." His comment to me was, "It sounds too black and will never crossover."

Well, Robbie is white. So, I said, "In other words, music can't crossover, like Michael Jackson or Prince..." I started naming all of these artists that can go in every single genre but Capitol at the time, they just didn't get it, really didn't get it and Ava's record, to me, was a crossover smash.

It was called *Streetcar Named Desire* and I thought it was absolutely terrific. I loved it.

And there was a person at that time named Frankie Crocker, who, I think, was the most respected DJ in the world of black music. Unfortunately, at that time, there was also a lot of payola in every genre but particularly in the black music area. It was obvious that if you wanted something played, you had to pay for it.

So, Frankie calls me; he doesn't know me. He calls me out of the clear, blue sky because he sees my name on the record somewhere. He calls the label, asks for my name, gets me on the phone. A super nice man. He says, "You're Bobby Colomby. Are you involved in this record with Ava Cherry?"

I said, "I'm not the producer, but I'm involved. I helped a little. Why?" He said, "I think this is a number one record. This is an incredible record. I love this record and I'm going to play it."

He was sending me a signal. *Go to your label and tell them they're never going to get a better jump-start than this.*

He wasn't asking for anything. He didn't say, *"Give me money."* It was purely because he discovered the record and found it infectious and wonderful. With that, he played it, he wasn't kidding. He started playing it on the biggest R&B station there was. And the rest of that label could not get it together to follow it and to spread it and make it a big record. That, if nothing else, could tell you how weak they were.

And that happens. There are labels that go up and down in success. If they get a better team together, they have success.

I was involved in a group at Epic Records, before I went to Capitol, that they didn't want anymore. They really wanted me to get rid of them. I could tell. I had comments from the head of the department saying, "I wish we could get rid of this deal," and I'm thinking, *I'm an artist and I would have to be at the receiving end of that type of feeling as an artist*, and I thought, *Oh, man, this is terrible.*

I went in and I couldn't get rid of them. I couldn't just drop them. I felt awful about the whole concept. I got involved and put together a team of people that I thought would help them to create a successful record. The people in my department out here were brand new in the business. I had been a drummer in a band; I had nothing to do with being in the record company world. They were kind of pissed off that I got the job that they all wanted. So, the second I came out here from New York, they were sniping at me. They had smiles on their faces but they were trying to screw me in every way they could.

Every project I was involved in, they tried to make it relevant in their way. And the A&R department, which is supposed to tell marketing and promotion what the hits are—we just make records, we sign these acts. Here, go for it.

In this particular case, I went into the studio with the group and helped them put together an album that I thought was really good. But at the first A&R meeting, all these people that didn't like me, I started to realize that they were just killing the record:

"That's no good. Why did you make this record? You shouldn't have made this record,"

I'm thinking, *I've been involved in records and sold over five million albums. These people have the same credibility as my dry cleaner. Why am I listening to them? Why am I even at this meeting?*

It got to the point where I started to feel that this is not a good fit, which was obviously the case, and that's why I went to Capitol Records after a year-and-a half.

The group put out the first single; no one lifted a finger to help the band, but it was kind of a hit in England and then one promotion guy in the world of black music named Paris Eley called me and said, "You got a hit on this album" and I think he took it upon himself to prove it. He asked me to make an edit because it was a very long track and I did. The first song that was a hit was "Blame it on the Boogie" and the second was called "Shake your Body (Down to the Ground)." Imagine if I had dropped that band. That's my point. So, it takes somebody with passion who gives a crap and a label to make something happen.

This guy was solely responsible for breaking and bringing back the Jacksons, because they were dead as a doornail at that time. They were a cartoon show, literally.

So, there was no one at Capitol for Ava. I wasn't an A&R guy. I wasn't in marketing. I wasn't in promotion. I didn't run the label. She didn't have that advocate within the label to take this lead that they got from Frankie Crocker, *"Take it and make it a hit record."*

She should have been a gigantic star, but like Lisa Fischer, and some other people I know, Sy Smith, who are ridiculously talented, they realized that they would have to put a band together, which is expensive. You rehearse and go out on the road without any support. You can't do it. So, when you get a job with David Bowie or Luther, or in the case of Lisa Fischer, the Rolling Stones, all these artists that are so good, but to organize your own career without financial backing is literally impossible. It's so expensive. You've got to pay musicians. Rehearse. And then you've got to try to get gigs without a hit record.

But the Rolling Stones said, *"How would you like to make a ton of money instead of losing a ton of money?"* And it wasn't a tough sell. She said thank you very much.

(The late Frankie Crocker came to fame in the late 1970s as program director of WBLS, the seminal black music radio station out of New York. He originated the phrase "urban contemporary" and used it to describe his diverse set lists.)

Streetcar Named Desire was unique to itself. You couldn't find another record and say, "It sounds exactly like that one." You couldn't. And anytime you have something which is on a short list—in other words, here are the thirty songs that sound like this—that's an opportunity for a long career because then you're establishing your own sound, your own groove, point of view. That's very unusual and she had all of that.

Working with Bob Esty was terrific. He's an extremely talented person who knew what he was doing musically. He had a concept and a point of view and knew how to get results, and again, there weren't many people who could do that at the time, and most importantly, besides the fact that he was very skilled, was that he really got Ava. He understood who she was as an artist. A record is just that. It's a record of who you are at that point in time. It's like you're making a record in a diary of *"Today, I'm experiencing the following."* A record for an artist is a recording of, hopefully, the musical integrity at that time. And he got Ava. He really knew how to deliver a record that represented her.

I can't tell you how many times I've seen an artist and heard the record and said, "My God, it's got nothing to do with them." It's easy for me to say stuff because I didn't have to go through the kind of gauntlet that most artists have to go through. I'm saying, an artist who would do something that wasn't who they were, was forced to do something and accepted that in some sad way and really, I'm not the guy to pass judgment—they almost deserve what they get—because an artist should say, "That's not who I am," because if it's a hit record, that doesn't represent who I am. I'm misrepresented. I'm going out there pretending to be something I'm not.

Some artists, like Donna Summer, she's a wonderful, wonderful girl and a perfect singer. She got into the disco thing because she liked it, but ultimately as a platform for her Christian point of view, thinking, *You know what? Give me the power to tell a story and let me get to the point where I can tell a story and I'll tell the story.*

Insofar as evaluating music from a drummer's perspective…

I don't think I pick stuff apart that way. I listen to the overall. I almost never played on albums that I produced because I figured there was always a better drummer I could hire.

In terms of defining qualities that Ava possesses…

The obvious and first one you look for is vocal skill and a sound that was unique, and she had that, and yet, she was able to be a background singer. Background singers that have very unique tones, they don't work out because then they stick out and they take attention but she had enough ability on her instrument to blend. Many artists that have a unique sound can't do that and she can. That worked for her. That's number one.

She had an extraordinarily rambunctious personality. I felt like she'd be someone, that if she walked in the room would probably not get ignored, but she did it in a really good way, in a nice way. I mean, you could do that by being obnoxious but she wasn't, she was great.

And optically, visually, I think she had a very interesting look that once you saw, you probably wouldn't forget, so that combination in terms of what can make an artist, it was all there. And as a record, I thought it had everything.

Again, the hardest thing to do, and a really good producer knows how to do this, is you get the soul of the artist on a record. You actually hear a record, and then if someone says, "Can you tell me who this person is?" You can describe who they are: their personality, point of view, their attitude, if they're solid or fun-loving...It's all on a record.

****

Picture Me, Capitol Records, released in 1987

Picture Me *received assistance from rock giants. Glen Ballard, acclaimed co-writer and producer of Alanis Morissette's* Jagged Little Pill *in the mid-90s, co-wrote three tunes and was one of the multiple keyboard players on this recording. Guitarist Jon Butcher contributed two co-writes and two of his own. Luther Vandross arranged vocals and harmonized with Alyson E. Williams, David Lasley and Gene Van Buren.*

Highlights include Ava's rendition of the title song in which she persuades her lover to gaze at her image on the "silver screen" and "the VCR." On "Beautiful Thief," her vocals graduate from grainy and raw to silky-smooth.

Good Intentions
Beautiful Thief
Keep Me Satisfied
Intimate Sin
For Your Pleasure
A Love So Tough
Communicate 1-2-1
Majic Castle
Last Lover

The title co-write by Ava and Mauro Malavasi (Change, Aretha Franklin, Andrea Bocelli) is a swooning, synth-lit proclamation. In "You Are," Ava's whispered melody undulates and appears in stark contrast to the throbbing instrumentals. "Forget Me Nots" is a Patrice Rushen cover, but Ava's rendition proves more elusive and soulful than that of her predecessor. "Gimme Gimme," also co-written by Ava and Malavasi, shimmers with arresting textures that surface intermittently from the call and response format.

AVA

Luther helped produce *Spend the Night*. I wrote most of the songs on there, except for the ones written by Damon Wiley. I loved that record so much and there were so many good songs on there. We just decided to do it at the last minute and it was really cool.

Mauro Malavasi is the one who did "Gimme Gimme" and "You Are." We recorded those in Bologna, Italy, where I spent three months. There were those mom-and-pop restaurants where the ladies were making that fresh pasta every day. Italian food is the best food in the world. I like Chinese, I like French, but the Italians? Forget it. Nobody can touch them. We used to go from province to province and in each place, the food was more incredible.

I had been working with a French manager named Claude and he was the one who suggested working in Italy with Mauro, who had been working with Luther Vandross on the Change records. He did that way, way back before European artists were working with black artists from here. He also produced opera records with Luciano Pavarotti. He was considered, and I'm sure still is, a very revered maestro in Italy.

So, we would write lyrics. The arrangements were beautiful, especially the strings. I really love recording like that because Mauro was used to doing opera. He was used to recording very moving music and on "You Are" and "Gimme Gimme," the music was beautiful, so I really enjoyed working with Mauro so much.

Mauro lived in a fascinating location. There were all of these ancient grounds beneath his house. When excavators dug below the surface, they found artifacts such as statues from the time of Julius Caesar.

29.
THE ASTRONETTES SESSIONS

*D*avid Bowie produced The Astronettes Sessions *in 1973-1974. The album was retitled and released in 1995 and 2010 as* People from Bad Homes, *which was also a lyric from the Bowie ballad,* "Fashion."

The album included the Beach Boys classic "God Only Knows," a cover of "Highway Blues" by Manchester, England's Roy Harper and Bruce Springsteen's "Spirits in the Night," as well as the American classic "I'm In the Mood for Love." "I Am a Laser" ultimately served as the prototype for "Scream Like a Baby" on Bowie's 1980 album Scary Monsters.

AVA

The album was released without being mixed. Those were demos. Tony Defries released them. The reason he did that was because David produced the record and he knew that people would buy it because David produced it.

Believe me, it was a big surprise to me when I saw that album in the '90s. When someone told me, "It's in the record store," I was so angry.

First of all, Tony Defries was not supposed to have had possession of the masters. David told me that he was putting the masters in the vault and that Tony would not be able to touch them, but then Tony got the masters and did what he wanted. He just mixed what was already on tape, but the vocals were not finished; none of it was finished. It was hit or miss.

Then I was angry at David. I said, "I thought you weren't going to let him just take them and do whatever he wanted to do with them."

I wanted so sue Tony but I didn't have the finances and he was like, "Sue me." And he released them again in London about seven years later.

But there were a couple of songs on there that were really great, like

"Highway Blues" and "I'm In the Mood for Love". A lot of people liked "I Am a Laser," but for me, if we had finished the project, that would have been the ideal situation.

And David never explained how Tony got those masters. I was trying not to be mad at him, but it just wasn't cool. Tony just took that material and did what he wanted with it. I wish I would have taken more control over my career.

If I redid the material, of course, I would do it differently. But I can't imagine who would produce it. I don't think anyone would produce that same kind of thing, but there were a couple of songs that I would redo.

✱✱✱

In 2018, Ava released "Straight from the Heart," which shot to No. 5 in the U.K. charts. Her love of dance music had been cultivated much earlier, of course. She recalls touching base with the late Frankie Knuckles, who, besides creating his own unique sound, was largely responsible for popularizing the Chicago style of "House," which also caught on internationally.

AVA

I performed at the Garage, Frankie's popular club in Chicago, during the time of my very first record, "You Never Loved Me," which is a disco classic, co-produced by Curtis Mayfield. I had first met Frankie, often called "the Godfather of House," in New York—we didn't hang out a whole lot together then, but he did a remix of my song and put it on one of his records because he loved it so much.

It's a small world—for Luther, Frankie released some great remixes, especially one called, "Power of Love." Luther and Frankie actually grew up in the same New York neighborhood.

Every time Frankie saw me, he'd say, "Ava, I love that record." He was a brilliant producer and DJ. He really revolutionized what House music sounded like and I really miss him. So many producers copied his style, but Frankie really brought it. I had a lot of respect for Frankie, his groundbreaking recording techniques and his energizing music.

There are few genres that Ava hasn't been keen to explore. Here are a few examples of more contemporary projects...

30.
KEEPING IT CURRENT

AVA

Doing rap isn't new to me. Way back when I recorded "Gimme Gimme," I explored the genre. It was not my thing back then, but I'm doing it now. I'm working with Boogie Wonda and Keith on a club, hip hop dance track. They're a production team but they rap, too, and I could tell that my new track needed a rap.

When I was working on the singing parts, I suggested that we do about an eight or sixteen-bar rap and they thought that was cool, so basically, they worked with me on the timing and where exactly I needed to place the rap on the track. That's what I'm getting ready to do next week. Boogie Wonda and Keith worked with me, essentially, on how slow or fast I should rap.

It's so much fun. I'm loving these guys. When they first sent me the tracks, they sent me, like, ten tracks. They map it out for you. They just have their ear to the street. They do their homework and they listen to what's going on. I got a chance to pick from an assortment of great tracks. They always try to make each track better or different. I have a lot of respect for these guys.

The track that I'm rapping on is "Be Nice but Get the Money" and it's got really cool music in the background. I don't really love the rappers that I hear right now. My favorites were Snoop Dogg and Eric B. I love the old school rappers. Those are my guys.

The new generation? I won't really say that I don't like them because I don't listen to rap that much, but I prefer the cool, swilling-the-gin-and-juice and listening to Snoop Dogg. That's the kind of rap I like—rap right now is a little too aggressive. They shout a little too much for me. I like the cool.

I don't like to stay in the same place. I like a challenge. I've always been good with languages. I speak fluent French. With Portuguese, I was told the words and I wrote it down phonetically, exactly the way I heard it. Rap is a new challenge and, of course, so is singing and recording in another language, but rap is a little different because with Portuguese, it's still singing—the bossa nova that I recorded has a release date of March 2019.

Over the years, I've had the opportunity to reimagine some of my favorite music. For example, I was asked to redo the backing vocals on the tracks from Sly and the Family Stone's 1969 release, *Stand!* (Cleopatra Records), a psychedelic funk treasure, which included "Stand" and "I Want to Take you Higher." I arranged the vocals and wrote the song "Plain Jane" which, unfortunately, did not get released.

But overall, I've always been a daredevil. I'm not afraid to try something new. Like when I went to find David, I went with two-hundred dollars in my pocket to Monaco, the most incredible place in the world.

I'll always remember how my mother shook her head in disbelief. "Ava, you're going to Monaco with only two-hundred dollars in your pocket?"

"Yeah, I am," I told her and, of course, she didn't see me until eight months later. I've never been afraid to take chances or to take risks in my career. I've never been afraid to try something new; to reinvent myself. I believe that's part of the key. Anybody who is afraid to reinvent themselves, they can have success, but why would they want to just stay like that instead of venturing out to do more and be more of a success?

People can be envious in this business. Some people don't want you to succeed and some people have tried to shut me down. When I first heard some negative comments, it hurt me that somebody would say things like, *"You shouldn't do things at this point in your life"*; that you might be too old to do something…We don't usually hear these comments about men.

I have a thick skin, though. I realized that people would only be saying this if they didn't have the courage to do something themselves and they didn't want you to do it. On the other hand, I never tried to discourage anyone who believed in themselves. I would be encouraging you.

So, my skin became very thick after hearing such comments once or twice. Everybody wasn't saying it to me at the same time; just one or two people said it, but I realized that those people were kind of jealous that I still looked great, that I was still doing what I wanted to do, or sometimes it's just a matter of misery loves company. When people are not in the place that they want to be, they don't want to see you there either, so I just took it like that.

The more the world discouraged me, the more I put myself out there; the more they dished it out, the more I took chances. After a while, I even took these negative comments as a dare. Watch me. See what happens.

"You really have a lot of chutzpah. You keep on going no matter what. You've come through it all, brilliantly. You look great. I'm so glad you're here doing it." I've also had so many people cheer me on.

Until they start throwing dirt in my face, I'm always going to be doing something. I'll never give up. The successful people want to keep you there. They're going to keep dangling that carrot. The money in touring is big. I consider myself old-school. You had to be on your notes.

The late actress, Betty White, while still in her nineties, was still going strong and making people laugh. I loved that about her. That positivity was so incredible.

If I could speak to an up-and-coming artist, I would say this—

Don't ever give up on yourself. If you keep at it long enough, you're going to win. Don't listen to what other people when they try to tell you to stop; just don't listen to it. Block it out. If you fail, pick yourself up. Dust yourself off. I've always felt fearless. I feel so ready for the future. New things are coming at me that I never thought at this time of my life would be coming to me and happening.

Ava's status in popular culture continues. This exhibit premiered in London before coming to Chicago, where she was asked to appear as a special guest speaker...

31.
DAVID BOWIE IS

D AVID BOWIE IS *took place at the Museum of Contemporary Art in Chicago from September 23, 2014 to January 4, 2015. But even before MCA chief curator, Michael Darling, daringly picked up the phone to inquire about the possibility of the exhibit coming to Chicago, British locals enjoyed the debut in London in March 2013. There, the phenomenon was coordinated by Victoria & Albert Museum curators Victoria Broackes (Head of Exhibitions for the Department of Theatre and Performance) and Geoffrey Marsh (director of the Department of Theatre and Performance). Thereafter, the ambitious team combined efforts with Michael Darling to showcase the exhibit in Chicago, the first American city to be offered this rare opportunity. It would not be until March 2, 2018 (closing July 15, 2018) that the show would run in the borough of Brooklyn.*

In a pennyblackmusic.co.uk interview published on June 9, 2014, Darling responded to several questions I posed concerning the behind-the-scenes logistics of the Chicago DAVID BOWIE IS *exhibit as well as how he attained first-city access.*

MICHAEL DARLING

When we heard about the show we immediately got in touch with the V&A and just started negotiating some dates with them, and from the very beginning negotiated the idea that we wanted to be the first venue if it was really going to work for us. So, I think it was about being timely and aggressive and, of course, I think they realised that this was a major market for the show to be seen in. So, we definitely had that working for us.

We had about seven weeks of down time between the show that preceded the Bowie show and the Bowie show opening, and that's about the longest that we've ever had between shows—the first show happened pretty quickly and then that left about six weeks just to set up the Bowie show. That's pretty extensive for us. Usually, those turnarounds are more like three or four weeks. It's really a lot of time, a lot of manpower to make it happen.

When asked whether he felt the exhibit would be creating a link between generations, Michael replied:

Yeah, that's the other thing that really made sense for us with this exhibition is how Bowie was so far ahead of the curve in terms of ideas about gender identity and sexual preferences and the fluidity therein and how we're in that kind of that post-gender moment right now in America, and in culture especially, I think, in terms of shows like *Orange is the New Black*, the TV show, and just how mainstream ideas about transgender identity issues are right now. To think back that here Bowie was testing those boundaries thirty or forty years ago made this show really relevant for us in that way too."

As for costume choices:

The ones he did with Kansai Yamamoto are some of my favourites. They're just really theatrical. You can see how they are both homages to Japanese culture but also very much of their time. They are these glam rock artifacts, very showy, very over-the-top and very androgynous. It's interesting how he navigated those different two reference points in a way.

Darling responds, too, to a question about David's involvement prior to the exhibit:

That part has been really interesting. He's been involved in that he allowed us access to all of his archives and gave the green light to the idea of the show, but beyond that he's really left this up to the Victoria and Albert museum curators to make the selections and create the structure for the exhibition and hasn't been showing up for the openings or press previews or anything. So, he's really stepping back and allowing the work and the career to speak for itself and not turning this into a media circus around his actual presence, which I think has also been a very smart move on his part.

It gives the show a certain amount of objectivity and makes it feel less of a kind of vanity project and so, or course, we'd love for him to show up, but that really hasn't been part of the way that this has all been structured. We don't anticipate him being here for the opening or anything like that, but we do hope that, since he lives in New York, Chicago's not so far...

So, maybe he can just pop over at some point just to check it out. Darling added that after Chicago, DAVID BOWIE IS would go to Paris at The Cite de la Musique.

A September 2014 press release from the MCA stated, "In conjunction with the exhibition DAVID BOWIE IS, the Museum of Contemporary Art Chicago is offering an eclectic mix of Bowie-related talks, events and performances." As such, local and national acts came aboard to drum up excitement prior to the actual opening.

Singer/songwriter Bryan Ferry and curator Michael Bracewell kicked off events with a discussion about fame, music, and creative inspiration in anticipation of the exhibition DAVID BOWIE IS. Ms. Broackes and Mr. Marsh discussed Bowie's extensive body of work and fielded audience questions. A concert at Chicago's popular Daley Plaza featured the Sons of the Silent Age, "the leading David Bowie cover band," led by Chris Connelly (Ministry and the Revolting Cocks) and Matt Walker (Morrissey and Smashing Pumpkins).

Featuring advanced sound technology, costumes from the 1980 Floor Show, footage from D.A. Pennebaker's Ziggy Stardust and the Spiders from Mars: The Motion Picture (1973) and a detailed analysis of David Bowie's gender-bending discography, the exhibit attracted audiences of all ages.

In a Bowie diary excerpt pertaining to a joint project with the late John Lennon, Ava was significantly referenced:

"Today, I introduced Ava to a Beatle and we are going to Electric Lady to record "Fame."

Ava also created a buzz during the MCA's lecture series. On October 7, Nick

Fraccaro and Paul Durica, co-authors of Pocket Guide to Hell, *discussed David Bowie's "many connections to Chicago, including his relationship with soul singer Ava Cherry and his involvement with Mercury Records' publicist Ron Oberman." Ava was there, too: posing with fans, stirring up memories and fueling pop culture fantasies.*

When asked to appear at a Chicago Bowie tribute, Ava couldn't wait...

32.
SONS OF THE SILENT AGE

METRO, *Chicago, Illinois, March 4, 2016*

AVA

I was really honored to perform at the Metro Show because they put on a David Bowie show every year, not just after David died; they did this show when he was still alive. The Sons of the Silent Age do the show every year because they're a basic Bowie tribute band, and so when I was asked by the band and METRO owner, Joe Shanahan, to do the performance, I was really honored because the Metro is a great place to perform and so many great artists have performed there.

I was a little nervous because after David had passed there was so much emotional energy going on—I was getting so many social media contacts, people crying and saying "he made my life feel like something when he was around and now I feel like I don't want to live and I'm so unhappy. Please talk to me because you had a connection to him…"

It was really gut-wrenching to me. I could see that people saw him as such a soothing influence. David changed their lives in so many ways, whether they were gay, straight, black or white or whatever. My involvement led to black people listening to him, because back at the Apollo, I'd hear, "David Bowie?" They didn't know who he was.

So, performing at METRO was an incredible experience. I rehearsed with the band for about two weeks before the show at Matt Walker's house in the suburbs. He's the drummer.

They were all wonderful musicians and I just enjoyed playing with them so much. They were a full-spectrum band and it was wonderful, too, because of that. It's fun to work with a couple of musicians, but they were elaborate. They had horns and everything.

I invited some friends to the club who had not seen me perform for a while. Like I said, I was a little nervous, but excited. METRO had put my name on the marquee as a special guest. I wanted to channel David that evening for all the people that were there, too, and loved him.

Vocalist Sinead O'Connor had been asked to perform, too, but at the last minute. She was in town and was staying with the drummer of the Sons of the Silent Age. I was excited to meet her because she was a great artist in her day, although I think she was going through something at the time, which felt a little strange at our meeting.

We got to the theater and were waiting for the different acts to go on. I was backstage getting ready and was told I only had about ten minutes until I went onstage. I always prepare mentally to go onstage. I learned that from David and Luther. I learned to center myself and not get involved in too much activity. I learned to concentrate on how I'm going to present myself at the performance.

I'm standing at the side of the stage waiting for the last song to finish.

The guys were doing half a set before I came on to sing "Young Americans" with them. I'm standing there, my hands were sweating and I was still a little nervous, wondering how the audience was going to receive me. It had been such a long time since I'd performed with Bowie.

I look over and hear them talking. Sinead is on the other side of me. I look at her and give her a smile. I was kind of wanting her to give me a smile back before I went onstage. But she just kind of stared at me.

I was back there praying, hoping to do my best. I had been looking at her, hoping to get some encouragement from another artist. I think she was a little upset because her name wasn't on the marquee but she didn't arrive until the last minute. It certainly wasn't intended to be a slight to her but she tends to take things defensively.

They were introducing me as "Longtime confidant, pop culture influence…Miss Ava Cherry." They said my name and people started to scream. Oh, my God. I can't tell you how touched I was because I didn't know what to expect. When that happened, I looked at Sinead and then went running out there."

It wasn't about my ego, about them saying my name. It was about my appreciation for how they welcomed me so enthusiastically. There were 1,100 people smiling in that room. They were coming up to the stage with their hands out, cheering, and I felt so touched and so happy. I just went into performance mode the minute I felt that energy and when they started to play the music.

My first song was "Moonage Daydream." As I sang, the audience started to wave their hands back and forth. I also sang my original song, "That's How Loneliness Goes" and finally "Young Americans." After the show, many people came up to me and said, 'Your energy made the show so great.' My ex came to see me and said, "Wow. I hadn't seen you perform for a long time, but you were really in your element." The response was wonderful. The METRO staff gave me a bottle of champagne, which they had ready for me.

METRO owner Joe Shanahan was so sweet to me. He was also celebrating that he had survived cancer. A lot of people were there who related to the cause because David had died of cancer. It was a very emotional event. I felt myself channeling David, just as I had hoped. As I

© Bobby Talamine

was singing "Moonage Daydream." I was feeling all of that energy that was so positive. It was just a great, great night.

On March 4, 2016, The 9-piece Sons of the Silent Age performed a David Bowie Tribute Concert at METRO, a popular North Side venue owned by Windy City native Joe Shanahan. Rehearsals had already begun in December of 2015, but during rehearsals in early 2016, all concerned learned the sad news that David Bowie had passed on January 10, two days after his birthday. Joe and the musicians had to decide how best to deal with this devastating news: Cancel the show or celebrate David Bowie's legacy.

The following interviews were conducted with SOTSA drummer Matt Walker (Garbage, Smashing Pumpkins) and Metro owner, Joe Shanahan, who had worked with Ava Cherry for the first time. In December of 2016, in the midst of rehearsals, Matt received word that David Bowie died. The band still went on with the show. Were they initially ambivalent?

MATT WALKER

We were actually rehearsing at the exact time he died, and without knowing, we definitely felt the air molecules change. But his passing only strengthened our resolve to bringing his sound, vision and spirit to the

226

stage in a way we felt honored his bold artistry.

Matt explains the mission of Sons of the Silent Age, in regards to the selection of material, and the challenge of narrowing down material when the Bowie canon offers such abundance.

SOTSA initially began as a dual purpose of me and Chris (lead vocalist Chris Connelly) indulging in our desire to perform Bowie's music, and also to benefit the Pablove Foundation (pediatric cancer charity). In order to do his music justice, we assembled quite a large band, and it became clear in the first few rehearsals that there was a wonderful alchemy between all of the musicians. The first show, which featured guest Shirley Manson of Garbage, was both a joy and a huge success, and a clear indicator that we should continue (not to mention that there were so many more songs we all wanted to play!).

© Bobby Talamine

We've since devoted ourselves to equally showcasing his most well-loved songs as well as his more challenging, commercial work. Choosing the songs for each show is very difficult as there's a seemingly endless library of incredible music to choose from.

We tend to choose material, in part, by designing the shows around themes, such as the recreation of an iconic record top to bottom (such as *Low, Station to Station, Scary Monsters*) or eras (*5 Year 69-74, The Best of*

Berlin). We often perform songs that Bowie never did live.

Was it challenging to come up with the right set list given that the audience emotions/expectations would most likely run very high due to David Bowie's unexpected death?

We played *Station to Station* as our first set. But yes, choosing the songs for the second set was a bit daunting. Our expectations are always the most difficult to meet, but there was definitely some stardust in the air that night carrying us along.

Matt comments on what it was like to rehearse and perform live with Ava.

Like many Bowie fans, we were most familiar with Ava from her work on *Young Americans*. Rehearsing with her was great because she's very sweet, but at the same time, she's a hard worker and focused, just as we are.

Rehearsal time is often short and the material is quite sophisticated. Ava has so much experience working with singers and it was a pleasure to see her expertise at work. And even in rehearsal, she sings with all of her heart and soul. Then, there was the element of Bowie having just passed and knowing her history with him, which just added to the already reverential air.

From the moment Ava came on, she was definitely in command of the stage, and I could feel the band rally behind her. She's an old school performer and isn't afraid to walk the tightrope, changing things up in the moment. Her style is as wild and adventurous now as it ever was. I think the majority of the audience wasn't prepared for such a powerful performance. They loved her whole set, but when we played "Young Americans," you could feel Bowie's presence in the air.

SOTSA, Metro, Chicago, Illinois, 03-04-2016, Set 1

1. Station to Station
2. Golden Years
3. Word on a Wing
4. Tvc15

5. Stay
6. Wild is the Wind

SOTSA, Metro, Chicago, Illinois, 03-04-2016, Set 2

1. Speed of Life
2. Ashes to Ashes
3. Under Pressure
4. Ava/Moonage Daydream
5. Ava/Jean Genie
6. Ava/That's How Loneliness Goes
7. Ava/Young Americans
8. Sons of the Silent Age
9. Fashion
10. Panic in Detroit
11. Fame
12. Let's Dance
13. Sinead O'Connor/Sorrow
14. Sinead/Life on Mars
15. Ziggy Stardust
16. Space Oddity
17. Starman
Encore:
18. Heroes
19. Lazarus

© Bobby Talamine

Joe Shanahan, music executive and owner of Chicago's METRO, looks back on this bittersweet tribute and reveals what it was like to meet Ava after years of being a fan.

Joe Shanahan interview: Wednesday, January 30, 2019, Re: March 4, 2016, METRO, Chicago

Was it difficult to make the decision to go on with the show?

No, it might have actually re-centered and refocused it. The community lens was kind of positioned one way before David's passing. Once he passed, I think that Chris (lead singer Chris Connelly) and Matt (Walker) and myself, there was, for lack of a better term, a real come-to-God moment. He meant so much to each and every one of us that, when we look at SOTSA, I don't look at it as a cover band, I have always looked at it as a tribute to David and with these very, very accomplished and very successful musicians that will dedicate and not just go out and perform, not just spend the rehearsal time but demonstrate the kind of thoughtfulness that goes into picking the right record, picking the right era, and not just,

"Oh, let's go out and do some covers, we'll do some glam hits," it's really more of a sojourn into an era that many remember very well in their lives as they were growing up with Bowie.

I am a cancer survivor and I was coming out of my treatment approximately at that time. That particular year, the beneficiary of the proceeds was the University of Chicago, which was where I was treated for cancer. It was for my doctors and my nurses that we did some fundraising as well as, most importantly, consciousness-raising about cancer and about cancer treatment and cancer research. For me, it was really important because I was able to give back. Chris and Matt both said, "Yes, Joe. We're feeling this."

The interesting piece of this is about Char Walker, Matt Walker's wife, who is a cancer nurse at North Shore Health Network. Char and I become a whole lot closer because she's in the health world and she surrounds herself with doctors and people that are trying to treat this disease. It is treatable, it's not always successful, but in my case, it was successful. So that's what takes on the gravity of that year.

There were people who were part of the tribute aspect of the Bowie world or the Bowie perspective. Ava was someone who lived it so there begins another language, another conversation. And that's where I think it got very interesting.

When she walked into my office, I was almost in tears. What I felt, my internal tuning fork went off so profoundly because she worked with him. And I saw her perform with David several times in the '70s. I was old enough to see that Young Americans/Diamond Dogs tour. She was involved with David at that time. I remember specifically the Arie Crown Theater. It was what they were calling the Young Americans/Diamond Dogs Tour. He didn't quite have the moniker because he kind of changed his mind as the production values rolled out but I remember an unbelievably striking woman in white, really short hair, so as a young man, I fell in love. There she was. She was the diva.

And on the record, of course, with Luther Vandross, Robin Clark and Ava, I was infatuated as a teenager. I went to any and all of those Bowie shows and I would travel from Chicago to St. Louis or Detroit or to Milwaukee, wherever David was doing something in the Midwest, I would convince my friend: either steal your parents' car or gently borrow it for a day or take a train.

It was such a part of my world, sometimes I would even hitchhike to some of these shows. I hitchhiked to a show in Nashville, from where I went to school, which was in Carbondale. You're getting the big, deep story from me because David Bowie was so influential in my life.

And here she walks into my office and calls me "darling." I'm telling you, I nearly fell over. Oh, my God. And she's an interesting woman. There's lots of twists and turns and ebb and flow with her personality and her presentation and in what she does. But I know, from my own personal stand, there was a photo taken of Matt, Chris, myself and Ava in the little theater at Metro at what we call The Top Note. I know it ended up in the *Tribune* or one of the media outlets here in town. I opened up the newspaper on Thursday morning and seeing our picture there with Ava Cherry was incredible and so momentous for me, because I had never met her, although I did meet David in that timeframe.

There were some chance meetings, which were interesting, certainly when he came back to town to do *The Elephant Man*. He was around the club scene quite a bit so we would hang out from time to time, going to some of the local clubs and local restaurants. My Bowie radar was good and I kind of knew where he'd be going. I would just sort of show up, a fly on the wall! Not creeping on him, but you know... Then, it became a thing where there'd be a drink and short conversation, so I had my moments through and with him.

And then years later, Billy Corgan (Smashing Pumpkins) invited me to a show that David was doing out at the Rosemont Horizon and a proper introduction was made back then. He started to remember the whole era of being back in Chicago with *The Elephant Man* and with Iggy.

I think that people realized that she worked with Bowie. I think they realized that that was a real thing. I think there was a moment where they thought, *Oh, Ava Cherry*. A little education. It's not like Mick Ronson walked onstage, even though he's dead. Or Tony Visconti walked onstage or Adrian Belew, a lot of the players that were intricate to that story. But what I don't think was missed was that people that go to this kind of event, their Bowie encyclopedia is pretty well-tuned and Ava was David's girlfriend.

She took him to the Apollo for the first time. During that *Young Americans* recording in Philadelphia, she had sway over him, for sure, both physically, mentally, spiritually. And I think people knew that. Once the story was told in the media, people came to see it.

"What's she going to do?"

She basically covered a lot of the *Young Americans* stuff and then still did some of the grand hits, which, of course, she learned because they did that material when they were touring together. She sang "Fame," which was David's first No. 1 hit in America. "Young Americans" is one of my favorites. They call it "plastic soul." She and Matt and Chris worked up a pretty solid *Young Americans* set.

What was also wonderful on Ava's part was that she went to the meet and greet with all the doctors and all the nurses that were from the University of Chicago, as well as the North Shore Health Network. On that particular morning, there was a combination; both were well-represented, and Ava came down and took photos with everybody and talked to everybody. She was so gracious as far as her time and because she understood the depth of the fact that someone that was so important in her life and in her musical career, physically, spiritually and mentally, had died that year and this was her way of celebrating some of his life.

We buddied up over the few days that she was with us, during rehearsals and during the show itself. I never got tired of her calling me darling, so that was always a plus. Ava says that word, "darling," like nobody else. Meeting Ava Cherry was a real pleasure and a real treat.

33.
PORTRAIT OF AVA: MARK WARDEL

*M*ark Wardel, aka TradeMark, is a contemporary artist based in London whose influences include pop art and New York street art of the 1970s and 1980s. He is acclaimed for his deep exploration of identity and urban subcultures and is closely aligned with the international club scene, as a unique image designer and cultural trend setter. As a super fan, Mark's initial interest in all things David Bowie began at the Blitz club; many of the portraiture subjects that helmed from that club's heyday, Steve Strange, Princess Julia and Boy George, shared his fascination with Bowie.

Mark was heavily involved in the V&A DAVID BOWIE IS exhibit in London, for which he designed 300 "Silver Duke" Bowie life mask sculptures. Ava's presence at the Chicago-based exhibit held at the Museum of Contemporary Art was a major draw during the opening weeks. It seemed almost serendipitous that the two like-minded individuals would find common ground in Mark's unique visions. The following excerpt is of an interview with Mark Wardel in which he talks about his attraction to David Bowie and Ava Cherry and how he chose to commemorate them through his vivid artistry.

MARK WARDEL, December 11, 2018

What led to your desire to create a contemporary oil and acrylic portrait of David Bowie and Ava Cherry?

I've been a huge David Bowie fan since 1972, when I was fourteen and fifteen and followed him ever since, really. He was the biggest influence in my life. When he went off to America around 1974-75 and he was away from Britain for about two years, basically I used to cut out any reports about him in the music press over here. I had this picture that I based the painting on in my scrapbook from 1975.

I always loved it and always thought that David and Ava made an amazingly cool and stylish looking couple so I always really liked the picture.

Had you known Ava prior to painting the picture?

No. I kind of got in contact with Ava on social media. We were chatting; she'd seen other work that I'd done and I said that I wanted to do a painting. She said that this was her favorite painting as well. It was her favorite picture of her and Bowie and my favorite picture of her and Bowie, so I decided that that was the one I was going to go for.

Other works center on individuals or groups. Were you specifically interested in Bowie and Ava because they were a couple?

No. I didn't do it because it was a couple, I just did it because they both looked so amazing. It was just a picture that I'd always really loved. I hadn't really intellectualized the reason behind it or anything like that. It was just literally because it was such a great image and was a lot different from what I had done a lot of—I was doing something slightly new and slightly different, using an old image that I really loved.

The faces were depicted in a very warm and genuine manner. The clothing was less realistically rendered, almost like an afterthought.

Absolutely. I always planned it to be like that. If it's not a picture that I've taken, I don't really like to just genuinely copy 100-percent accurately what someone else has done. I always try to change things. On a lot of my paintings, I've switched heads on people and things like that so they're never genuinely just a straight-forward copy from an existing photo. Obviously, I didn't want to change any heads around on this one because I wanted it to be Ava and David Bowie. But what I decided to do is stylize it so that you get a realistic rendering of the faces, which are more modeled, and then it leads on into more of almost a line drawing. Partly it was an exercise in style; two different styles of painting done together.

Partly it was to take the original painting away from being a slavish copy of the original photograph. By doing that, you create something different. If you look at the actual photograph and then you look at the painting, you can see that it's not a straightforward copy.

Sometimes photos show a couple looking very much like a posed couple. They deliberately pose for the camera, as if to show that they are indeed together, their eyes lock or they're holding hands, etc. This was an unusual image for that reason.

They were distinctly themselves and they both had a similarly stylish and extreme look that looked well together but it was like an image of a couple that weren't completely dependent on each other. They were really strong characters. It didn't look as if there was an imbalance in the relationship. It was like two striking, strong people.

On your website, there is the finished portrait and an earlier sketch.

As with a lot of paintings, it's always a good idea to try them out as sketches. I tried the sketch out to see how my idea would work of stylizing the faces-against-the-bodies idea. That meant that If you did it as a smaller sketch first, you didn't waste time; it took quite a long time to paint the large canvas, which is quite big, and I kept changing things and whatever.

It just made sense to do a small version, because you get to know the details. I knew Bowie's face very well, I'd done pictures over the years, but I hadn't done so many of Ava so it was kind of an exercise for me, I had to familiarize myself with the structure of her face and all of that. So, you work it out on the sketch, really, before you go to a large painting.

Did your perception of Ava change at any point during this process?

I've been aware of Ava Cherry since 1973 when she first started appearing in the press. She was a person that I'd been aware of for a very long time. I didn't know her personally but I felt like I kind of knew her. I always knew what I wanted to do, really, so it didn't really ever change. That was really my intention and that's how it worked out. That was the intention that I'd always had.

The original photograph was taken backstage at a Rod Stewart concert at Madison Square Garden in March 1975. There are quite a few pictures, interestingly, from that actual party of David Bowie and Ava Cherry, but there's not very many pictures of that particular shot which I've always liked. If you Google it, you'll see a lot of different pictures of that event but not so many of that particular image. So, I had to use it as a reference and it was a very small image, only about an inch-and-a half high, to base it on. It was quite difficult to convert an inch-and-a half picture, which was kind of like a press shot, a newsprint, into a six-foot-high painting.

Ava's reaction to the finished product...

Ava was very pleased; she really liked it. The photograph has been around since 1975 but the painting is new. It was literally done this year.

Can you elaborate on the influence of David Bowie and Ava Cherry, in terms of how you see this portrait being categorized within a larger body of work?

I've always been associated with David Bowie. When I left art school in 1978 and came to London, I met his PR lady and I gave her a picture which I'd done in art school and six months later, I got a hand-written letter from David, who was then in Berlin, thanking me for the picture and everything. When they did the big V & A Bowie Exhibition in 2013, I did life masks of him and he actually bought two for his collection.

There's always been a Bowie connection and one of my aims has always been to do an exhibition of my Bowie-related artwork and life masks. I was going to focus on my favorite period, which is his most enigmatic, which coincided with when he and Ava were in a relationship, which was in 1974 and 1975, so my exhibition was going to really focus on that particular era of Bowie and it's something that I'm still planning to do. There's been a bit of Bowie overkill since he's died so I didn't want to exhibit it in the immediate aftermath of his death because there were a lot of people cashing in and doing things and I didn't want to be part of that feeding frenzy. I decided to wait on that and it's something that I will be doing. That painting will hopefully be part of an exhibition at some point over the next couple of years, focusing on that period when Bowie and Ava were together.

Do you foresee depicting Ava as part of any future projects?

Ava is planning to come to London to do some press and possibly some performances and we're going to use that painting and a new portrait that I'm planning to do of her, as she is now, as part of the press campaign that she's going to do. There are various contexts in which that work can be used or will be used.

What has been Ava's influence in the U.K.?

Ava Cherry's look has been a big influence on fashion here. I sent her a picture that I took in the London tube station a couple of weeks ago. There was some big, new, fashion campaign with a model who had the Ava Cherry '70s look, with very short, bleached hair and everything. It's kind of a timeless look. It still influences things to this day in certain ways.

Part of David Bowie's fascination with Ava was that she epitomized U.S. Soul culture.

34.
AVA'S CHICAGO SOUL: PAUL TRYNKA

Esteemed British journalist Paul Trynka, former editor of Mojo *from 1999 to 2003, wrote* Starman: David Bowie *in 2011. His other books include rock biographies* Sympathy for the Devil: The Birth of the Rolling Stones *and* The Death of Brian Jones *(2014) about the late Rolling Stones guitarist and* Iggy Pop: Open Up and Bleed. *Here, he responds to comments and queries regarding Ava Cherry and David Bowie.*

PAUL TRYNKA, January 23, 2019
The thing is, David only knew about Chicago or American soul culture secondhand. It always had this mysterious *oeuvre* for him, right from when he went to the department store down the road on Bromley and listened to the Gramophone. He and his friends used to see records and buy them randomly or go in and check them out as Gramophones. He'd always been in love with this mysterious, magical, yet soulful music. Ava was a key person who epitomized that because it wasn't just about her singing, it was about her background, her dad, the whole thing, so I think she had a very magical *oeuvre* on him for that reason.

In Starman, *you offered some general impressions of Ava Cherry and the Astronettes material, i.e., "I Am a Laser" and "I Am Devine." Was David's desire to record Ava sincere?*

That collection was part inspirational and part mess, it was all over the place. David had this amazing work ethic that he maintained for a long time but then it started to fracture. A lot of that had to do with MainMan and he was trying to do too many things at once. I guess that what happened with his mindset was affecting him as well. He was basically shooting off in lots of different directions and being pressured by a lot of different people and just starting to crack a little bit along the way. That's the magic in the record, I think, but it never quite came together. It was never finished, so I think there was a raw bit to it. There were a lot of people to deal with and Ava was a better singer than Jason Guess, in my mind, so there was a bit of a disconnect between Ava and the Astronettes but it's a fascinating artifact. It's a shame actually that it wasn't executed perfectly. Quite a few of David's projects weren't executed properly during that period. If you look at Iggy Pop, David tried to give him a fair shake; he didn't really help him at all.

Has Ava strongly impacted David Bowie's legacy?

I don't think David would have made that leap into American Soul culture to the same degree without her. You can't come up with a percentage or a rational analysis of it all; he walked into a lot of venues and he was a very, shy person and wouldn't have done that without her.

Also, if you look at what happened during the early *Young Americans* tour, it was a mess. There was a very nasty atmosphere around the place. A lot of people said that it was Ava and Carlos that gave it a sweet edge. Without them, who knows what would have happened? David would have been even more fried. I think it's impossible to disentangle all of the threads of what she was responsible for or what she wasn't responsible for but she was a key part of his look, a key part of helping him get through and she was a key part of helping him discover this original soul culture. She was important, but you can't really put a figure on it.

In Starman, *you stated: "The new material, notably "1984/Dodo" was dense and intriguing," What else does you recall about the legendary 1980 Floor Show?*

I think David at that point was going from one aesthetic to another so *Diamond Dogs* was a darker, spookier version of the *Aladdin Sane* concept. It went beyond the London construct; what he was reaching for was something that was much more transatlantic. It wasn't perfectly done though it does have magic to it. There were English players that were trying to sound American; people like Mark Pritchett, and with Mick Ronson, it was one of his last collaborations. To me, it sounded slightly raw, slightly messy and slightly unfinished which adds to the magic.

Why have you cited Ava as a frequent source in your Bowie biographies?

For me, I had more of an interest in Ava than in a lot of the other MainMan characters. Ava was an important interview for me because she was sort of a lodestone. Some people don't necessarily have an agenda. They see what's happening. They can tell the difference between what they know about and what they don't know about. She had respect for David but her head wasn't necessarily turned by him, if that makes sense. Some people back in the day didn't really have an agenda. They were just decent people, doing their work and Ava was definitely one of those.

With Ava's opinions, I trusted them and I followed them. There were a few people that I was trying to bounce opinions off of, could it have been this or that? Was it A or was it B? There weren't that many people who knew David well, there would only be a couple from each time period and Ava was definitely one of those. And apart from that, I enjoyed talking to her. She was just honest without any real agenda and could remember a lot, as well, whereas some other people don't actually remember and they make up a story of what might have happened, which happens to quite a surprising degree.

A lot of people were bitter, but Ava wasn't bitter at all. Why should anybody be bitter? The fact is, everybody was a consenting adult who went into all of that and Ava had a clarity and integrity. She's enjoyable company and a good singer.

Can you comment on Ava's vocal quality?

Ava has more than just a Chicago soul voice. She has modernity to it, as well. When I think about singers like Grace Jones and Ava, I think in terms of their not having an over-engineered or overblown or over vibrato-ed soul voice. I think in terms of a natural voice and Ava always seemed to me to have that kind of voice, a modern aesthetic, and that's why it works with electronic instrumentation as well, moving forward and beyond the 1980s.

35.
CATCHING UP:
DAVID BOWIE EVENTS ABROAD
& LATEST PROJECTS

With a natural gift for language, it's no surprise that Ava enjoys venturing out into international circles, first in her modeling career and then by recording and entertaining in Latin America.

(A record was released in Portugal in November of 2018 and the rest of the world, Brazil and the States, etc. heard it in March and April of 2019.)

AVA

When I was invited to Encierra, Portugal to do the Bowie Tribute with Jorge Vadio, I was especially excited because I had not worked much with those people that had done a Bowie tribute, like guitarist Earl Slick and pianist Mick Garson. Jorge had done the tribute before with Mike Garson and was telling me all about it.

When I got there, I discovered how wonderful Portugal was—it was full of beautiful, beautiful people and wonderful, wonderful food and gorgeous landscaping. We got there and rehearsed for about a week before the show, which was actually an outside festival which took place at the edge of town with a beautiful stage. They took such good care of me. Before I go onstage, I'm a picky eater, so I asked them if they could make me a soup; they made me this beautiful soup with squash, carrots and spinach, and afterwards, some lovely fish.

During that week, we went to a Fado House, where all of these famous Fado singers sang. The reason that I loved it was because it reminded me of Flamenco because of the singers' depth of emotion. They use their voices to convey emotion much more so than other singers I've heard who sing in Portuguese.

The Fado people invited us to dinner. We met two very famous female Fado singers and a few males. I especially loved the female singers and heard the love of their country in their phrasing.

Note: *"Fado" refers to a traditionally structured Portuguese song that conveys a deep sense of longing and centers on themes such as poverty or seafaring. The genesis of this genre goes back to the early 1800s.*

The recording that we did in Portugal was released at the end of November 2018 in Brazil because November and December are their summer and the setting of the song took place at the beach. So, it was recorded in Portugal in November of 2018 and the rest of the world, Brazil and the States, etc. would hear it in March and April of 2019.

Learning to sing in Portuguese was really an experience. I can sing in a few different languages such as French and Spanish, but I was asked to do the recording a day after we finished the show at the outdoor festival and at first, I thought, "Oh, I'm tired."

But Jorge said, "Please, just do this duet with me." One of my all-time favorite songs is "The Girl from Ipanema" by the incredible Brazilian composer Antonio Carlos Jobim. I said that if I do it, I want to do it like Astrid Gilberto would do it, who was the vocalist who brought it to fame. So that's exactly what I did.

Now, usually I go to a foreign country and learn the language very fast, or at least the pronunciation. But I found learning Portuguese to be very, very difficult. Jorge said that he wanted me to sing the choruses in Portuguese and I said, "Okay, but you're going to have to help me."

Finally, I asked him to sing it to me phonetically, exactly the way it sounded, and I wrote it down, exactly how it sounded to me. And that's what I'm singing. I was concerned about the outcome, but Jorge assuaged my fears. He told me, "The people love how you sound in Portuguese." He said it was sweet and innocent-sounding.

36.
RIGHT FROM THE HEART

Another project in the works is my dance track, "Right from the Heart" which reached No. 5 in the U.K. charts. Truthfully, "Right from the Heart" took a while, a few months, to get done. I was working with an agent in London, Lady Jackie Periera. She had suggested that I do a dance track over there. She said that even though I was known as working with Bowie, I could get a new audience with a dance song, which was right.

I'm excited about my new record, because I just got signed to the biggest recording label in Europe, Defected/Glitter Box. They signed me to do a brand-new song which I recorded in February in New York. They called me up from London and asked me to send them the track because they wanted to see if I could write—everybody can't write and they don't know me that well, so I sent them what I wrote and they were so excited after hearing what I'd come up with. The producer on that project is Luke Solomon and the owner of the label is Simon Dunsmore.

I was so excited when "Right from the Heart" shot up the U.K. charts to No. 5.

Lady Jackie came to Chicago over Christmas and we tried to work with a producer from here but the producer did not have the sound that she was looking for and the genre that she promotes out of in Europe. She said that she would have to put me together with a British producer back there. That's the way she envisioned getting the song together for that genre. So, she paired me with Lee Hepworth and he came up with the track.

I had already done some vocals which I sent on to him, which he put together with the track. The theme was my idea. It was such a heart-felt thing. It took a while to get done because there were a lot of ups and downs. It wasn't easy to do. First of all, Lady Jackie had been looking for the right person to do the track and then when she found the right person, we haggled about how many vocals were going to do on it. I remember being unhappy that of all the vocals I'd done, only about a quarter of those vocals went on the record. They told me the DJs wouldn't play it if there were too many vocals on it, but I didn't believe that and I still don't. I think that they have to have a leader to play other things, but I'd heard of a lot of records that have full vocals. I think there's a difference between what's on the radio and a situation where the DJs are trying to program music.

Like I said, I did my vocals here in Chicago. My engineers know exactly what I want and they always give me exactly what I need. I produce my own music. Lee wrote the music for this record which was combined with the vocals that I sent him.

I work with a lot of studios but the one I worked with on this project was Flip the Switch. It's a small studio, but the engineer, DMan, whom I do a lot of vocals with on a lot of projects, knows how to get the right sound for me. I am always the producer of my vocals, but he's an engineer who knows how to mix and master and make whatever you're singing sound good on the track.

37.
A NIGHT OF STARDUST! & A DEEPER VISION:
AVA CHERRY'S GLOBAL AND ARTISTIC LEGACY

January 2019

*P*art of Ava's trajectory has involved reconnecting with long-term David Bowie fans, connecting with newbies and continuing to perform his most beloved songs to all concerned. As such, she was excited to attend and perform at the third annual "Philly Loves Bowie Week," advertised along with the caption, "Celebrating the City of Brotherly Love for The Starman" at the annual A Night of Stardust. This 2019 event took place between January 4-13. Ava happily returned the following year, but the 2021 event was cancelled due to the Covid-19 pandemic.

The proceeds from the related Bowie Silent Auction were slated for the Cancer Center at Children's Hospital of Philadelphia, in David Bowie's memory. Other vendors generously came forth, too, such as jewelry designer Beren Weil, who contributed "Bowie-themed guitar pick earrings" and "guitar picks purchased from the DAVID BOWIE IS exhibit in Brooklyn, NY."

Houston's Yasmin Cespedes donated an aluminum and leather "David Bowie Aladdin Sane collar necklace." Another Texas talent from Austin, Kayci Wheatley, parted with a "Bowie bomber jacket" for the charitable cause.

The maelstrom of events included a special screening of a documentary about Bowie's recording rituals as they related to the Sigma Kids at the PFS Roxy Theatre: a "Starman" Karaoke night at Johnny Brenda's and a Bowie-based quiz sponsored by Patti Brett, Sigma Kid extraordinaire and owner of Doobie's Bar in the Rittenhouse area.

Ava performed on January 11, which is the day after David Bowie died. She noted that every act there performed with the band that they hired for the event.

Weeks before the engagement, she conceptualized her outfit and finally decided that she would be decked out "in silver that night; very 'stardust' and very glam rock for David."

AVA

I love "Rebel Rebel," especially because I was sitting at the piano when David wrote it. It was just the two of us there, as he was coming up with the words. That song has a special place in my heart, actually.

We were at the Olympic Studio in London at the time (in Barnes). I remember that day very well because the band recording in the studio next to us was Bad Company. That was where they recorded their famous *Bad Company* album which was a huge success for them—they were actually recording the track, "Rock Steady" next door.

I've always been a huge Paul Rodgers fan. I love Paul Rodgers. There were some great vocalists coming out of England at that time. We had a chance to hear some of the songs before they got released.

So, there we were, sitting in the studio in the dark. David said, "I've got a song idea" and started coming up with a few lyrics. I might have added a few words like, "boy, girl." I didn't get credit but I came up with one or two words to help him with it. He was still writing it down, so we didn't actually record that day.

Believe me, I had no idea that that song was going to be a hit. Sometimes you sit there and come up with a few words. He wrote the song but I know I gave him one or two words. I felt the basic groove, but I didn't know what kind of track he was going to put under it. That's why I didn't know if it was going to be a "serious" song: because David was just picking out chords on the piano, so I really didn't know what it was all about, but I thought it was cute.

Here's how I feel about the Bowie tributes. I'm committed to doing whatever I'm asked to do to commemorate David and his music through songs that I loved by him and songs that I believe he would want me to tribute.

The original concert date had been changed as Mick had to undergo emergency heart surgery in April of 2019. For Chicagoans, that change yielded a flood of memories, as their national tour would begin in the city where the Stones jump-started their careers at the recording studio at 2120 S. Michigan, Chess Records, which now serves as a museum and hosts the Blues Heaven Institute. The company was owned originally by The Chess Brothers, but the late Marie Dixon, wife of the late songwriter Willie Dixon, had the foresight to purchase the building after promising her husband that she would use the space to educate musicians and entertain locals.

****

AVA

My life in entertainment has come full circle. Throughout the highs and lows, I've retained memories of fabulous relationships with David Bowie, Luther Vandross...I love Keith and I love Mick. Whenever they perform in Chicago, they give me backstage passes.

On the second night of the No Filter tour on June 25, 2019 at Chicago's Soldier Field, when the Stones played 20 songs, Keith invited me backstage. He wore a wonderful smile. He looked up and said, "Oh, Ava." He was dressed casually and greeted me warmly. He gave me a very warm hug and introduced me to the other people in the room. His manager, Jane Rose, led me to the dressing room and snapped our photo.

You could feel the energy in the 60,000-seat football stadium. Fans were not only excited to be there, they were heartened to see that Mick had made such a remarkable recovery. As he strolled the ramp in a jeweled jacket, many of us held our breath, but not for long, as the Stones put on a two-hour show and Mick showed absolutely no signs of fatigue.

I'm always impressed by the overall professional quality of their shows and the vivid imagery they flaunt from the video screens and this night was no different, except that in times past, fans held up lit matches when demanding an encore, and this time, they held up cell phones.

I was so happy to reconnect with my old friend after all of these years. I really enjoyed the backstage camaraderie. There has always been such a high level of respect between us. I gave Keith some cologne. After such a longstanding friendship, our reunion felt warm and fuzzy, forming the perfect circle to an already incredible relationship.

After spending so many years in a competitive industry, here is my takeaway. I talked about it earlier, but I have to state it again: I listened to the people who were really successful. I took chances. I was brave. I was never afraid. Those feelings have lingered. I've been able to do things that I'd never done before, learn something that I didn't know before. Perhaps it all harkens back to the beginning of my career. My hunger to succeed. My inner drive.

Looking back to my years with David Bowie and Luther Vandross, I feel their energy all the time. My astrologer told me that they would always be in my karma for the rest of my life and that there would always be a strong connection between us.

Postscript

In March 2020, I did a Nu-Disco single and related video called "Testify Love" on producer Pepper Gomez's Chicago/Miami-based record label Wake Up! Music that did really well and, like last year's rendition of "Let's Dance," "Testify Love" has been positively acclaimed in, among other magazines, people.com, where writer Jordan Runtagh called my latest original "enthralling."

Here are some other dance track reviews:

Regarding "Testify Love": Ralph White, at hotindienews.com, said on March 18, 2020 "As her music fills your ears, imagined images of what it must've been like to be on the crowded dance floor of the long-gone Studio 54 fills your mind, and haunts you like forgotten ghosts on a moonless night."

Ondeckmagazine.com, April 19, 2020, "Ava Cherry Returns with Testify Love": "It's a bit of musical magic that's destined to become a classic in its own time."

Aupium.com, April 21, 2020, "Ava Cherry Makes Love Look Fabulous in New Video 'Testify Love'": "She chants with high-tempo splendor as the shimmering cascades of synths induce us into the dance floor."

Eatsleepbreathemusic.com voted in "Testify Love" for Song of the Day and described it as: "laced with mesmerizing vocals and hypnotic lyrics, this song will get you off your feet."

Exhimusic.com on April 23, 2020 exclaimed: "In this time of disquiet and stress, it's especially gladdening to hear Cherry's message of perseverance and survival."

Regarding the related video: "The video showcases Cherry giving it her all in a captivating performance on stage, and also footage of her singing joyfully in the middle of the city" ("Dance-Pop/Soul Veteran Ava Cherry Delivers a Triumphant New Tune/Video").

On Aprll 13, 2020, Karen Benardello, of shockya.com ("Ava Cherry's Testify Love Music Video Review") observed: "The strong vocals that are featured throughout the track are reminiscent of some of Cherry's fellow pop powerhouse contemporaries, including Tina Turner, Toni Braxton and Patti La Belle.

In "Ava Cherry Paying Tribute to David Bowie with Her Version of 'Let's Dance,'" Tracy Heck, of rocklife.com on January 10, 2020, underscored

Ava's ultimate mission: "My calling is to make people feel soothed and feel some emotion through the music, particularly happiness and love."

At the end of March, in 2021, I released a CD of never-before-released songs and a few that may be known. I'm also involved in a documentary about my earlier years with David Bowie.

Annually, I've performed at the Bowie celebration held live in Philadelphia which was cancelled due to the pandemic, but I participated in the January 8 global stream *A Bowie Celebration: Just For One Day!* So, for that January extravaganza, I arranged and sang the backup vocals for "Heroes" and also sang backup on "Fame" and "Young Americans." It was exciting to re-release my debut album, *Ripe,* in August of 2020.

As far as surviving the pandemic, I am so saddened by the number of people in my country and in the world who died from this pandemic. I'm looking forward to happy days again; people being able to show love and affection again to each other, to be together. As musicians, we suffered so much, besides the people who passed, we suffered the most in the pandemic. We were not able to soothe people in terms of live performance; we were really put down in our ability to perform live.

And I wish, that after this terrible pandemic, the world can get together and show our love for one another and especially through music. Love from me, always, and hope this is food for thought for everyone.

Bibliography

Books:

Broackes, Victoria, Marsh, Geoffrey. *David Bowie Is the Subject*. V&A Publishing, London. 2013.

Dickerson, James. *Women on Top: The Quiet Revolution That's Rocking the American Music Industry*. Billboard Books, New York, 1998.

Doggett, Peter. *The Man Who Sold the World: David Bowie and The 1970s*. HarperCollins, New York. 2012.

Edwards, Henry and Zanetta, Tony. *Stardust: The David Bowie Story*. McGraw-Hill, New York, 1986.

Jones, Dylan. *David Bowie: The Oral History*. Three Rivers Press, New York. 2017.

Marcic, Dorothy. *Respect: Women and Popular Music*. Texere Press, New York, 2002.

Pareles, Jon, et. al., *The Rolling Stone Encyclopedia of Rock & Roll*, Revised for the 21st Century. Fireside, A Rolling Stone Press Book. New York, London, Toronto, Sydney. 2001.

Ribowsky, Mark, *Signed, Sealed and Delivered: The Soulful Journey of Stevie Wonder*, Wiley, 2010.

Robinson, Lisa. *Nobody Ever Asked Me About The Girls: Women, Music and Fame*. Henry Holt and Company, New York, 2020.

Seymour, Craig. Luther: *The Life and Longing of Luther Vandross*. HarperCollins, 2004.

Spector, Ronnie/Waldron, Vince. *Be My Baby*. Harmony Books, New York. 1990.

Spitz, Mark. *Bowie: A Biography*. Crown Publishers, New York. 2009.

Stambler, Irwin. *The Encyclopedia of Pop, Rock and Soul.* St. Martin's Press, New York, 1989.

Stokes, Tucker, Ward. *Rock of Ages: The Rolling Stone History of Rock and Roll.* Rolling Stone Press, New York. 1986.

Taylor, Billy, Teresa L. Reed, *The Jazz Life of Dr. Billy Taylor*, Indiana Univ. Press, 2013.

Trynka, Paul. *David Bowie: Starman.* Little, Brown and Company. New York, 2011.

Periodicals:

Rolling Stone, April 1, 1974
New York Times, August, 1987

Websites:
www.pennyblackmusic.co.uk.
www.bowiewonderworld.com

Devitt, James. "The Black Women Behind Rock and Roll," (Interview with Maureen Mahon), nyu.edu, November 23, 2020.

Giorgis, Hannah. "The Final Word on Tina Turner," The Atlantic Magazine, March 27, 2021.

Joseph, Chante. "Back to Black: how the Music Industry Reckoned with Race this Year, guardian.com, December 28, 2020.

Pareles, Jon. "Pop View; Who Decides the Color of Music?" The New York Times, May 17, 1987, (nytimes.com),

Sharif, Hamza, 20-Feet-From-Stardom, socialistreview.org.uk/390/20-feet-from-stardom, April 2014.

Acknowledgments

Ava and Lisa wish to sincerely thank interviewees: Patti Brett, Ms. Erma Cherry, Bobby Colomby, Chris Connelly, the late Bob Esty, Marla Kanevsky, Catherine Layton, Joe Shanahan, Toni Shimek, Paul Trynka, Matt Walker, Mark Wardel and Tony Zanetta.

The following interview excerpts/interviews conducted by Lisa Torem were reprinted from pennyblackmusic: Michael Darling, Earl Slick, Tony Visconti and Woody Woodmansey. Extreme gratitude to: John Clarkson and Christopher Torem for editorial commentary.

Thank you, Ava and Eliza.

Lisa

About the Authors

Ava Cherry is a singer, producer and fashion icon. Her personal and professional collaboration with international superstar David Bowie in the 1970s fostered a strong soul influence on Bowie's hit album *Young Americans*. She was also instrumental in the evolution of the proto-New Wave band The Astronettes. Cherry's formative years on the Chicago black music scene shaped her soul music sensibilities that would later influence the work of numerous artists following in her footsteps. Cherry was later a backup singer for Luther Vandross and eventually struck out on her own to launch a solo career. She is currently enjoying a resurgence on the international music scene.

Lisa Torem, a native Chicagoan, holds a B.A. in Education with a Major Concentration in Music and an M.A. in Applied Linguistics from Northeastern Illinois University. She taught English as a Second Language and English at local schools and colleges.

A musician and playwright, Torem wrote original music about pioneering American women for Scott Foresman Co. and her one-act play, *Dog Sharing*, was produced at a New York theater. Her original multicultural tape, *Singlish*, won a Parents' Choice award and select songs were performed by American Women Composers at the Chicago Cultural Center.

Torem writes reviews and features for multiple music outlets, including *Popmatters*, *American Blues Scene*, the *Chicago Reader* and pennyblackmusic.co.uk., for which she is a staff writer. She has conducted more than 100 interviews with high-profile and rising stars. Torem received a fellowship for the Summer Literature Seminar held in Tbilisi, Georgia in 2018 and was also invited that year to attend Sicily's annual Bread Loaf conference. Her previously co-authored book is *Through the Eye of the Tiger* with Jim Peterik (2014).

CPSIA information can be obtained
at www.ICGtesting.com
Printed in the USA
BVHW031146240122
627023BV00013B/173/J